Reserved Words in Standard Pascal

Reserved words have special meanings in the Pascal language and cannot be used as identifiers.

AND	DO	FUNCTION	NIL	PROGRAM	TYPE
ARRAY	DOWNTO	GOTO	NOT	RECORD	UNTIL
BEGIN	ELSE	IF	OF	REPEAT	VAR
CASE	END	IN	OR	SET	WHILE
CONST	FILE	LABEL	PACKED	THEN	WITH
DIV	FOR	MOD	PROCEDURE	TO	

Note: Some Pascal compilers treat FORWARD as a reserved word.

Standard Functions

Seventeen functions are predefined in Standard Pascal:

Function	Computes	Example
Abs	Absolute value	Abs(-3.1) = 3.1
ArcTan	Arc tangent (in radians)	ArcTan(1.0) = 0.785398
Chr	Character	Chr(65) = 'A' in ASCII
Cos	Cosine (angle in radians)	Cos(3.1415926) = -1.0
EOF	End of file	EOF(InFile)
EOLn	End of line	EOLn(InFile)
Exp	Power of e	Exp(1.0) = 2.71828
Ln	Natural log	Ln(2.0) = 0.693147
Odd	Oddness	Odd(3) = True
Ord	Ordinal value	Ord('A') = 65 in ASCII
Pred	Predecessor (of ordinal)	Pred('B') = 'A'
Round	Nearest integer	Round(-3.8) = -4
Sin	Sine (angle in radians)	Sine(3.1415926) = 0.0
Sqr	Square	Sqr(-3.0) = 9.0
SqRt	Square root	SqRt(2.0) = 1.41421
Succ	Successor (of ordinal)	Succ('A') = 'B'
Trunc	Integer part	Trunc(-3.8) = -3

Standard Procedures

Thirteen procedures are predefined in Standard Pascal:

Procedure	Description
Dispose(*Pointer*)	Deallocates storage cell pointed to by *Pointer*.
Get(*FilePointer*)	Advances *FilePointer*, then copies next file component into *FilePointer^*.
New(*Pointer*)	Allocates new storage cell and stores its address in *Pointer*.
Pack(*UnpackedArray*, *FirstSubscript*, *PackedArray*)	The *FirstSubscript* element of *Unpacked-Array* is copied into the first position of *PackedArray*, and so on.
Page(*FilePointer*)	Advances the output device to a new page before printing the next line of the file.
Put(*FilePointer*)	Appends the buffer variable *FilePointer^* to the file, then advances the pointer.
Read(*FilePointer*, *VariableList*)	Reads data from the specified file into the listed variables. If *FilePointer* is not given, the standard Input file is read.
ReadLn(*FilePointer*, *VariableList*)	Reads a line of data from the specified Text file into the listed variables. If the file pointer is not given, the standard Input file is read.
Reset(*FilePointer*)	Opens file associated with *FilePointer* for reading only.
Rewrite(*FilePointer*)	Opens file associated with *FilePointer* for writing only.
Unpack(*PackedArray*, *UnpackedArray*, *FirstSubscript*)	Copies first element of *PackedArray* into the *FirstSubscript* position of *Unpacked-Array*, and so on.
Write(*FilePointer*, *ExprList*)	Writes the values of the listed expressions to the specified file. If *FilePointer* is not given, the values are written to Output.
WriteLn(*FilePointer*, *ExprList*)	Writes the values of the listed expressions to the specified Text file, then writes <EOLn>. If *FilePointer* is not given, the values are written to the standard Output file.

THE **STRUCTURES** AND **ABSTRACTIONS LABS**

Experiments in Pascal
and Turbo Pascal

WILLIAM I. SALMON
University of Utah

IRWIN
Homewood, IL 60430
Boston, MA 02116

Cover painting: Paul Klee, Submersion and Separation, 1923
8¾ x 11 (22.2 x 27.9); watercolor and gouache
Collection of the Arts Club of Chicago, Arthur Heun Bequest
Reproduced by permission.

Senior sponsoring editor: Bill Stenquist
Designer and compositor: Impressions, Inc./Bill Salmon
Project editor: Karen J. Nelson
Production manager: Mary Jo Parke
Cover designer: Image House, Inc.
Printer: Edwards Brothers, Inc.

ISBN   0-256-10352-6

The programs in this book have been included for instructional use only. They have
been carefully tested but are not guaranteed for any particular use. The author and the
publisher accept no liabilities for the use of the programs.

MS-DOS is a trademark of Microsoft Corporation.
Macintosh and Apple are trademarks of Apple Computer, Inc.
Turbo Pascal is a trademark of Borland International, Inc.
THINK Pascal is a trademark of Symantec Corporation.

Printed in the United States of America
  2 3 4 5 6 7 8 9 0 EB98 7 6 5 4 3 2

**Dedicated to
Alfred R. Armstrong,
who taught lab technique and a whole lot more.**

Preface

Computer science must be learned by doing. After all, computer scientists are in the business of inventing software and hardware, and the only way to learn inventing is to invent—over and over again. So, while some of computer science can be learned in the classroom or by reading books, most of it is learned during long hours of tinkering with the machinery.

This manual is intended to provide some guidance during those long hours. It provides hands-on, step-by-step guidance through the experimentation required during a first course in computer science, running parallel to the *Structures and Abstractions* textbook. The labs provide much of the help that might be expected from a lab assistant, leading students through the first steps in running an operating system and Pascal environment, learning the syntax of the Pascal language, and solving problems of increasing complexity. This manual is suitable for both self-study and for guided lab sessions with an instructor.

Three kinds of labs

Three types of labs are provided, and all are intended to be hands-on experiences. In the early stages, there are a few labs that introduce the student to an operating system or Pascal package to be used in the course. These labs are necessarily specific to a particular software product. For example, labs 1.1, 1.3, 5.1, and 10.3 are specific to Turbo Pascal® and MS-DOS® computers, while labs 1.2, 1.4, and 5.2 are specific to THINK Pascal® and the Apple® Macintosh® computers.

Most of the labs, however, are system-independent, and great care has been taken to use only ISO Standard Pascal except in file operations, where some system-specific operations are necessary. There are numerous labs that lead students through experiments with the subtleties of Pascal syntax, to emphasize the constant need to see and understand what really happens, as opposed to what a book says should happen.

Finally, there are "lab projects," which are programming projects similar to those assigned in the textbook, but which lead the way through the problem-solving and program-building processes, leaving a piece of the problem to be solved by the student. These projects are intended as practice, to prepare for the full-blown programming assignments in the textbook.

For the instructor

This manual provides many more labs than can be used in a typical course, and more types of labs than a typical instructor will want to cover. This allows for different audiences and different styles of teaching. My hope is that a typical course will find some labs quite easy, some quite hard, and some in between. Individual instructors will have to choose appropriate labs for their particular courses.

For the student

Before working through a lab, you should be familiar with the material listed in the prerequisites. *The labs do not substitute for the textbook!* Also, it is a good idea to read all the way through the lab material before sitting down at the computer to do the work. In this way, you will know when you start what needs to be done, what files will be needed from the accompanying disk, and what is expected of you. If you plan carefully for each lab, you will learn more from the experience.

While working the experiments, don't try to cut corners. To learn the material, you must experience it firsthand and feel its meaning unfold as you work. The lab experiences themselves are not only important, but *vital* to your understanding of the subject.

After completing a lab session, go back over it in your mind and summarize for yourself the major results and what they mean. If the meaning is still not clear to you, perform more experiments until it is. This kind of review, coupled with constant experimentation, is the key to learning science.

The accompanying disks

Packaged with this manual, you will find two floppy diskettes. The 5.25-inch disk contains source code (and in a few cases, object code) for use with Turbo Pascal, versions 5.x and 6.0, on MS-DOS computers. The 3.5-inch disk is for Apple Macintosh computers running THINK Pascal, versions 3.x and 4.x.

However, the source code on these disks almost always conforms to the International Standard for Pascal, and can be ported to other machines virtually without change. The only exceptions are:

1. In opening files, there is no standard way to associate an external filename with a file pointer, so you will have to adjust this to suit your compiler.

2. In Lab 8.1, an ELSE clause is used in a CASE structure. (It's called OTHERWISE in THINK Pascal.) If your Pascal system will not allow a default clause, you will want to alter or skip this example.

The disk files are simple ASCII text, and porting to other computer systems should be simple in most cases.

Acknowledgments

I would like to thank the students in my courses for all the questions, suggestions, comments, and criticisms over the years; I hope I have benefited from them. I also want to thank the following reviewers, whose criticisms and suggestions have improved the choice and presentation of material in this manual:

Matthew Dickerson, Middlebury College;

David E. Leasure, University of Kansas;

John Lowther, Michigan Technological University;

Jack Mostow, Rutgers, The State University of New Jersey;

George Novacky, University of Pittsburgh;

Lou Steinberg, Rutgers, The State University of New Jersey;

Phillip Tomovitch, SUNY at Stony Brook;

Chris Van Wyk, Drew University;

Barry Wittman, Rutgers, The State University of New Jersey.

Suggestions for improvements are always welcome; I can be reached at the following e-mail addresses, or through the publisher.

William I. Salmon
Internet: salmon@cs.utah.edu
CompuServe: 71565,135

Table of Contents

The first number refers to the corresponding chapter of *Structures and Abstractions*. Labs marked as projects lead to significant out-of-class assignments. Pages are numbered separately in each lab.

1.1 Using MS-DOS
1.2 Using a Macintosh
1.3 Using Turbo Pascal
1.4 Using THINK Pascal

3.1 Program Structure

4.1 Real Numbers, Roundoff Error, and I/O
4.2 Modularity and Hierarchy

5.1 Using the Turbo Pascal Integrated Debugger
5.2 Using the THINK Pascal Integrated Debugger

6.1 Animating a Function

7.1 Experimenting with Integers
7.2 Experimenting with Characters

8.1 Booleans and Conditionals
8.2 Top-Down Design of a Calendar Function (Project)

9.1 Studying Loops with the Debugger
9.2 Completing the Calendar Program (Project)

10.1 Testing Loop Invariants
10.2 Checking Text for Readability (Project)
10.3 Profiling Nested Loops in Turbo Pascal

11.1 Animating Recursion
11.2 How Many Ways to Make Change? (Project)

12.1 Experimenting with Subranges and Enumerations

13.1 Experimenting with Arrays
13.2 A One-Dimensional Cellular Automaton (Project)

14.1 Drawing High-Resolution Sierpinski Curves (Project)

15.1 Records

16.1 Files
16.2 Turing Machines (Project)
16.3 Eliza (Project)

18.1 Animating Sorting

19.1 Pointers and Linked Lists

Appendices

Lab 1.1:
Using MS-DOS

Materials required: IBM PC-compatible computer, equipped with MS-DOS (version 3.x, 4.0, or 5.0) and either two floppy drives or a hard drive and at least one floppy drive. Also, a blank floppy disk and a copy of the floppy disk that came with this lab manual.

Concepts: Operating system; booting; formatting; directories and subdirectories; filenames and pathnames.

Lab techniques: Learning by experimenting.

Prerequisite: Basic computer literacy, but not familiarity with MS-DOS. Chapter 1 of *Structures and Abstractions.*

What is MS-DOS?

The most common software to control an IBM Personal Computer® or IBM-like clone is produced by the Microsoft Corporation, and called the Microsoft Disk Operating System, or MS-DOS® for short. Many people just call it DOS (pronounced "doss"). As explained in Section 1.4 of the text, the operating system controls the hardware of the computer system and provides a user environment in which programs can be conveniently run. The following is a series of experiments to introduce you to this environment. We assume that you have at least two disk drives in your machine—either two floppy drives or a floppy drive and a hard drive.

Loading MS-DOS from a hard disk

When you turn on the computer's power, MS-DOS is not yet running; it must be loaded into the computer's memory from external disk storage. (This is one reason it is called a *disk* operating system.) In some computer systems, MS-DOS is loaded automatically from a hard disk, and all you have to do is to turn on the machine and wait for it to load. Your instructor will tell you if this is the case with your machine, or you can turn on your machine and see what happens.

Loading MS-DOS from a floppy disk

In other computer systems, MS-DOS is loaded into memory from a floppy disk. If your system does this, you must insert an MS-DOS floppy disk into a particular floppy disk drive before switching on the power. Your instructor will tell you which drive slot to use on your machine.

Loading MS-DOS is called *booting* the system

Whether your machine loads MS-DOS into memory from the hard disk or from a floppy, the loading process is called **booting** the computer. (Short for "bootstrapping.") The process starts with some instructions wired into the ROM circuits of the computer, telling the computer how to start up and how to load further operating system instructions from the appropriate disk. After MS-DOS has been copied into main memory from a disk, the operating system takes control of the machine, displaying first (on some systems) a request for the current date.

```
Current date is Mon    1-01-1992
Enter new date  (mm-dd-yy): _
```

If you see this message, key in the current date in the mm-dd-yy format requested. If you make a mistake before pressing Enter, backspace through the error and retype the characters. When the date is correct, press the Enter key. (Highlighting indicates the user's input.)

```
Current date is Mon    1-01-1992
Enter new date  (mm-dd-yy): 11-12-92
```

If you enter an illegal date or a date in an incorrect format, DOS will display the message Invalid date and then give you another opportunity to enter the date. After it accepts a valid date, DOS will ask for the current time. Key in the current time in the format requested and press Enter:

```
Current date is Mon    1-01-1992
Enter new date  (mm-dd-yy): 11-12-92
Current time is  0:01:01.00
Enter new time: 3:30
```

Many computer systems store the date and time permanently in battery-backed memory, even when turned off. These systems will not automatically display the messages shown above, but will display them when you give a DATE or TIME command. The method for giving such commands will be described shortly.

Whether or not the system asks you to give the date and time, you will eventually see, as the final act of booting, the name of the operating system and the name of the active disk drive.

```
MS-DOS Version 5.00
Copyright (C) Microsoft Corp. 1981-1991
C:\>_
```

The hard disk is usually called drive C: (the colon is part of the drive name). If you are using a floppy-disk-only system, the final line will be A:\> instead of C:\>. (If you don't see the colon and backslash, read the next paragraph.) Whichever letter appears, it is the name of the currently-active disk drive. A typical modern personal computer system includes two floppy disk drives, called A: and B:, and a hard disk, called C:. The message C:\> does two things: it identifies the active disk drive, and it is a request for a command—a **prompt**, as we call it in computing.

(On some networked systems, you may see a more complicated prompt, indicating that the system has initially placed you inside one of the subdirectories on the disk. If so, don't worry about it right now; we'll cover subdirectories later. Just enter the command CD \ and press return, and you should see a prompt like the one shown.)

Displaying the full prompt

If your system boots with a prompt of the form A> or C>, change it so that it will display the current subdirectory as well as the drivename. Enter the command PROMPT PG, with a space between the command word PROMPT and the parameters PG, then press Enter. Here's what you should see:

```
C>PROMPT $P$G
C:\>_
```

Changing the active drive

The cursor now rests after the prompt, waiting for you to key in an operating system command. One of the simplest commands is to change the active disk drive.

If you booted on hard drive C:, give the command to switch to floppy drive A:. To do this, press the A key, *followed by a colon*, then press the Enter key. Write in the space below what you see after doing this:

_____

_____

If you booted on floppy drive A:, give the command to switch to floppy drive B:. To do this, press the B key, *followed by a colon*, then press the Enter key. Write in the space on the next page what you see after doing this:

_____

_____

Explanation

If there is a disk in the requested new drive, you will see the prompt for that drive, indicating that you have successfully switched over. However, if there is no disk in drive A:, you will get the famous MS-DOS error message

```
Not ready error reading drive A
Abort, Retry, Ignore? _
```

Any rational person would expect that by keying a for Abort, you could recover from the error. But no, that would be too simple for MS-DOS (except for versions 5.x under some circumstances). On MS-DOS versions before 5.0, there are only two ways to recover from this error: either put a formatted disk in drive A: and key r for Retry, or reboot the machine. Just in case you don't have a formatted disk to put in drive A:, we'd better practice rebooting the machine when all else fails.

Rebooting the machine

When you have so thoroughly locked up the machine that you cannot recover from your error, you can usually **reboot** the system by keying Alt-Control-Delete; that is, hold down both the Alt and Control keys while pressing Delete. This is sometimes called a **warm boot**—rebooting with the machine already turned on. If this method doesn't work, you need to take more drastic action: turn off the computer's power, wait a few seconds, then turn the power back on. This is called a **cold boot**. (Some machines provide a special reset button for performing a cold boot.)

Perform a warm boot at this time, to see what it's like. Report your observations below:

_____

_____

Formatting or initializing a floppy disk

Before you can store data or programs on a new floppy diskette, the diskette must have some initial data written on it, marking the sectors and directory areas. This process is called **initializing** or **formatting** the diskette, and it is performed by a FORMAT command, giving the name of the disk drive to be used. For example, to format a diskette in drive B: while C: is the active drive, the command would be

`C:\>FORMAT B:`

After giving this command, you will see the message

```
Insert new diskette for drive B:
and strike ENTER when ready_
```

Place a new diskette in drive B:, press Enter, and you will see drive B:'s light come on, indicating that the drive is writing on the diskette. Eventually, you will see a message asking if more diskettes are to be formatted. Answer Y or N for Yes or No, respectively, and press Enter.

WARNING: FORMATTING A DISK ERASES ANY PREVIOUS CONTENTS! THEREFORE, YOU SHOULD FORMAT ONLY NEW DISKETTES OR DISKETTES WHOSE CONTENTS ARE NO LONGER NEEDED.

You should format a brand-new disk at this time, for use in the following experiments. Report your observations below:

_____

_____

_____

_____

Filenames

Data and programs are saved on mass storage in the form of files: sequences of symbols collected together under a single name. In MS-DOS, a **filename** can consist of up to eight upper- or lowercase letters and/or digits, and can contain the special characters

```
! @ # $ % & ( ) - _ { } ' '
```

In addition, a suffix called an **extension** can be added to the filename, creating what is called a file specification or **filespec**. The extension can contain up to three of the same kinds of characters, and must be separated from the filename by a period. The following are legal filenames:

```
REPORT1.TXT     MYFILE     FISH(91).MS
44BONUS.DOC     44.40      Z
```

The following are illegal for the reasons shown. *Note that the filename/extension cannot contain embedded blanks.*

```
REPORTING.TXT   Filename has more than eight characters.

.TXT            No filename.

FISH 91.MS      Embedded space not allowed.

FISH:DOC.MS     Colon not allowed in the filename.
```

MS-DOS reserves some filenames for its own use, and you should not attempt to use these names yourself:

```
AUX      COMm     LPTn     PRN
CLOCK$   CON      NUL
```

(Here, m is a digit in the range 1-4 and n is a digit in the range 1-3.)

Furthermore, some filename extensions have special meanings in MS-DOS or Turbo Pascal, and you should not use these extensions without knowing what you are doing:

.BAK   The extension used by many applications programs for saving an earlier version of text as a backup.

.BAS   Used to identify source code files in the BASIC language.

.BAT   Used to identify a batch file; that is, a text file containing a sequence of MS-DOS commands to be executed one after another when the filename is issued as a command.

.CHK   For files created by CHKDSK.

.COM   A command file; a program that can be run by invoking its name.

.EXE   An executable file. Like a command file, it can be executed by invoking its name.

.MAP   Used to identify link-map files created by the linker.

.PAS   A Pascal source code file used by Turbo Pascal.

.REC   Used to identify files created by RECOVER.

.SYS   A system file for internal use by MS-DOS.

The disk directory

MS-DOS maintains on each disk a directory of the files stored on that disk, listing for each file its name, size in bytes, and date and time when last modified. To see the directory listing for a disk in a given drive, just enter the command DIR, followed by a space and then the name of the drive. The name of the drive is optional if you want a directory of the currently active drive. Here is an example in which the active drive is C: but the user wants to see the directory of a floppy disk in drive B:. Suppose there are three files on the disk in drive B:, called CURLY.PAS, MOE.PAS, and LARRY.TXT:

```
C:\>DIR B:
 Volume in drive B has no label
 Directory of  B:\
CURLY    PAS       357    3-24-91    3:53p
MOE      PAS       357    3-25-91    2:03p
LARRY    TXT      1024    3-31-91   10:23a
        3 File(s)     359424 bytes free
C:\>_
```

Check the directory of your *active* disk drive, and copy in the space provided below what you see on the screen. If there are more than about five directory entries, just list a couple of the first- and last-listed entries.

_____

_____

_____

_____

_____

_____

_____

Copying particular files from one disk to another

Some of our later experiments will require files from the floppy disk accompanying this lab manual. You should copy a few of these files to your active drive at this time. To do this, use the `COPY` command, specifying the file to be copied. The syntax is

```
COPY FileToBeCopied
```

Again, there must be a space between the command word and its parameter.

First copy the `SIMPLE1.PAS` file from the lab manual disk to your active disk. If `C:` is your active drive and the lab manual disk is in drive `A:`, the exchange should look as shown below. Note that we need to tell MS-DOS where to find `SIMPLE1.PAS`, so we specify the lab-manual-disk drive as part of the filename, using a backslash to separate the drivename from the filename. The destination drive needn't be specified because we are copying to the active drive.

```
C:\>COPY A:\SIMPLE1.PAS
        1 File(s) copied
```

Similarly, copy the `SIMPLE2.PAS` file to your active drive. Afterwards, request a directory listing of your active drive, and show it in the space provided below. Remove the lab manual disk from its floppy drive.

_____

_____

_____

_____

_____

_____

_____

_____

Checking for a particular file or group of files

You can request a listing for a particular file by giving its name. Suppose you check the listing for the SIMPLE1.PAS you just copied to your active drive:

```
C:\>DIR SIMPLE1.PAS
 Volume in drive C has no label
 Directory of  C:\
SIMPLE1 PAS        357    3-24-91    3:53p
        1 File(s)     15424359 bytes free
C:\>_
```

You can also ask for a listing of all files having the extension .PAS:

```
C:\>DIR *.PAS
 Volume in drive C has no label
 Directory of  C:\
SIMPLE1 PAS        357    3-24-91    3:53p
SIMPLE2 PAS        357    3-25-91    2:03p
        2 File(s)     15424359 bytes free
C:\>_
```

Here the "*" is called a **wildcard**, and it stands for any group of characters. The filespec *.PAS means "any file having any name followed by .PAS." So we got a listing of all files with the .PAS extension. This wildcard option works with most other MS-DOS commands, too.

There is also a single-character wildcard, the question mark. For example, to ask for a listing of all files with the name SIMPLE and then a single character, and with the .PAS extension, you can command DIR SIMPLE?.PAS:

```
C:\>DIR SIMPLE?.PAS
 Volume in drive C has no label
 Directory of  C:\
SIMPLE1 PAS        357    3-24-91    3:53p
SIMPLE2 PAS        357    3-25-91    2:03p
        2 File(s)     15424359 bytes free
C:\>_
```

Copying to a new floppy

Insert your *newly-formatted* floppy diskette in drive B:. (Use drive A: if you don't have a drive B:.) Make the floppy drive active and then copy the two SIMPLE files from C: to the floppy. Here's one way to do it:

```
C:\>B:
B:\>COPY C:\SIMPLE1.PAS
        1 File(s) copied
B:\>COPY C:\SIMPLE2.PAS
        1 File(s) copied
```

There is an easier way to do the same thing, using a wildcard. Show how to do it in the space provided below:

_____

_____

Try out this method and prove that it works. Note: If you already copied SIMPLE1.PAS and SIMPLE2.PAS in two stages as shown above, the wildcard method will overwrite those copies with new ones, which won't hurt anything.

Subdirectories

When you have many files on a disk, it is helpful to group the files according to their subjects, like putting files in folders in a filing cabinet. MS-DOS provides subdirectories for this purpose. To make a subdirectory on the currently active disk, give the "make directory" command MD, followed by a space and then the name of the desired subdirectory. For example, if the currently active drive is B: and you want to create on B: a subdirectory for storing Pascal source code and another subdirectory for storing the manuscript of this book, you might give the following commands:

```
B:\>MD PSOURCE
B:\>MD MSS
B:\>_
```

You can check to see if the subdirectories are really there:

```
B:\>DIR
 Volume in drive B has no label
 Directory of  B:\
SIMPLE1 PAS      357    3-24-91    3:53p
SIMPLE2 PAS      357    3-25-91    2:03p
PSOURCE    <DIR>         4-02-91   11:17a
```

```
MSS          <DIR>       4-02-91  11:17a
       5 File(s)     357376 bytes free
B:\>_
```

Do this on your floppy disk, and then display the directory. Copy below the resulting directory listing:

_____

_____

_____

_____

_____

_____

_____

_____

Now the disk has a hierarchical structure. Within the directory, there are two new, empty subdirectories. (Figure 1)

Moving around in the subdirectories

The drive prompt B:\> indicates that you are now in the directory of floppy disk B:, but outside of its subdirectories. This means that, unless you say otherwise, all commands you issue will pertain to files located in the B: directory. To move to one of the subdirectories, use the change-directory command CD. For example, to move from the B: main directory to the PSOURCE subdirectory on that disk, you would give the command

B:\>CD PSOURCE

Because you earlier gave the PROMPT PG command, the prompt now shows your location in the hierarchical directory structure:

B:\PSOURCE>

The name of your present location is B:\PSOURCE. This name

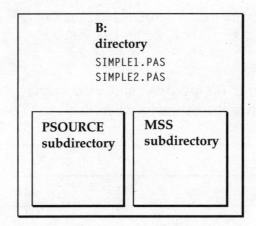

FIGURE 1. The B: directory contains two subdirectories. There are two files in the B: directory itself, but none in the subdirectories.

specifies the path by which you arrived in this subdirectory, and is called the **pathname** of the subdirectory. If you now ask for a directory listing, you find that the subdirectory is empty:

```
B:\PSOURCE>DIR
Volume in drive B has no label
Directory of B:\PSOURCE
.           <DIR>       4-02-91   11:17a
..          <DIR>       4-01-91    4:53p
      2 File(s)   357376 bytes free
B:\PSOURCE>_
```

Here is something we haven't seen before. There are no files listed—just two directories, named ".", and "..". These marks are shorthand for directories relative to the current directory—that is, the PSOURCE directory we are now in:

.   stands for "the current directory."

..   stands for "the directory of which this one
         is a subdirectory."

So if you ask for a directory listing of ".." you will see a listing of B:, which is the directory containing the PSOURCE directory.

```
B:\PSOURCE>DIR ..
 Volume in drive B has no label
 Directory of  B:\
SIMPLE1 PAS         357     3-24-91    3:53p
SIMPLE2 PAS         357     3-25-91    2:03p
PSOURCE      <DIR>          4-02-91   11:17a
```

```
MSS          <DIR>        4-02-91   11:17a
        5 File(s)      357376 bytes free
B:\PSOURCE>_
```

Try moving in and out of the subdirectories on your disk, using the commands listed above. Keep experimenting until you are comfortable with these commands.

The root directory

Another directory name used in MS-DOS is "\," all by itself, which stands for **root directory**. The root directory is the main directory of the disk, the parent of the highest-level subdirectories. On our example disk, the root is B: itself:

```
B:\PSOURCE>DIR \
 Volume in drive B has no label
 Directory of  B:\
SIMPLE1 PAS       357    3-24-91     3:53p
SIMPLE2 PAS       357    3-25-91     2:03p
PSOURCE       <DIR>      4-02-91    11:17a
MSS           <DIR>      4-02-91    11:17a
        5 File(s)      357376 bytes free
B:\PSOURCE>_
```

Subdirectories within subdirectories

You are still in the PSOURCE subdirectory. Suppose you make two new subdirectories within PSOURCE:

```
B:\>PSOURCE>MD OLDP
B:\>PSOURCE>MD NEWP
```

Now a directory listing shows the new second-level subdirectories:

```
B:\PSOURCE>DIR
Volume in drive B has no label
Directory of B:\PSOURCE
.             <DIR>      4-02-91    11:17a
..            <DIR>      4-01-91     4:53p
OLDP          <DIR>      4-02-91    12:53p
NEWP          <DIR>      4-02-91    12:53p
        2 File(s)      355328 bytes free
B:\PSOURCE>_
```

You now have the hierarchical directory structure of Figure 2.

To move down to the `OLDP` subdirectory, you again use the change directory command:

```
B:\PSOURCE>CD OLDP
B:\PSOURCE\OLDP>_
```

You are now in the `OLDP` subdirectory, whose pathname is `B:\PSOURCE\OLDP`.

Perform all of these operations on your floppy disk. Do not continue until you have completed them.

Exercises

Suppose your root directory for drive `B:` contains a subdirectory called `ONE`, which in turn contains a subdirectory called `TWO`. To begin with, you are in the root directory. Then you change to subdirectory `ONE`. Here is what you see:

```
B>CD ONE
B>_
```

Why don't you see the name of the subdirectory in the new prompt?

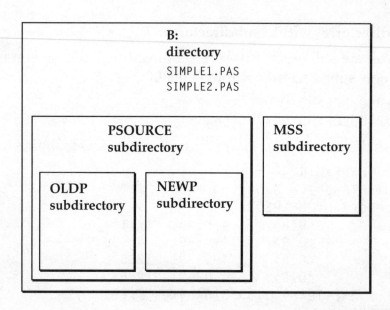

FIGURE 2. *The B: directory is parent to the two subdirectories PSOURCE and MSS. Within the PSOURCE subdirectory, there are now two subdirectories called OLDP and NEWP.*

At this point, if you give the command "DIR .", what directory will you see?

If you give the command "DIR ..", what directory will you see?

Copying files into the current subdirectory

Suppose you want copies of the files SIMPLE1.PAS and SIMPLE2.PAS in your OLDP subdirectory. You can copy them to the current subdirectory with the command

```
B:\PSOURCE\OLDP>COPY \SIMPLE1.PAS
        1 File(s) copied
B:\PSOURCE\OLDP>COPY \SIMPLE2.PAS
        1 File(s) copied
B:\PSOURCE\OLDP>_
```

Here the name \SIMPLE1.PAS means "the file named SIMPLE1.PAS in the root directory."

It is simpler, however, to use a wildcard to copy all files with extension .PAS in one operation:

```
B:\PSOURCE\OLDP>COPY \*.PAS
B:\SIMPLE1.PAS
B:\SIMPLE2.PAS
        2 File(s) copied
B:\PSOURCE\OLDP>_
```

You now have two files in the OLDP subdirectory. (Use DIR to check this.) The complete names of these files include their path-names:

```
\PSOURCE\OLDP\SIMPLE1.PAS
\PSOURCE\OLDP\SIMPLE2.PAS
```

Copying to another subdirectory

Suppose you want to copy a file to the PSOURCE subdirectory while you are in the OLDP subdirectory. To do this, you use a form of the COPY command in which you specify both the source and the destination of the file to be copied. The form of the command is

```
COPY <SourceFilePathname> <DestinationFilePathname>
```

For example, if you want to copy the file SIMPLE1.PAS into the PSOURCE subdirectory, but you want the copy to have the filename ASSIGN1A.TXT, you would give the command as follows. *Note that pathnames cannot contain embedded blanks.*

```
B:\PSOURCE\OLDP>COPY \SIMPLE1.PAS \PSOURCE\ASSIGN1A.TXT
        1 File(s) copied
B:\PSOURCE\OLDP>_
```

If you now ask for a directory listing of the parent subdirectory of the current OLDP subdirectory, you see the new file ASSIGN1A.TXT:

```
B:\PSOURCE\OLDP>DIR ..
Volume in drive B has no label
Directory of B:\PSOURCE
.             <DIR>      4-02-91   11:17a
..            <DIR>      4-01-91    4:53p
OLDP          <DIR>      4-02-91   12:53p
NEWP          <DIR>      4-02-91   12:53p
ASSIGN1A TXT     357     3-31-91   10:23a
        3 File(s)    352923 bytes free
B:\PSOURCE\OLDP>_
```

Deleting files

Now that you have copied the original files into subdirectories, suppose you want to delete the original files from the root. You can change to the root directory and then delete the files one by one. *WARNING! BE SURE THAT THE DELETION COMMAND IS CORRECT BEFORE YOU PRESS THE ENTER KEY!*

```
B:\PSOURCE\OLDP>CD \
B:\>DEL SIMPLE1.PAS
B:\>DEL SIMPLE2.PAS
B:\>_
```

A faster method is to delete all files by using wildcards for the filename and for the extension. This is potentially such a dangerous command that DOS asks for confirmation before carrying it out:

```
B:\>
Are you sure <Y/N>?Y
B:\>_
```

If you now ask for a directory listing, you will see that the files have been erased from the root directory, but the subdirectories and their contained files remain. In the space below, draw a diagram of the directory structure after performing all of the described operations.

Summary of common MS-DOS commands

In the following summary, items in angle brackets indicate where parameters are to be inserted.

`CD <target directoryname>`
Change directory: make the named directory active.

`CD ..`
Change directory: activate the parent of the present subdirectory.

`CD \`
Change directory: make the root directory active.

`CLS`
Clear the screen.

`COPY <source> <destination>`
Copy the source file(s), placing the copy at the named destination. Source and destination are both pathnames.

`COPY <source>`
Copy the source file(s), placing the copy in the active subdirectory, with the same filename.

`DATE`
Set the current date.

`DEL <filename>`
Delete (erase) the named file. *WARNING! Once you give this command, you will be unable to recover the file by ordinary means!*

`DIR`
List items in the active directory.

`DIR <directoryname>`
List items in the named directory.

`DIR <directoryname> /P`
List items in the named directory, pausing at the bottom of the screen if there are too many files to show at once.

`DISKCOPY`
Make a copy of an entire disk. *WARNING! This erases previous contents of the destination disk!*

`EDIT`
Invokes a full-screen editor. (DOS 5.x)

`FORMAT <drivename>`
Format the disk in the named drive. *WARNING: This erases previous contents!*

`HELP <command>`
Provides information about a DOS command. (DOS 5.x)

`LABEL <drivename>`
Give a name to the disk in the named drive.

`MD <directoryname>`
Make a new subdirectory having the given name.

`PRINT <filename>`
Print the named file.

`RD <directoryname>`
Remove (delete) the named subdirectory.

`REN <oldname> <newname>`
Rename a given item.

`TIME`
Set the current time.

`TYPE <filename>`
Display the named file on the screen. (Only works with text files.)

`UNDELETE <filename>`
Restores a deleted file under some circumstances. (DOS 5.x)

Wildcards

`*`

Means all filenames or all extensions. For example, `*.*` means all filenames and all extensions; `*.PAS` means all filenames with the `.PAS` extension; `S1.*` means all files with the name `S1`, no matter what the extension.

`?`

Stands for any character at the indicated position. For example, `SIMPLE?.PAS` means any file having a seven-character filename starting with `SIMPLE`, and having the `.PAS` extension.

Important key commands

To abort a running program: Control-C.
To send end-of-file: Control-Z.
To reboot the machine (warm boot):   Alt-Control-Delete.
To print the current screen on paper: PrtScr

Using a mouse or trackball

PC software is becoming visual, using a point-and-select method for giving commands. This is done with a pointing device like a mouse or trackball. With such a device, there are three important techniques: clicking, double-clicking, and dragging.

To **click** on a screen object, you move the pointing device until the tip of the screen pointer lies on the desired object, then you click the left mouse button. (This is called **left-clicking.**) This technique is usually used to select an object on the screen so that some task can be performed.

Double-clicking is the same, except that you click the left mouse button twice in rapid succession. This technique is often used to open and close windows on the screen.

To **drag** a screen object, you left-click on the object but then hold the device's button down while moving the screen pointer. This technique is used to move objects on the screen or to select from pull-down menus.

In most software, the righthand mouse button either does nothing or can be set up to perform some other function, like requesting on-line help. Further information on this subject will be found in your software manual. Also see Figure 3.

Redirecting I/O to the printer

MS-DOS provides an easy way to make a paper record of a run, a process called **echo printing**. (This may not work on a network, however!) At the DOS prompt, key Control-P or Control-Print-Screen to turn on echo printing. Then all inputs and outputs appearing before the next Control-P or Control-PrintScreen will be copied to the printer as well as the screen. (To use this with a Turbo Pascal program, you must first save the executable code for the program as a .EXE file. This is done by selecting "Destination Disk" from Turbo's Compile menu before compiling and linking. Then exit the Turbo environment to perform the echo printing.)

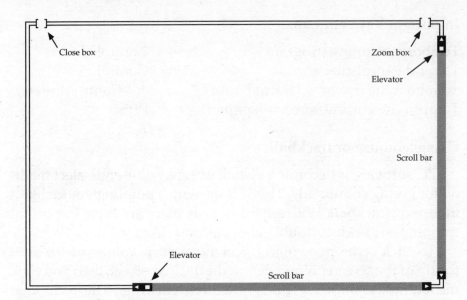

FIGURE 3. Mouse control points in a typical MS-DOS window. To close a window, left-click on the close box. To make the window larger or smaller, left-click on the zoom box. To scroll the contents of the window, either click in the vertical or horizontal scroll bar or drag that bar's elevator box.

If you want to send only a program's outputs, but not its inputs, to the printer, you can make use of the MS-DOS output redirection operator, ">." Here is an example in which `PROG1.EXE` is run, with its outputs redirected to the printer:

```
C:\>PROG1 >PRN
```

This method can also be used to send outputs to a text file:

```
C:\>PROG1 >ASSIGN1.TXT
```

MS-DOS also provides an input-redirection operator denoted by "<." Here is an example in which `PROG1.EXE` is executed with its inputs coming from the `INDATA.TXT` file and its outputs going to the `OUTDATA.TXT` file:

```
C:\>PROG1 <INDATA.TXT >OUTDATA.TXT
```

Where do I learn more?

MS-DOS is a complicated study in itself; whole books have been written about it. One of the best introductions is Van Wolverton's *Running MS-DOS*, fifth edition (Microsoft Press, 1991).

Lab 1.2:
Using a Macintosh

Materials required: Apple Macintosh® computer, with either two floppy drives or a hard drive and a floppy drive. Also, a blank floppy disk and a copy of the floppy that came with this lab manual.

Concepts: Operating system; booting; formatting; folders; files.

Lab techniques: Learning by experimenting.

Prerequisite: Basic computer literacy; read Chapter 1 of *Structures and Abstractions*. If you have it, this is good time to run the "Tour" disk supplied by Apple.

What is an operating system?

The set of programs that controls the computer hardware, providing the user environment in which programs can be conveniently run, is called the *operating system*. The operating system for Macintosh computers is loaded into main memory from a floppy or hard disk, and is therefore called a disk operating system. (On other computer systems, but not usually on the Mac, this is abbreviated DOS and pronounced "doss.") Different computer systems have different operating systems; the Mac's operating system is well-known for its visual appearance and its use of a mouse or trackball as a pointing device. The following is a series of experiments to introduce you to this environment. We assume that you have at least two disk drives in your machine—either two floppy drives or a floppy drive and a hard drive.

Turning on the machine

On the smaller Macs with integral monitors, like the Mac Plus, the SE, and the Classic, you turn on the machine with the power switch located on the rear of the machine. In Mac II–series machines, the On switch is located at the top right of the keyboard.

Loading the operating system from a hard disk

When you turn on the computer's power, the operating system is not yet running; it must be loaded into the computer's memory from external disk storage. In many Macintoshes, the operating system is loaded automatically from a hard disk, and all you have to do is to turn on the machine and wait for the system to load. Your instructor will tell you if this is the case with your machine, or you can turn on your machine and see what happens.

Loading the operating system from a floppy disk

In Macintoshes lacking a hard disk, the operating system is loaded into memory from a floppy disk. You can tell if your machine is like this: turn on the machine. If your Macintosh shows only a picture of a floppy disk, you must insert a system floppy disk into one of the disk drive slots. (It doesn't matter which slot you use.)

Loading the operating system is called *booting* the system

No matter whether your machine loads the operating system from the hard disk or from a floppy, the loading process is called *booting* the computer. (Short for "bootstrapping.") The process starts with the instructions wired into the ROM circuits of the computer, telling the CPU how to start up and how to load further

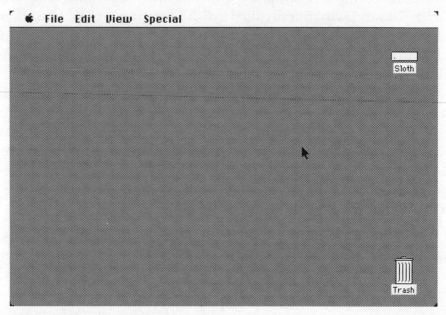

FIGURE 1. This symbolic picture of a desktop is an example of what you might see after booting a Macintosh from a hard disk named "Sloth." At the top left, you see five menus of commands. At the lower right is a trash can for discarded items. At center right is a mouse pointer representing the relative position of the mouse on your desktop. This machine was last shut down with the Sloth disk's window closed, so you can't see what's stored in the disk. Another possible startup screen is shown in Figure 3.

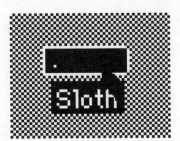

FIGURE 2. *If you can't see what is stored in the Sloth disk, move the mouse pointer so its tip lies within the Sloth icon, then press the mouse button twice, in quick succession. (This is called "double-clicking.") The icon will "open up" to show a window containing icons for the objects stored in the disk, as shown in Figure 3. If the machine was last shut down with Sloth's window open, the window will be open when you boot the machine.*

operating system instructions from the appropriate disk. Once the operating system has booted, a picture of your metaphorical "desktop" appears on the screen, displaying icons (symbolic pictures) of the disks loaded into your machine, menus of commands, and a trash can for throwing away whatever you don't want. This is shown in Figures 1–3. At this point, your computer is under the control of an operating system program called the Finder.

The desktop metaphor

As the operating system is copied into memory from a disk, the screen first displays a "Welcome to Macintosh" message, then displays a stylized picture of the *desktop*, as shown in Figure 1 or Figure 3. The desktop is an iconic representation of the top of a desk surface, viewed from above, with various objects lying on it. You can drag the objects around on your desktop, open them up to see what's inside, and give commands selected from the menus. We will describe these operations one by one.

You point with a mouse

To perform the various desktop operations, the Macintosh uses a mouse as a pointing device. A mouse is, of course, a palm-sized box with a rolling ball or optical sensor on the bottom and one or more switches on the top. By moving the mouse around on your table or desk surface, you signal the computer to move a pointer around on the screen. (See Figures 1 and 2.) In place of a mouse, some Macintoshes are equipped with a trackball, which is like an

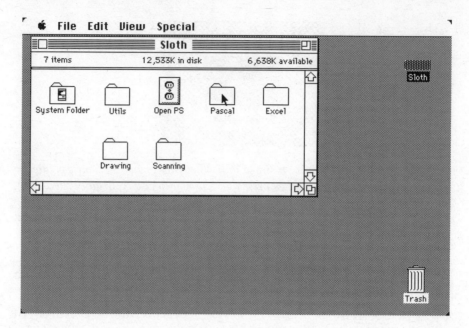

FIGURE 3. *After booting your system, you may see a screen like this, in which the boot disk's icon is already open, showing a window into the disk contents. The disk's window shows the disk's name at the top. Inside, there are icons for programs, documents, and folders containing other programs, documents, and folders. If your system booted to a screen like Figure 1, you can double-click on the disk icon at upper right to see a window like the one shown here, as explained in Figure 2.*

upside-down mouse. A trackball remains in one place on your work surface; you roll the ball with your thumb or fingers.

The mouse pointer on the screen looks like an arrow when you are performing graphical operations. The *tip* of the arrow is the precise spot at which you are pointing: when you want to point at an object, *the tip of the arrow must lie within that object*. As you will see later, the arrow changes to an "I-beam" when you are editing text. In that case, the vertical and horizontal bars of the I-beam indicate a character position in the text.

Clicking, dragging and double-clicking

The mouse or trackball is used for three basic operations—selection, moving, and opening. To *select* an item for some operation to be performed, you move the mouse pointer tip onto the icon, then, while holding the pointer there, click the mouse button once. The icon will darken to indicate that the object has been selected. This mouse operation is called *clicking* on the object.

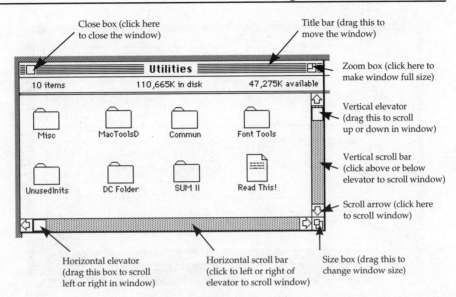

FIGURE 4. *Each window contains icons for its own controls. With the help of the mouse, you can move the window, close it, scroll it, or change its size.*

To *move* an icon to a new position on the screen, you click on the object but then hold the mouse button down while moving the mouse pointer to the desired position. The selected object will move with the pointer. When the icon is in the desired position, release the mouse pointer. It feels like you are dropping the icon in the new position. This mouse operation is called *dragging*.

When you want to *open* an icon to see what's in it, or open a program in order to run it, you *double-click* on the icon. This means that you click twice in rapid succession. If the second click is delayed, the effect will be the same as if you single-clicked. Double-clicking is illustrated in Figures 2 and 3.

The window metaphor

When you want to see the contents of an icon, you open a *window* into it, either by double-clicking on the icon (the easy way) or by means of the **Open** command in the **File** menu. A window is a display rectangle that can show the contents of an object. Windows are controlled with the mouse, using various control tools attached to the window. You can open and close windows, change their shapes and sizes, and scroll their contents. See Figure 4.

There are various kinds of windows. When you are running the Finder and therefore looking at the desktop, windows are used to

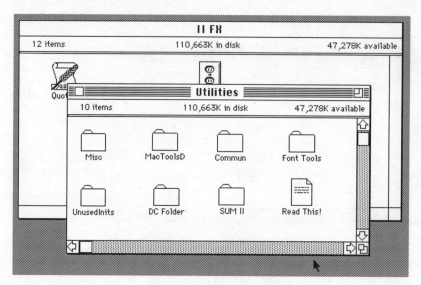

FIGURE 5. In this example, the Utilities window is active, as indicated by the lines visible in its title bar. The other window is inactive.

see the files and folders within disk icons. In other words, they are used to see what other computer systems call *directories* of files. But when you are running an application (a program), windows are used to see textual and graphical data being manipulated by the program.

The active window

More than one window can be open at a time, but only one window will be in use at a given moment. The *active window* is the one on which you are currently performing operations, and it is indicated by horizontal lines in its title bar. The active window will also lie in front of other windows that overlap it. See Figure 5.

If the active window has too many icons to be displayed at one time with the current window size, the window will display horizontal and vertical scroll bars. As indicated in Figure 4, the mouse can be used to scroll the contents of the window, or you can click on the zoom box to expand the window.

Opening folders

Inside the window of a disk, you will almost certainly see folders. A folder can hold files and other folders. To see what's in a folder, you double-click on it. This opens up a window showing the contents. As an experiment, look through the folders on your system disk and see if you can find a file called THINK Pascal. (Look for an icon with this name that is not a folder.) Record the location of THINK Pascal below:

_____

_____

_____

Opening a file

Once you find the THINK Pascal file, look carefully at the icon. Note that the icon contains a graphic, and doesn't look like a folder. Compare the icon to another in the same folder. There will probably be some non-folder icons that look different from the THINK Pascal icon. This is because there are two kinds of files on the Macintosh: there are *applications* and there are *documents* that belong to applications. The word "application" is Macintosh jargon for a *program*. THINK Pascal is an application, and it has a special icon—a computer with hands on the keyboard—reserved for that application. In the same folder, or in one of the folders inside, you will find icons with names like `Runtime.lib` and `Interface.lib`. These are documents containing code to be used with THINK Pascal, and their distinctive icons reflect that.

As an experiment, open the THINK Pascal application by double-clicking on it. You will be presented with a screen like one of those shown in Figure 6. If there is a dialogue box in the middle of the screen, click on the **Cancel** button in this box in order to close the box. Then hold down the **Command** key (the one at the lower left with a cloverleaf on it) and while holding it down, press the **Q** key. You are giving the **Command-Q** signal to quit the THINK Pascal application. This should send you back to the desktop view from which you launched the program. Describe your experience here:

_____

_____

_____

Now close the windows that you opened while searching for THINK Pascal, leaving only the disk window open.

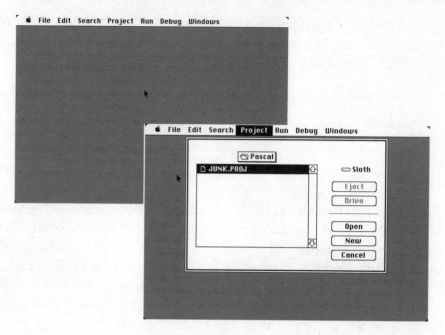

FIGURE 6. *When you open the THINK Pascal application, you will be presented with a screen like one of these, depending on how your THINK Pascal has been configured by previous users.*

Using a menu

In the previous example, you quit from THINK Pascal by giving a key-command, but you could have accomplished the same thing by using a *menu*. This business of menus will come up repeatedly, so let's try out one of the Finder's menus. (You *are* back on the desktop, aren't you? If not, return there now, as instructed in the previous paragraph.)

At the top of the screen are the five Finder menus. From left to right, they are the **Apple**, **File**, **Edit**, **View**, and **Special** menus. When you click on one of these, a menu drops down from the top of the screen and remains visible as long as you continue to press the mouse button. To select a command from the menu, drag down through the menu until your desired command is darkened, then release the mouse button.

Try an experiment. Click on one of the folders visible in the open window. This selects the folder. Then pull down the **File** menu and select **Open**. Note that the effect is the same as if you double-clicked on the folder: the folder opens up and you see a window into its contents.

Now with the folder open, select **Print Directory** from the **File** menu. (First make sure that your printer is turned on.) What happens? Your instructor may want you to turn in the results.

Not all menu commands are active at a given time

Note that in a typical menu, some of the selections are "grayed." Such selections are not available at the moment because they don't apply under the current conditions. Try an experiment. Close all the open windows on the desktop and then click in the blank central area of the screen to deselect all disks. Now pull down the **File** menu. Which menu commands have become unavailable because you have no active window and no active disk?

Formatting or initializing a floppy disk

Before you can store data or programs on a new floppy diskette, the diskette must have some initial data written on it, marking the sectors in which data can be stored. This process is called **initializing**, **formatting**, or **erasing** the diskette. *WARNING! FORMATTING A DISKETTE ERASES ANY PREVIOUS CONTENTS! THEREFORE, YOU SHOULD FORMAT ONLY NEW DISKETTES OR DISKETTES WHOSE CONTENTS ARE NO LONGER NEEDED.*

You can format a brand-new diskette or one that has been used previously. When you load a brand-new diskette into a disk drive, the Macintosh will detect the new disk and lead you through a sequence of questions about formatting. You reply to the Mac's questions by clicking on the appropriate buttons and entering a name for the disk. See Figure 7.

The Mac will ask permission to format the diskette. Once you give permission, the Mac may ask—depending on the type of disk drive you have—whether to format both sides of the disk, or only one. Normally, you format *both* sides. Finally, the Mac will ask you to name the diskette.

You should format a brand-new diskette at this time, for use in the following experiments. Report your observations below; your machine may behave differently from the figure, depending on the model of disk drive you are using.

Did your system behave as shown in Figure 7? If not, describe what happened:

_____

_____

_____

_____

_____

_____

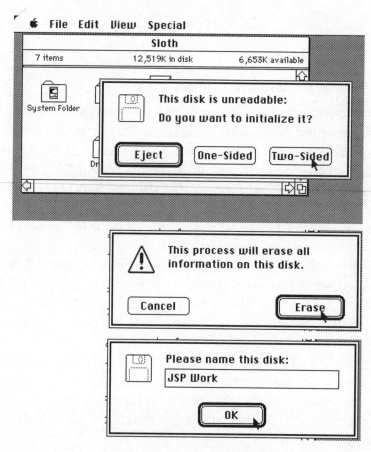

FIGURE 7. When you insert a new, unformatted floppy disk in a drive slot, the Macintosh recognizes that the disk is unreadable and leads you through a sequence of dialogue boxes as it asks you what to do. You reply by clicking on the appropriate buttons.

Erasing a previously-initialized disk

You can also format a previously-formatted disk, in which case *the previous contents are lost*. To do this, insert the diskette into a disk drive—it doesn't matter which—and make sure the disk's icon is selected. (If it is, it will darken.) Then drag down the **Special** menu at the top of the screen, down to the **Erase Disk** command. When this command is darkened, release the mouse button. You will then be presented with a dialogue like the one at the bottom of Figure 8.

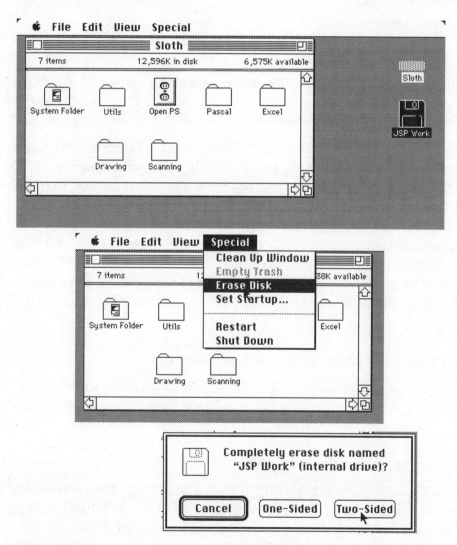

FIGURE 8. The sequence of steps in reformatting (erasing) a floppy disk. (1) Click on the disk's icon to select it. (2) Select Erase Disk from the Special menu. (3) Click on the appropriate box to tell the Mac whether you want a single- or double-sided floppy. Normally, you will want a double-sided floppy.

Files and filenames

Data and programs are saved on mass storage in the form of files, which are sequences of symbols collected together under a single name. On the Macintosh, a *filename* can consist of up to 32 upper- or lowercase characters, including spaces and most symbols. However, a filename cannot contain a colon (:) because colons are used in specifying the path to reach a file within nested folders, as in *DiskName:FolderName:FolderName:FileName*. The following are all legal filenames:

```
StuffAndNonsense          Down Home 10/21
Stuff and Nonsense        Spending $148.95
Simple1.pas               1234
```

Note: Folder names have the same rules as filenames.

Creating a new folder

To create a new folder, select **New** from the **File** menu. You can accomplish the same thing more quickly by keying **Command-N**. The Command key is the one near the lower left corner, marked with the cloverleaf symbol. To enter Command-N, hold down the Command key while pressing the N key briefly. A new folder will appear on the screen, with the name Empty Folder. This folder will automatically be selected, as indicated by its dark color. Just enter the name you want to give the folder and then press Return or click the mouse outside of the folder. Your new name will be given to the folder.

Changing the name of an existing folder or file

To change the name of a folder or file, click on the icon to select it, then enter the name that you want it to have. Then press Return or click somewhere else, and your new name will be in effect.

Changing *part* of the filename

If you need to change only *part* of a filename, click on the icon to select it, then drag through the erroneous portion of the filename. This portion alone will be darkened, indicating that it is the only portion selected. Then type in the correction. The new letters will replace the old ones.

Deleting a file or folder

To delete a file or folder, you simply drag its icon into the trash can icon, and release the mouse button. The trash can will swell to show that something's inside. The deleted item is not yet gone, however: if you double-click on the trash can, you can see that your item is inside. To get rid of the item—that is, to make the operating system forget it existed—you empty the trash. You can do this manually, by selecting **Empty Trash** in the **Special** menu. Otherwise, the trash will be emptied automatically when you shut down the computer, start up a program, or eject a floppy from which items were discarded.

Changing the window view

The objects in a window can be displayed in several forms. The default form of display is in the form of detailed icons, as we have seen so far. However, if there are many objects in the window, the detailed icons may take up too much space on the screen. Therefore, the Mac also lets you display the objects as smaller icons or a list of names. Click on a window to make it active, then pull down the **View** menu. Select various forms of display and see what they look

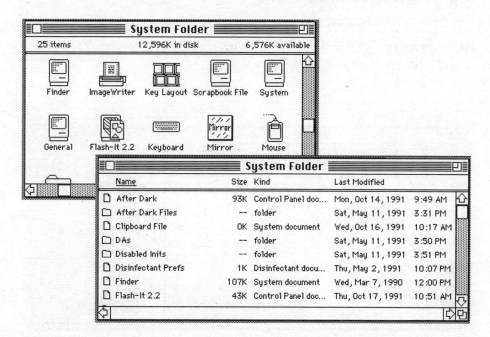

FIGURE 9. A System Folder, as it looks when displayed with Icon View, and again with Names View. The viewing mode is controlled from the View menu.

like. Figure 9 shows a window as it looks when displaying icons, then again when displaying a list of names. For most purposes, viewing files by **Name** is the most useful choice. Once you select a viewing mode, it remains in effect for that window until you make another choice.

Copying particular files from one disk to another

Some of our later experiments will require files from the floppy disk accompanying this lab manual. You should copy a few of these files to your boot disk at this time. To do this, insert the Lab Manual floppy into one of your floppy drives. When the disk has been loaded, open its window by double-clicking on the disk icon, if necessary. Then double-click on the LM1 folder to open it.

First copy the SIMPLE1.PAS file from the lab manual disk to your boot disk. Just drag the SIMPLE1.PAS icon from the LM1 window to the disk icon for your boot disk. Then release the mouse button to "drop" the file onto your boot disk. (Figure 10.) Alternatively, you can drag the icon into the boot disk's window, and release it there.

Copying several files at once

Copying several files is done in the same way, but first you must select all of the files to be copied. There are two ways to make multiple selections:

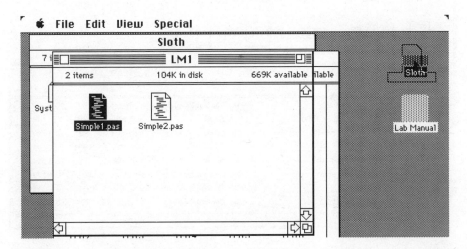

FIGURE 10. *Drag the Simple1.pas file icon from the LM1 window to your boot disk icon and release it there. This is how you copy a file from the Lab Manual disk to your boot disk.*

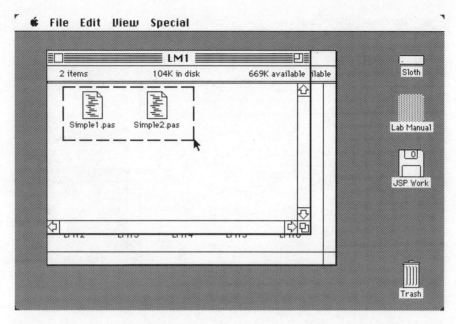

FIGURE 11. Icons that are grouped together can be selected together by lassoing them. Start at the upper left and drag down toward the lower right until the dotted selection rectangle encloses the icons to be selected.

1. Click on all of the files while holding the Shift key down.

2. If the files are shown as icons and the icons are grouped together, you can lasso all of them, by dragging from a point above them and to the left, down to a point below them and to the right. As you drag down and to the right, you will see a dotted *selection rectangle* form. When this rectangle encloses all files you want to copy, release the mouse button. (See Figure 11.)

Copying a file into a folder

To copy a file into a folder, drag the file's icon onto the folder, so that the folder darkens, then release the mouse button.

Copying an entire floppy disk, using two floppy drives

You should make an extra copy of the floppy disk that accompanies this lab manual. After all, something could happen to the original, and you don't want to damage your only copy. It's far better to make a copy right away and put the original away in a safe place, away from heat and magnetic fields.

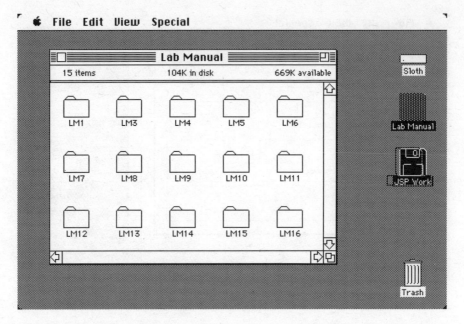

FIGURE 12. *If you have two floppy drives, you can copy one diskette onto another one directly. Just load the two diskettes into the floppy drives and drag the original diskette's icon onto the copy diskette's icon.*

Format another blank disk and name it LabMan. (If you feel this is sexist, name it LM or LabWoman or something.) Insert both this blank disk and the original Lab Manual disk into floppy drives. You should then see both disk icons on the screen. Drag the disk icon for the original Lab Manual disk over onto the disk icon for the new disk, and release it there. (Figure 12.) You will see a dialogue box asking you whether you really want to replace the contents of Lab Man with the contents of Lab Manual. If you say yes, the copying process will proceed, making Lab Man a duplicate of Lab Manual.

Copying an entire floppy disk, using a single floppy drive

If you have only one floppy drive, you won't be able to copy diskettes as easily as if you had two. Here's the fastest way to do it, assuming that you have a hard disk:

1. Drag your floppy disk icon onto your hard disk icon or into the window for your hard disk. This will *not* destroy the previous contents of the hard disk, but will create a new folder on the hard disk, containing the contents of your floppy. The folder will have the same name as the original floppy.

2. Remove the original floppy from the disk drive.

3. Insert a newly formatted floppy into the drive or format a new one now.

4. Copy the contents of the floppy folder to the new diskette. To do this, open the folder on the hard disk, key Command-A (for **Select All**), then drag the selected files into the new disk's icon or window.

MultiFinder

The Finder allows you to have only one application loaded into RAM at a time. On Macintoshes with a lot of RAM, you have the option of running a more powerful version of Finder, called MultiFinder. MultiFinder, as you can guess, lets you load multiple applications into RAM and switch instantly from one to the next. (Don't try this on a system with less than 2 Megabytes of RAM; in fact, 4 Megabytes would be better.) Either Finder or MultiFinder is loaded into memory as the machine starts up, according to the settings specified with the **Set Startup...** selection in the **Special** menu. After changing the settings, the Macintosh must be restarted in order for the changes to take effect.

You can tell at a glance if your machine is currently running MultiFinder. If it is, you will see an icon in the upper right corner of the screen, indicating what program is currently being used. By clicking on this icon, you can switch instantly among the programs currently loaded into RAM.

How to restart the machine if a program crashes

Every once in a while, a program may go haywire and *crash the operating system*. To be specific, the machine may lock up and refuse to respond to the mouse or the keyboard. You may even see a "bomb message" on the screen—an operating system error message with a picture of a bomb with a lit fuse. (How cute!)

In such a situation, you must restart your machine: that is, reset the hardware and reboot the operating system. There are three ways to do this, depending on the nature of the error and the model of Macintosh you are using.

1. If you have a bomb message on the screen, just click the Restart button displayed with the message.

2. Otherwise, press the Restart button—the frontmost of the pair of buttons on the side of your machine. (This is the front half of what Apple calls the "programmer's switch," in tacit admission that programmers crash their systems more than other computer users.) Unfortunately, not all Macs are equipped with a programmer's switch.

3. If you can't use methods 1 or 2, shut off the power to your machine, wait ten seconds, then start it up again.

Shutting down the machine

When you are finished using your Macintosh, *don't just turn off the power!* Instead, exit from any programs you are running and return to the desktop. From there, select Shut Down in the Special menu. This command will terminate any running programs and save the configuration of the desktop before shutting off the machine.

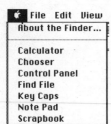

The Apple menu in brief

The Apple menu (at the top far left of the screen) displays the desk accessories (DAs) installed in your system. These are frequently-needed utility programs that can be run in upper memory even when you are running another program. Because there are ways to install and deinstall many desk accessories, your Apple menu may not look like the one shown here. We show a typical assortment of standard desk accessories.

About . . .
Gives information about the program currently running. When you are on the desktop, this will say **About the Finder . . . .**

Calculator
Provides a pop-up four-function calculator.

Chooser
A program that sets up the Macintosh to talk to whatever printer you have installed. Run this program whenever you try to print, but get no printer dialogue box.

Control Panel

Used to control many of the Macintosh's hardware and operating system parameters, like the time, the desktop background, the beep, and so on.

Find File

Used to find files when you can't remember where they are buried in the folders. Just give it a filename or part of a filename, and set it running by clicking on the Run button. After your filename appears in the box, click on it to see where it is in the folder system.

Key Caps

Displays the characters corresponding to the keys of the keyboard, when using the currently-selected font.

Note Pad

Used for recording short messages that you might want to see later.

Scrapbook

Used for saving multiple chunks of text or diagrams copied or cut using the commands in the edit menu. These saved items can later be cut or copied from the scrapbook and pasted into other documents.

The File menu in brief

New Folder (equivalent to **Command-N**)
Creates a new empty folder, initially named Empty Folder. The folder appears in the window that is currently open.

Open (equivalent to **Command-O** or **double-clicking**)
Opens the currently selected object. If the object is an application (a program), this command runs the program.

Print
Prints a document. This command is available only when the selected object is a printable document.

Close (equivalent to **Command-W**)
Closes the selected object. If the object is the currently running program, this command terminates the program.

Get Info (equivalent to **Command-I**)
Displays information about the currently selected object, including size in bytes, date of creation, and so on.

Duplicate (equivalent to **Command-D**)
Creates a copy of the selected object, with the name `Copy of....`

Put Away
When an object has been pulled from a folder out to the desktop or placed in the trash, this command can be used to put it back where it came from. (After the trash has been emptied, it's too late . . . .)

Page Setup
Selects page layout for printing.

Print Directory
Prints a list of all objects in the currently selected window or folder.

Eject (equivalent to **Command-E**)
Ejects the selected floppy diskette, leaving its icon on the screen. Note: Floppies can also be ejected from the two disk drives by keying **Commmand-Shift-1** and **Command-Shift-2**.

The Edit menu in brief

Undo (equivalent to **Command-Z**)
Reverses the effect of the previous editing command.

Cut (equivalent to **Command-X**)
Removes selected text and places it in the Clipboard.

Copy (equivalent to **Command-C**)
Copies selected text to the clipboard.

Paste (equivalent to **Command-V**)
Inserts a copy of the contents of the clipboard at the current insertion point.

Clear
Discards the selected text.

Select All (equivalent to **Command-A**)
Selects all objects in the current window.

Show Clipboard
Displays a window into the clipboard.

The View menu in brief

by Small Icon
Displays objects in current window as small icons, but gives no information about them.

by Icon (the default)
Displays objects in current window as large icons, but gives no information about them.

by Name
Lists objects in current window sorted by name. Also shows their sizes, types, and dates/times of last modification.

by Date
Lists objects in current window by name, sorted by date/time of last modification. Also shows their sizes and types.

by Size
Lists objects in current window by name, sorted by size. Also shows their types and dates/times of last modification.

by Kind
Lists objects in current window by name, sorted by type. Also shows their sizes and dates and times of last modification.

The Special menu in brief

Clean Up Window
Arranges the icons in the current window in an orderly fashion.

Empty Trash
Discards the contents of the trash can. *After this command is given, it is too late to retrieve items from the trash!*

Erase Disk
Reformats the selected disk.

Set Startup . . .
Designates the currently selected application (program) to run automatically when the Macintosh is started up.

Restart
Resets the hardware and reboots the system. The same effect can be achieved with the programmer's button on the side of the machine.

Shut Down

Closes any open applications, saves the desktop configuration, and shuts down the machine. *Use this method to shut down your Macintosh—don't just turn off the power!* If you just turn off the power, the desktop configuration will not be saved and the desktop will have to be rebuilt the next time you turn on the machine.

Where do I learn more?

The Macintosh is a user-friendly machine. Now that you know how to perform the basic operations, you can usually figure out the others by experimentation. When you need more help, however, you should look in the Macintosh Reference Manual that comes with your machine. Another useful source is *The Macintosh Bible*, by Sharon Zardetto Aker and Arthur Naiman, published by Goldstein & Blair. This sprightly book is revised frequently.

Lab 1.3:
Using Turbo Pascal (Versions 5.0/5.5/6.0/TPW)

Materials required: MS-DOS computer system equipped with Turbo Pascal, version 5.0, 5.5, 6.0, or Turbo Pascal for Windows (TPW). Also, a floppy disk on which to save your work.

Concepts: Turbo Pascal IDE; editor; compiler; linker; syntax error; source code and machine code.

Lab techniques: Learning to use the Turbo environment by experimentation; using the compiler to check for simple syntax errors.

Prerequisites: Lab 1.1; Section 1.6 in the Turbo edition of *Structures and Abstractions* (Section 1.5 in the ANSI edition).

To start Turbo from DOS, boot up your machine and load the Turbo disk. If necessary, move to the subdirectory containing the Turbo program. Then key in the command TURBO and press the Enter key. The Turbo Integrated Development Environment (IDE) will appear on the screen. If are using version 5.0, 5.5, 6.0, or Turbo Pascal for Windows, the screen will look more or less like Figure 1.

FIGURE 1. The initial screen in Turbo Pascal version 6.0. Versions 5.0 and 5.5 lack the Search, Window, and Break/Watch menus; Turbo Pascal for Windows lacks the Debug menu and the command list at the bottom of the screen. The bars and boxes are for mouse operations, as shown in Figure 3 of Lab 1.1.

There is a **menu bar** across the top of the screen and a **list of commands** across the bottom. In between, there is a large **editing window** in which you create and edit your Pascal source code.

Taking a cue from the commands list, press the F1 function key and you will see a help message explaining the purpose of the editing window. When you are finished reading the message, press ESCape to make it go away. Wherever you are in the IDE, you can press F1 for help, then ESC to go back to what you were doing.

To use the menus, press the F10 function key. The last-used menu will light up, indicating that the menu is now active. Press Enter to pull the menu down. Use the left and right arrow keys to move to other menus. Try this out for a minute, to familiarize yourself with the contents of the menus. Notice two things:

- The title of each menu starts with a highlighted or capitalized letter. When editing, you can press the **Alt** key and this letter to activate the corresponding menu. Within a menu, each item contains a highlighted letter. While the menu is active, this letter is a shorthand way of issuing the corresponding command. We will discuss some examples shortly.

- The most used menu items also list a function key. The function key is the fastest way to issue the corresponding command while editing, and doesn't require using the menus.

These are the two shorthand methods for commands in Turbo Pascal 5.0/5.5. Look around in the menus until you have a general idea what they do.

Using a mouse or trackball in version 6.0 and TPW

With the newer versions of Turbo, you can also navigate by means of a pointing device:

- Version 6.0 and Turbo Pascal for Windows allow commands to be selected from menus by means of a pointing device like a mouse or trackball. You **left-click** on a menu to pull it down, then **drag** down to a menu selection to issue a command. (See Lab 1.1.)

Creating a simple program

Let's see these methods in action as we create a simple program. Return to the editing window by pressing ESC or by clicking the mouse in the edit window. Now the blinking cursor is in the large editing window, as it was when you first started Turbo. This window is the area in which you create and edit your Pascal source code. For practice, key in the following program:

```
PROGRAM Simple ( Output );
BEGIN
    WriteLn( 'Will this really work?' )
END.
```

If you are using Turbo for Windows (and *only* then), you will need to add an extra line to your program:

```
PROGRAM Simple ( Output );
USES WinCRT;
BEGIN
    WriteLn( 'Will this really work?' )
END.
```

If you are using Turbo for Windows, remember the extra line USES WinCRT; *you will have to add it to all Pascal programs that use text I/O.*

Enter the Pascal code just as you would in other text editors or word processors. If you make a mistake, backspace or delete through it and retype. (You can position the cursor with the arrow keys or mouse.) When you finish, the screen should look as shown in Figure 2 on the next page.

When you are satisfied that the Simple program is correct, you should save your source code in a disk file. You can do this by means of the File menu at the top of the screen. If you are not using a mouse, press **Alt-F** (that is, hold down the Alt key while pressing F) for the **File** menu, which will drop down from the top of the screen. Now press S for **S**ave. A window will appear, asking you to name your source code file. This is shown in Figure 3. When you have named your file (SIMPLE.PAS for example), press Enter and your file will be saved on your disk. Afterwards, you will find yourself back in the editing window. Carry out these steps now.

After your file has been named and saved in this way, you can resave your later edits even more quickly by simply pressing the F2 key. Try it; your disk light will come on briefly, indicating that the file is being saved again. (The file-naming window does not appear

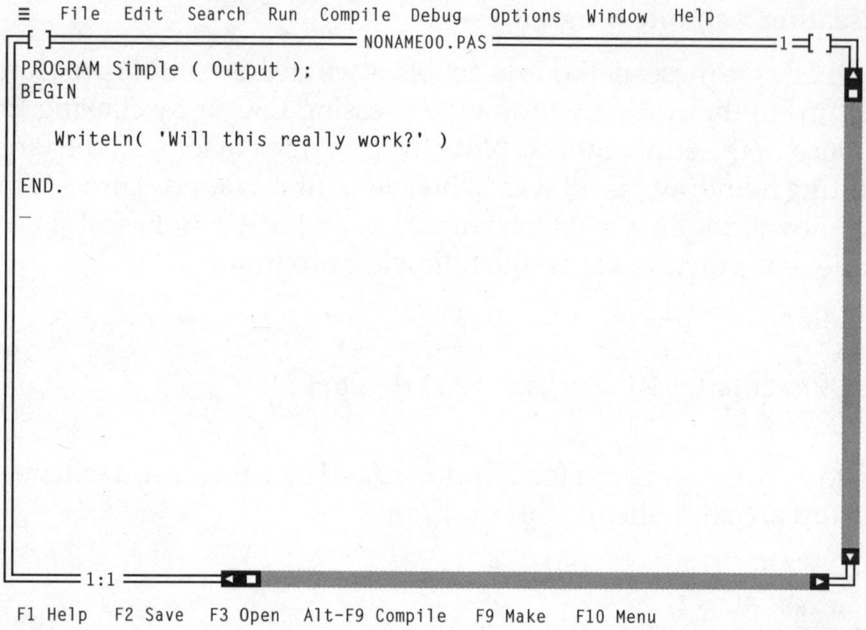

```
 ≡  File  Edit  Search  Run  Compile Debug  Options  Window  Help
┌[ ]══════════════════════ NONAME00.PAS ═══════════════════1═[ ]┐
│PROGRAM Simple ( Output );                                    ▲│
│BEGIN                                                         █│
│                                                              ║│
│   WriteLn( 'Will this really work?' )                        ║│
│                                                              ║│
│END.                                                          ║│
│_                                                             ║│
│                                                              ║│
│                                                              ▼│
└═══1:1══════◄■═══════════════════════════════════════════════►┘
 F1 Help  F2 Save  F3 Open  Alt-F9 Compile  F9 Make  F10 Menu
```

FIGURE 2. The screen as it looks in version 6.0 of Turbo Pascal, after entering the Simple program. Versions 5.0, 5.5, and Turbo for Windows look similar. Turbo for Windows requires an extra statement in the program, as explained in the lab.

because you have already named your file.) *Note: All Pascal source-code files should have the .PAS filename extension.*

In version 6.0 or Turbo Pascal for Windows, you can also save your source code by pulling the File menu down by left-clicking on it with a mouse or trackball, then dragging down to the Save option and releasing the mouse button.

Compiling, linking, and running your program

You can compile, link, and execute your program in one step by selecting the Run command from the Run menu. There are three ways to do this; try one of them now:

- Select the **R**un menu by keying Alt-R, then select the **R**un command by keying R.

- Simply press Control-F9; that is, hold the Control key down with one finger and press F9 with another finger.

- In version 6.0 or Turbo for Windows, pull the Run menu down by left-clicking on it with the mouse, then drag down to the Run command and release the mouse button.

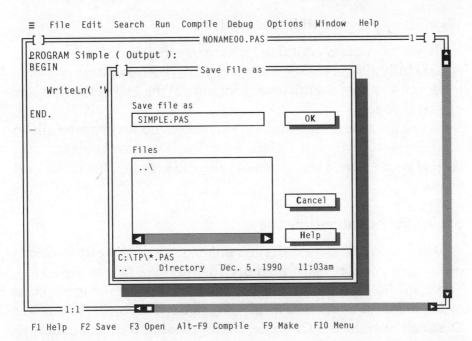

FIGURE 3. *After giving the Save command for a new file, the Turbo environment asks you for a filename. Key in the name as shown in the "Save file as" box, then key "K" or left-click on the "OK" button.*

If your program was keyed in *exactly* as shown, it will compile and link successfully and then run. You will briefly see the input/ output (I/O) window, containing the message

```
Will this really work?
```

On a fast machine using versions 5.0, 5.5., or 6.0, the I/O window will appear and then disappear so quickly that you will hardly see it. To make it reappear, key Alt-F5; that is, hold the Alt key down with one finger while keying F5 with another finger. After you have read the contents of the I/O window, press ESC to get back to the edit window.

In the space below, describe what happened when you first compiled your program:

_____

_____

_____

What if my program didn't compile?

If your program contained a syntax error, it did not compile successfully and an error message appeared. An example is shown in Figure 4, where a semicolon is missing at the end of the first line of Pascal code.

If you get an error message, examine your code very carefully to see how your program differs from the one shown above, and correct your errors. Then save your file and give the Run command again.

Saving the machine-code file

The Turbo Pascal compiler and linker normally save a program's executable code in main memory for the sake of greater speed. There are, however, occasions when you want the executable code to be saved in a .EXE disk file. To make Turbo do this, select **Destination** from the **Compile** menu, causing the destination to toggle (switch) from Memory to Disk. Then give the **Compile** or **Run** command, and Turbo will save an .EXE file for your program.

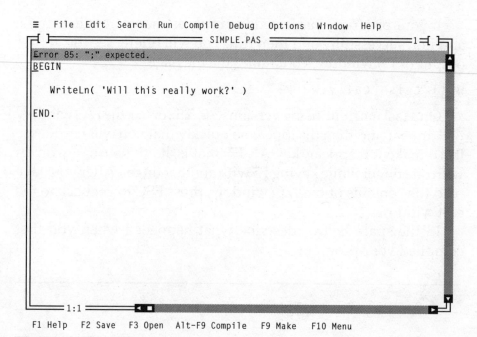

```
  ≡   File  Edit  Search  Run  Compile  Debug   Options   Window   Help
┌┤ ]═══════════════════════ SIMPLE.PAS ═══════════════════════1═┤ ]
 Error 85: ";" expected.
 BEGIN

    WriteLn( 'Will this really work?' )

 END.










 ═══1:1═══        ◄■ ►
 F1 Help   F2 Save   F3 Open   Alt-F9 Compile   F9 Make   F10 Menu
```

FIGURE 4. A missing semicolon at the end of the first line of code produced this error message at the beginning of the second line.

Quitting the Turbo environment

To exit from the Turbo environment, you can select e**X**it from the **F**ile menu, but the fastest way to exit is to key **Alt-X**; that is, hold the Alt key down while keying X.

Exercises

In the space below, show a sequence of key strokes (no function keys) that will open an existing source-code file:

_____

_____

_____

What function key will accomplish the same thing?

_____

In the space below, show a sequence of key strokes (no function keys) that will compile a program without executing it:

_____

_____

_____

What function key will accomplish the same thing?

_____

In the space below, show a sequence of key strokes (no function keys) that will quit from Turbo Pascal:

_____

_____

_____

What function key will accomplish the same thing?

After setting Destination = Disk on the compiler menu and then compiling, linking, and running the SIMPLE.PAS program, what machine-code file will have been saved to the active directory? (Give its name.)

When Jackson P. Slipshod compiles the following program in Turbo Pascal, he gets an error message saying Error 10: Unexpected end of file and the cursor appears at the position shown:

```
PROGRAM Simple ( Output );
BEGIN

    WriteLn( 'Will this really work?' )
END
_
```

What is Jackson's error? (How does Jackson's program differ from the one we said to key in?)

When Myra Meltdown compiles the following program in Turbo Pascal, she gets an error message saying Error 3: Unknown identifier and the cursor appears at the position shown:

```
PROGRAM Simple ( Output );
BEGIN

    WriteLn( Will this really work?' )
END
```

What is Myra's error? (How does Myra's program differ from the one we said to key in?)

Summary of Menu Commands
in Turbo Pascal, version 6.0

(Earlier versions are similar, but some menu entries differ)

FILE MENU (Alt-F)

Open (F3)	Displays a dialog box, allowing you to select an existing file for editing.
New	Opens a window for new source code, which will be named when you first save it.
Save (F2)	Saves the editing file in the selected window to disk. If the file has the default name of the form NONAMExx.PAS, you are asked to name the file.
Save As	Allows you to name and save a new file, or save an opened file under a new name.
Save All	Saves all modified files from all open windows.
Change Dir	Lets you specify a drive and directory as the current pathname from which files will be opened, and to which files will be saved.
Print	Prints the file shown in the active editing window.
Get Info	Displays information on the current file—its size, memory requirements, and so on.
DOS Shell	Lets you temporarily leave Turbo and return to DOS, so that you can enter a DOS command or run a program. To return to Turbo, give the EXIT command on the DOS command line.
Exit (Alt-X)	Exit from Turbo, remove Turbo from memory, and return to DOS.

EDIT MENU (Alt-E)

This menu provides cut, copy, and paste operations for use when editing text. The commands in this menu act on *selected text*. Text can be selected in five ways:

1. By holding down the Shift key and moving through the text with with the arrow keys in the numeric keypad.

2. By dragging with the mouse.

3. By placing the cursor at the beginning of the text to be selected, keying Control-KB, then placing the cursor at the end of the text to be selected and keying Control-KK.

4. A single word can be selected by placing the cursor in it and keying Control-KT..

5. A single line can be selected by double-clicking in it with the mouse.

Restore Line	Undoes the previous editing change.
Cut (Shift-Delete)	Removes a selected block of text, placing it in the Clipboard. (The hotkey command requires using the Delete key imbedded in the numeric pad.)
Copy (Ctrl-Insert)	Copies selected text into the Clipboard. (The hotkey command uses the Insert imbedded in the numeric pad.)
Paste (Shift-Insert)	Pastes contents of Clipboard into text window at the cursor position. After pasting, the Clipboard is empty. (The hotkey command uses the Insert imbedded in the numeric pad.)
Copy Example	Copies preselected example text from the Help window into the current window at the cursor position.
Show Clipboard	Displays the contents of the Clipboard.
Clear	Discards selected text without placing it in the Clipboard.

SEARCH MENU (Alt-S)
This menu lets you search for text and replace it.

Find (Alt-SF)	Finds a specified string.
Replace (Alt-SR)	Replaces a specified string with another specified string.
Search Again (Control-L)	Repeats the previous Find or Replace operation.
Go To Line Number	Prompts for a line number and takes you there.

Find Procedure	Prompts for a procedure or function name, then takes you there.
Find Error (Alt-F8)	Moves cursor to position of a run-time error. In order for this to work, the Debugging box must have been checked, using the Options/Debugger menu selection, before the program was compiled.

RUN MENU (Alt-R)

Run (Control-F9)	Runs your program. If breakpoints are enabled, runs to the next breakpoint. If the program has been changed, Turbo automatically recompiles and relinks it before running it.
Program Reset (Control-F2)	Resets execution during debugging, so that the next Run command will start execution at the beginning.
Go to Cursor (F4)	Runs the program to the line containing the cursor.
Trace Into (F7)	Runs the next statement in your program, updating the Watch window. Single-steps through subprograms, too.
Step Over (F8)	Runs the next statement in your program and updates the Watch windows. Runs subprograms without stopping in them—that is, it "steps over" subprograms.
Parameters	Allows you to send command-line arguments to a program, as though you were running it from the DOS command line.

COMPILE MENU (Alt-C)

Compile (Alt-F9)	Compiles the active editing file, but doesn't link and run it.
Make (F9)	Compiles and links the active editing file, making an EXE file. Automatically recompiles and relinks any parts of the program that have been changed since the last Make, including imported units.
Build	Unconditionally recompiles and relinks the program, regardless of whether it has been changed.

Destination	Lets you specify whether the executable code produced by compiling and linking will be saved in memory or on disk. (Choosing Disk also increases the amount of memory available for compiling.)
Primary File	Lets you specify which .PAS file will be used when you give the Build or Make command.

DEBUG MENU (Alt-D)

Evaluate /Modify (Control-F4)	Opens a dialog box for evaluating variables and expressions while your program is halted.
Watches	Opens a pop-up menu of commands to control the use of the Watch window. Here's the submenu:

> **Add Watch** (Control-F7) allows you to enter Watch expressions to the Watch window.
>
> **Delete Watch** (Del or Control-Y) deletes the active Watch expression.
>
> **Edit Watch** allows you to change the active Watch expression.
>
> **Remove All Watches** deletes all Watch expressions.

Toggle Breakpoint (Control-F8)	Sets or clears a breakpoint on the line containing the cursor.
Breakpoints	Opens a dialog box that allows you to specify a list of breakpoints, their line numbers, and the conditions under which they will break execution.

OPTIONS MENU (Alt-O)

Compiler	Displays a dialog box in which you can select compilation options, including **debugging options**, **range checking**, and the way in which **numerical processing** will occur.
Memory Sizes	Lets you configure the default memory allocation for a program.
Linker	Opens a dialog box in which you can control various linking parameters.

Debugger   Opens a dialog box in which you can choose the
                        kind of debugging code to be generated during com-
                        pilation and linking, depending on whether you
                        will use the integrated or stand-alone debugger.

Directories   Lets you tell Turbo where to find the files it needs
                        to compile, link, and save your code.

Environment   Lets you control the Turbo IIDE, specifying compiler
                        options, how the editor and mouse will work, and how
                        the screen will look.

Save Options   Lets you save the various settings you've made in the
                        Find and Replace dialog boxes, the Compile/Destina-
                        tion and Compile/Primary File options, and under the
                        Options menu.

Retrieve Options   Retrieves from TURBO.DSK the options previously
                        saved.

WINDOW MENU (Alt-W)
Controls the appearance of windows.

Size/Move   This command lets you use the arrow keys to move
(Control-F5)   the active window, or use Shift with the arrow keys
                        to size it. (However, these operations are more
                        easily performed with a mouse.)

Zoom   Zooms active window to full size, or back down again.
(F5)   (This operation can also be done with a mouse, by
                        clicking on the window's zoom box.)

Tile   Sizes and rearranges the open windows so that none
                        overlap.

Cascade   Stacks the open editing windows, so that the active
                        window is on top and the others peek out from
                        underneath.

Next   Chooses the next window in a cascaded stack,
(F6)   placing it on top and making it active. (This can also
                        be done with a mouse, by clicking on the desired
                        window.)

Previous   Chooses the previous window in a cascaded stack,
(Shift-F6)   placing it on top and making it active. (This can also
                        be done with a mouse, by clicking on the desired
                        window.)

Close   Closes the active window. (The window can also be
(Alt-F3)   closed with a mouse, by clicking on the window's
                     close box.)

Watch   Opens the Watch window and makes it active.

Register   Opens the Register window and makes it active.
                     This lets you watch the contents of the CPU registers.

Output   Opens an Output window and makes it active.
                     You can also switch from the editing screen to the full
                     output screen by means of Alt-F5.

Call Stack   Shows the stack of procedure calls used to arrive at
(Control-F3)   the procedure that is currently running. The current
                     procedure is listed at the top of the stack; the main
                     program is at the bottom.

User Screen   Switches from the editing window to the full output
(Alt-F5)   screen. You can return to the editing window by
                     pressing any key.

List   Shows a list of all windows currently open.
(Alt-O)

HELP MENU (F1)

Shows information about how to use Turbo's features. If the cursor is currently
positioned in a word in an editing window, help will be provided with language
syntax. In other circumstances, information will be displayed about the current
context.

Contents (F1)   Shows the Table of Contents for Help topics.

Index   Displays a dialog box of Help keywords. Choose one
                     by double-clicking with the mouse or by scrolling with
                     arrow keys and then pressing Enter.

Topic Search   Displays help with Pascal syntax at the position of
(Control-F1)   the cursor in the active editing window.

Previous Topic   Opens the Help window and redisplays the informa-
(Alt-F1)   tion you saw last time.

Help on Help   Explains how to use the Help system.
(F1)

Navigation in the Turbo Editor

You can move around in the file being edited with the help of a mouse or trackball, or you can use the hot keys shown below:

Action	Key
Up a line	Up-arrow
Down a line	Down-arrow
Up a screen	PageUp
Down a screen	PageDown
To beginning of file	Ctrl-PageUp
To end of file	Ctrl-PageDown
Move right one char	Right-arrow
Move left one char	Left-arrow
To beginning of line	Home
To end of line	End
To next window	F6
To previous window	Shift-F6

Selecting, Cutting, Copying, and Pasting

The following hot-key commands are especially useful in the Turbo editor:

Action	Key
Select text for operation	Shift-arrow
Select current word	Ctrl-KT
Copy selection to clipboard	Ctrl-Insert
Cut selection to clipboard	Shift-Delete
Delete selection	Ctrl-Delete
Paste clipboard	Shift-Insert

Compiler Directives in Turbo Pascal (Partial list)

The compiler can be given directives by inserting special comments in your source code. Such comments are not part of the Pascal language, but a way of controlling the actions of the Turbo compiler.

Directive	Default	Action
{$B+} or {$B-}	{$B-}	Do/don't require complete evaluation of boolean expressions.
{$D+} or {$D-}	{$D+}	Enable/disable generation of code for debugger.
{$E+} or {$E-}	{$E+}	Enable/disable software emulation of 80x87 arithmetic coprocessor.
{$I+} or {$I-}	{$I+}	Enable/disable I/O error checking.
{$L+} or {$L-}	{$L+}	Enable/disable generation of local symbol information for debugger. (Needed when debugging procedures and functions.)
{$N+} or {$N-}	{$N-}	Use/don't use 80x87 arithmetic coprocessor.
{$R+} or {$R-}	{$R-}	Enable/disable range checking.

The directives {$D-}, {$I-}, {$L-}, and {$R-} make object code smaller and faster, but they should not be used when you are compiling code that might require debugging.

How Turbo Pascal Differs from American National Standard Pascal (Partial list)

Only the first 63 characters of an identifier are significant.

A comment that begins with "{" must end with "}" and a comment that begins with "(*" must end with "*)".

A file is allowed to have components of a type that contains files.

A file variable does not have an associated buffer variable, referenced by means of the ^ suffix. Also, there are no predefined Get and Put procedures.

The requirement that a function assign a value to the function identifier is not enforced.

The requirement that the selector variable of a variant record part cannot be an actual variable parameter is not enforced.

Procedural and functional parameters are not allowed.

File variables that are arguments in Reset or Rewrite statements must have been assigned an external file name by means of a nonstandard Assign statement.

The standard procedures Pack and Unpack are not provided.

A FOR-loop control variable can be altered or threatened from inside the loop.

When Read or ReadLn reads from a text file an <EOLn> into a character variable, a carriage return (ASCII 13) is stored rather than a blank.

When Read or ReadLn reads from a text file an integer or real number, only a blank or control character will terminate the number.

A Write to a text file will be completed even if the string being written is longer than the specified field width.

The standard file variables Input and Output are not required as program parameters, even when used in the program.

The following nonstandard keywords are reserved:
     ABSOLUTE, EXTERNAL, IMPLEMENTATION, INLINE, INTERFACE, INTERRUPT,
     OBJECT, SHL, SHR, String, UNIT, USES, XOR.

Identifiers may contain underscores after the first character.

A CASE structure can have an optional ELSE clause. Correspondingly, the selector variable is not required to have one of the listed values.

The range of Integers is –32768... +32767. Integers can be written in hexadecimal, in which case they are prefixed by a $. The nonstandard types ShortInt, LongInt, Byte, and Word are provided.

Label, constant, type, variable, procedure, and function declaration parts can appear any number of times in a block.

The MOD operator performs a simple remainder, not a true modulo operation.

There are nonstandard real types called Single, Double, Extended, and Comp.

Turbo's nonstandard String type includes a dynamic length attribute. Thus, strings can vary in stored length during a run.

Characters and packed string arrays are compatible with Turbo's predefined String type.

Variables can be declared at an absolute memory address by means of an ABSOLUTE clause.

The type of a value can be changed by means of typecasting.

There are typed constants, which can be used to initialize variables of all types except files

The nonstandard @ operator extracts the address of an identifier.

String types can be read with Read and ReadLn and written with Write and WriteLn.

"Lazy I/O" allows interactive and noninteractive I/O to be treated identically.

Compilation units are supported. Each unit has an `Interface` part and `Implementation` part.

Data-Storage Representations in Turbo Pascal

Boolean	8 bits, with value 0 or 1
Char	8 bits, unsigned
Byte	8 bits, unsigned
ShortInt	8 bits, 2's-complement
Word	16 bits, unsigned
Integer	16 bits, 2's-complement
LongInt	32 bits, 2's-complement
Enumerated	8 bits, unsigned, for ordinal values 0 thru 255; otherwise, 16 bits, unsigned.
Real	48 bits, with 8-bit exponent and 1-bit sign.
Single	32 bits, IEEE format
Double	64 bits, IEEE format
Extended	80 bits, IEEE format
Comp	64 bits, 2's-complement
Pointer	32 bits, with offset in the low word and the segment in the high word.
Set	A bit-vector consisting of an even number of words (exception: set of 8 or less elements is one byte)
String of n chars	1-byte length field, followed by n character bytes. Maximum length is 256 bytes for String[255].

Lab 1.4:
Using THINK Pascal (Versions 3.0 and 4.0)

Materials required: Apple Macintosh equipped with THINK Pascal, version 3.0 or 4.0. Also, a blank floppy disk.

Concepts: THINK Pascal integrated environment; editor; compiler; linker; syntax error; source code and machine code.

Lab techniques: Using the THINK environment by experimentation; using the compiler to check for simple syntax errors.

Prerequisites: Lab 1.2; Section 1.5 of *Structures and Abstractions*.

Boot up your Macintosh and load the THINK disk, if it isn't already present. Move to the folder containing THINK Pascal. Double-click on the THINK Pascal icon. The THINK environment will appear on the screen, asking you to open a program project or to create a new one. The screen will look like the one in Figure 1.

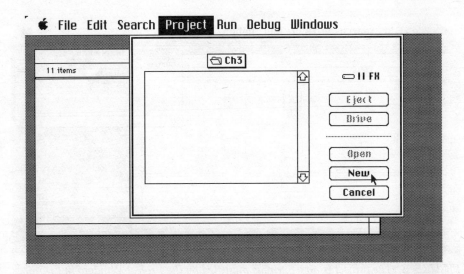

FIGURE 1. *The initial screen in THINK Pascal version 3.0, in which the user is being asked to open an existing program project or to create a new one. You are creating a new project, so you should click on the New button.*

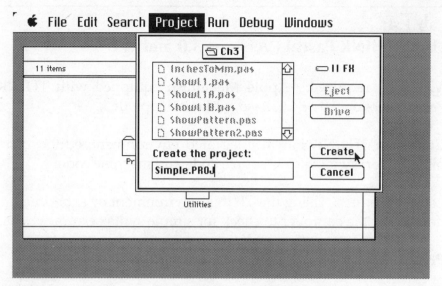

FIGURE 2. Enter the program project name (use a .PROJ extension) and click on the Create button.

Once you click on **New**, you will be prompted for the name of the new program project. This is shown in Figure 2. Key in the name Simple.PROJ. (We suggest the .PROJ extension for all project names, for reasons that will become apparent shortly.) The new project will open, as shown in Figure 3.

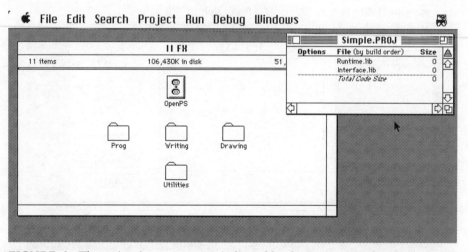

FIGURE 3. The project is now open, as indicated by the Project Window in the upper right corner. The Project Window shows the code files that will be compiled and linked to create a complete program. THINK Pascal has automatically included two files of machine code from the Pascal library, called Runtime.lib and Interface.lib. We have not yet written our source code. The icon in the extreme upper right is the THINK icon that displays under MultiFinder. You will not see it if you run under the Finder.

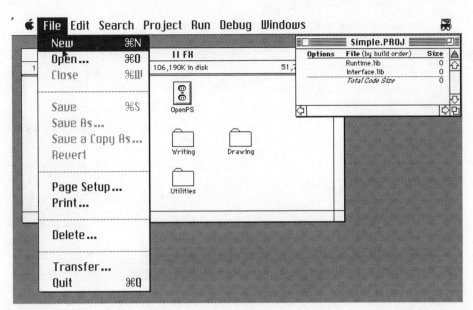

FIGURE 4. *Selecting the New command in the Files menu, in order to create a new file for our program's source code.*

The menu bar across the top of the screen shows seven menus containing THINK Pascal operations. Pull down the Files menu and select **New**, so that you can create a new file for the Pascal source code in your program project. This is shown in Figure 4.

- The most used menu items also list a function key. The function key is an alternative way to give a command. As you see from Figure 2B.4, Command-N gives the New (new file) command.

Creating a simple program

Let's see these methods in action as we create a simple program. Click inside the new source-code window just created. The text insertion point will appear in that window, marking where text will appear as you start to enter it. For practice, key in the following program:

```
PROGRAM Simple ( Output );
BEGIN
   WriteLn( 'Will this really work?' )
END.
```

Key in the Pascal code just as you would in other text editors or word processors. If you make a mistake, backspace through it and retype. (You can move the insertion point to the location of an error

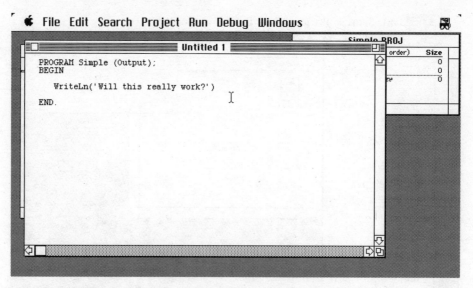

FIGURE 5. *The screen as it looks after entering the Simple program. The source-code file still doesn't have a name, so giving it a name will be the next step.*

by pointing with the mouse and clicking.) When you finish, the screen should look as shown in Figure 5 on the next page.

When you are satisfied that the program is correct, you should save your source code in a disk file by selecting **Save As ...** from the **File** menu. A window will appear, asking you to name your source code file. (Figure 6.) When you have named your file (Simple.pas

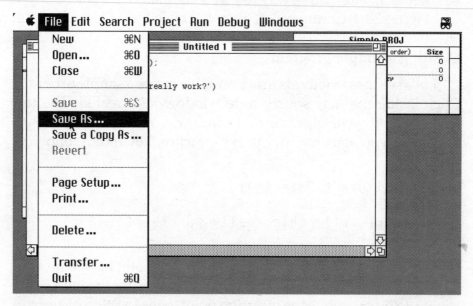

FIGURE 6. *Using Save As ... to give the source-code file a name and save it.*

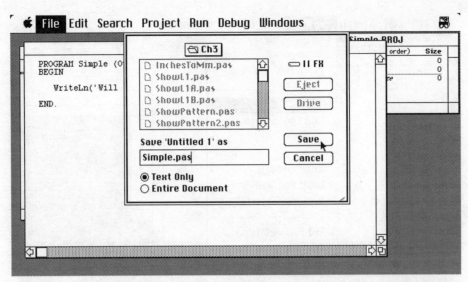

FIGURE 7. After you give the Save As . . . command, you are asked for a filename. Key in the name as shown in the "Save file as" box, then click on the Save button. After the file is copied to disk, the new name will appear at the top of the source-code window.

for example), press Enter or click on the **Save** button, and your file will be saved on your disk. (Figure 7.) After your source code has been named and saved, you can resave your later edits even more quickly by simply pressing Command-S, which is equivalent to the **File** menu's **Save** command.

Source-code file vs. the project file

Note the distinction between the source-code file, `Simple.pas`, and the project file, `Simple.PROJ`. The project file is where THINK Pascal keeps all the pieces of object code that are to be linked together, and also (unless you say otherwise) where it keeps the executable machine code that results from linking. Don't get the two files mixed up!

Adding your source code to the project

Before you can compile and link your program, you must tell the compiler and linker what code to use. In THINK Pascal, you do that by adding the source-code file to the project. If your source-code file is not already the active window, click on it to make it active. Then select **Add Window** from the **Project** menu. (Figure 8.)

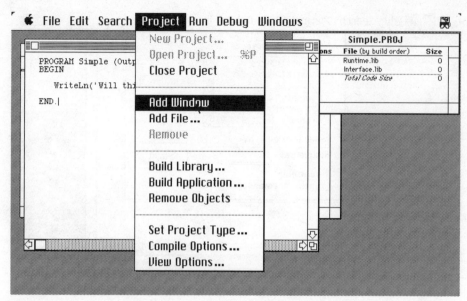

FIGURE 8. Adding the source-code file to the project. This tells the compiler and linker what code to use.

Compiling, linking, and running your program

You can compile, link, and execute your program in one step by selecting the **Go** command from the **Run** menu. But before you do this, open a Text window to contain the output from your run. Pull down the **Windows** menu and select **Text**, as shown in Figure 9.

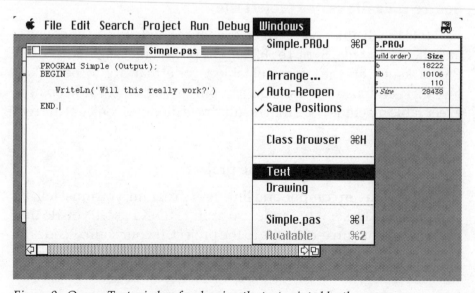

Figure 9. Open a Text window for showing the text printed by the program.

Then give the **Go** command from the **Run** menu, or equivalently, press **Command-G**. This is the command to compile, link, and run the program. The moment of truth has arrived. If your program was keyed in *exactly* as shown, it will compile and link successfully and then run. You will see the following message appear in the Text window:

```
Will this really work?
```

If no error messages appeared and the compiler and linker appeared to run correctly, but you still don't see your program's output, check to see if you have forgotten to open the Text window. If so, open it at this time. Your screen should look as shown in Figure 10.

In the space below, describe what happened in your case:

_____

_____

_____

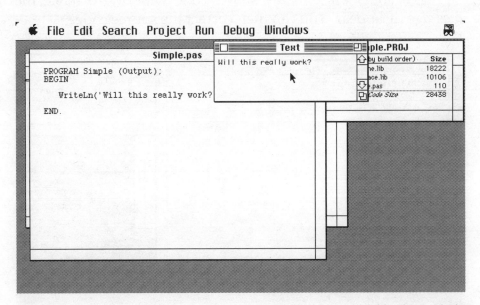

FIGURE 10. *If everything went well, your screen should now look like this, with the output from the program appearing in the Text window.*

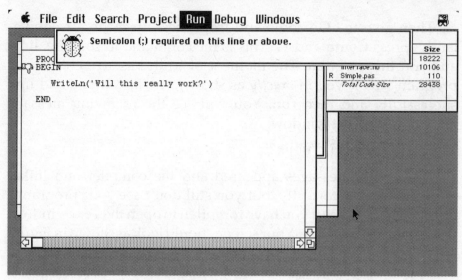

FIGURE 11. *A missing semicolon at the end of the first line of code produced this error message. Click in the source-code window to make the message go away, so you can see the offending line of code. You will then see what is shown in Figure 12.*

What if my program didn't compile?

If your program contained a syntax error, it did not compile successfully and an error message appeared. An example is shown in Figure 11, where a semicolon is missing at the end of the first line of Pascal code. Click in the source-code window to make the message disappear. You can then correct the source code.

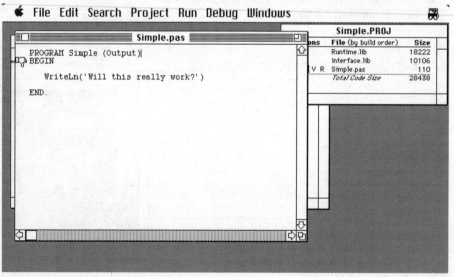

FIGURE 12. *After clicking in the source-code window, you will be able to see the location of the error and be able to correct it. Here the semicolon is missing from the end of the first line.*

If you get an error message, examine your code very carefully to see how your program differs from the one shown above, and correct your errors. Then save your file (**Command-S**) and give the **Go** command (**Command-G**) again.

Saving a clickable machine-code file

THINK Pascal normally saves the program's executable code in the project file. Then, when you reopen the project, you can run the program again without recompiling and relinking it. However, you can't run this executable code without opening the project, and you can't open the project without having the THINK Pascal application. If you need to supply an executable program to someone who doesn't have THINK Pascal, you will need to save your machine code as a standalone, clickable program. Such a program is called an *application* in Macintosh jargon. Pull down the **Project** menu and select **Build Application**. You will be presented with a dialog box, asking you for a name to give the application. You might, for example, call our example program `Simple App`. Whatever name you use, make sure is different from both your source-code and project files. If you use the same name as one of these, your application's machine code will replace your source code or project!

Quitting from THINK Pascal

To exit from the THINK Pascal environment, you can select **Quit** from the **File** menu, but the fastest way to exit is to key **Command-Q**. This works with most Macintosh software.

Exercises

(To answer the following questions, you must first experiment with the menus in THINK Pascal.)

In the space below, describe how the mouse can be used to open an existing source-code file:

_____

_____

_____

What key-command will accomplish the same thing?

_____

In the space below, explain how the mouse can be used to compile a program without executing it:

_____

_____

_____

What key-command will accomplish the same thing?

_____

In the space below, show how the mouse can be used to quit from THINK Pascal:

_____

_____

_____

What key-command will accomplish the same thing?

When Jackson P. Slipshod compiles the following program in THINK Pascal, he gets an error message saying `This statement or keyword doesn't belong here` and the cursor appears at the position shown:

```
PROGRAM Simple ( Output );
   WriteLn( 'Will this really work?' )
END
```

What is Jackson's error? (How does Jackson's program differ from the one we said to key in?)

When Myra Meltdown compiles the following program in THINK Pascal, she gets an error message saying `This doesn't make sense` and the cursor appears at the position shown:

```
PROGRAM Simple ( Output );
BEGIN
   WriteLn(_Will this really work?' )
END
```

What is Myra's error? (How does Myra's program differ from the one we said to key in?)

Summary of Menu Commands
in THINK Pascal, versions 3.0 and 4.0

(Earlier versions are similar, but some menu entries differ)

FILE MENU
(Some commands are visible only when the Option key is pressed.)

New	(Cmd-N)	Opens a window for new source code, which must be named and saved by means of the Save As comand.
Open...	(Cmd-O)	Displays a dialog box, allowing you to select an existing file.
Close	(Cmd-W)	Closes any selected window having a close box.
Close All (Option-Cmd-W)		Closes all open windows.
Save	(Cmd-S)	Saves the file in the selected window to disk.
Save All (Option-Cmd-S)		Saves the files in all open windows.
Save As...		Allows you to name and save a new file, or save an opened file under a new name. When changing the name of a file already added to the project, the name in the Project Window will automatically change.
Save a Copy As...		Saves a copy under a new name, but does not alter the filename in the project window.
Revert		Restores the last-saved version of the current file, discarding any changes made since the last save.
Page Setup...		Allows selection of paper size, print orientation, or reduction before printing.
Print...		Copies the current file to printer.
Print All (Option menu)		Copies all open files to printer.
Delete...		Allows you to delete a file from disk without leaving THINK Pascal.
Transfer...		Launches another application without first returning to the desktop, thus saving time.

Quit   (Cmd-Q)   Exit from THINK and return to desktop.

EDIT MENU

Undo   (Cmd-Z)   Reverses the last edit operation.

Cut   (Cmd-X)   Removes a selected block of text, placing it in the Clipboard.

Copy   (Cmd-C)   Copies selected text into the Clipboard.

Paste   (Cmd-V)   Pastes contents of Clipboard into text window at the insertion marker.

Clear   Deletes the selected text.

Select All   Selects all text in the current text window.

Show Clipboard   Displays the contents of the Macintosh Clipboard.

Source Options...   Lets you change the way the editor pretty-prints your source code. You can change fonts, tabs, etc.

Auto-Reformat   Lets you specify when the editor pretty-prints a line you have entered, either when you hit RETURN or when you enter a semicolon.

Projector Aware   Makes code useable with the Macintosh Programmer's Workshop Projector, a separate product used by developers.

SEARCH MENU
(Some commands are visible only when the Option key is pressed.)

Find (Cmd-F)   Lets you specify the string you are searching for. You will hear a beep if it isn't found.

Find Again (Cmd-A)   Searches for the next occurrence of the string specified with Find.

Find in Next File (Cmd-T)   Lets you search through the next file of the project for the specified string.

Find in All Files (Option-Cmd-T)   Lets you search through all files of the current project for the specified string. (Version 4.0)

Enter Selection (Cmd-E)	Takes the currently-selected text as the search string, after which you can use Find Again or Find in Next File to search, or Find... to set the search options.
Replace (Cmd-R)	Replaces string specified with Find command with specified replacement string.
Replace and Find Again (Cmd-D)	Replaces current selection with the specified replacement string, then finds the next occurrence of the search string, but doesn't replace it.
Replace All	Automatically replaces all occurrences of the search string with copies of the replacement string.
Show selection	Quickly scrolls text window to show insertion point or selected text.
Show Error	Quickly scrolls text to show position of downturned thumb, marking an error.

PROJECT MENU
(Some commands are visible only when the Option key is pressed.)

New Project...	Creates a new project and opens a project window containing Runtime.lib and Interface.lib by default.
Open Project... (Cmd-P)	Allows selection of an existing project.
Close Project	Closes the currently open project.
Add Window	Adds the current text-window file to the current project.
Add File...	Adds one file or library to the current project.
Add Files... (Option menu)	Adds multiple files or libraries to the current project. (Version 4.0)
Remove	Deletes from the current project the selecteditem in the project window.
Build Library...	Compiles and links your project and saves it as a library to be used by other projects.

Build Application   Compiles and links your project and saves it as a double-clickable application that can run without THINK, or as a library to be used by other projects, or as a compressed project (no object code).

Remove objects   Removes all object code from a project. This is used to make a project as small as possible for transmission to someone else.

Set Project Type...   Allows you to declare that your project will build a desk accessory, driver, or code resource instead of a normal application.

Compile Options...   Allows you to request machine code for the 68020 CPU and/or the 68881 numeric co-processor. Also allows you to specify the maximum size of sets of integers.

View Options...   Allows you to specify what appears in your project window, and the font used to show it.

Get Info...   Shows the code and data sizes for the files in the current project. (Version 4.0)

RUN MENU
(Some commands are visible only when you hold down the Option key.)

Check Syntax (Cmd-K)   Checks Pascal syntax of the current editing window.

Build (Cmd-B)   Compiles all files currently tagged for recompilation.

Check Link   Links the project without running it.

Reset   Resets a paused program so that the next Go, Go-Go, Step, or Trace will start at the beginning.

Go (Cmd-G)   Runs the program, first building it if necessary. If Go encounters a stop sign, it halts. You can give another Go command to resume execution. Choosing Go with the Shift key depressed causes THINK to fall into Macsbug just before returning from a subprogram.

Go-Go (Option-Cmd-G)   Runs the program, pausing at each stop sign to update the Observe and LightsBug windows. Holding the Shift key down while issuing this command causes a break to MacsBug just before returning from a subprogram.

Step Over
(Cmd-J)

Runs the next statement in your program and updates the Observe and LightsBug windows. Runs subprograms without stopping in them—that is, it "steps over" subprograms. Holding the Shift key down while issuing this command causes a break to MacsBug just before returning from a subprogram.

Step Into
(Cmd-I)

Runs the next statement in your program, updating the Observe and LightsBug windows. Single-steps through subprograms, too. Choosing Step Into with the Shift key depressed causes a break to MacsBug just before returning from a subprogram.

Step-Step
(Option-Cmd-I)

A continuous stream of Step Intos, running the program in slow motion. Choosing Step-Step with the Shift key depressed causes a break to MacsBug just before returning from a subprogram.

Step Out
(Cmd-U)

Runs the program until the next return from a subprogram. Choosing Step Out with the Shift key depressed causes a break to MacsBug just before returning from a subprogram.

Auto-Save

Automatically saves all changed files prior to running, without asking. The opposite of **Confirm Saves**.

Confirm Saves

Asks before saving changed files before running. The opposite of **Auto-Save**.

Don't Save

Tells THINK not to save changed files.
Useful when you want to quickly try out a change without overwriting the previous version on disk.

Run Options...

Allows selection of resource file, adjustment of parameters of text-output window, echoing to printer, and adjustment of stack and zone (heap) sizes.
See the manual for details.

DEBUG MENU
(Some commands are visible only when you hold down the Option key.)

LightsBug
(Cmd-L)

Opens a LightsBug debugger window.
Up to four of these windows can be opened at once, by using the shift key when opening the second through fourth. See discussion of LightsBug in Lab 5–1.

Instant

Opens a window for executing extra statements while your program is halted.

Observe	Opens a window for observing the values of expressions during program execution.
Show Finger	Activates the window containing the execution finger, scrolling it to show the position of the finger.
Pull Stops	Removes all stop signs from the current editing window.
Pull All Stops (Option menu)	Removes all stop signs from all files in the current project. (version 4.0)
Auto-Show Finger	Automatic version of Show Finger.
Stops In	Lets you place stop signs in your code. After choosing this command, stop signs are inserted by clicking in appropriate places in the left margin of the edit window.
Break at A-Traps	Tells THINK to halt execution just before a Macintosh A-Trap (a call to a Toolbox routine).
Use Second Screen	If you have two screen displays connected to your machine, this command puts the Instant, Observe, and LightsBug windows on the second screen. (V. 4.0)
Quietly Auto-Reset	This command causes an automatic program reset if if you modify your source code while debugging. (V. 4.0)
Monitor (Cmd-M)	Invokes the machine-level debugger, if installed. (Either MacsBug or TMON will work.)

WINDOWS MENU: opens and controls the appearance of windows.

(Project Name)	Makes the Project window active.
Arrange...	Arranges the open editing windows on the screen, either overlapping, tiled, side-by-side horizontally, or side-by-side vertically.
Auto-Reopen	Reopens a project's windows automatically when the project is reopened.
Save Positions	Saves positions of windows so that they will reappear in the same positions when the project is reopened.

Class Browser	Displays the Class Browser window, for use in object-oriented programming.
Text	Opens a window for display of standard output from Write or WriteLn statements. The window can also be opened by a ShowText call in your program.
Drawing	Opens a window for display of graphical output. The window can also be opened by a ShowDrawing call in your program.
(File Name)	Makes a given file window active.

Compiler Options in THINK Pascal

The Options column in the Project Window shows the settings of four compiler options used in debugging. These options are turned off and on by clicking on them. A box around the option-letter indicates that it is turned on. The options are:

D (Debug)	Compiler adds code to support single-stepping, tracing, and observing with the source-level debugger. Note: the debugger can be used only with code compiledwith this option.
N (Names)	Procedure names are inserted as labels into the object code, allowing easier debugging with machine-level debuggers like Lightsbug and Macsbug.
V (Overflow Checking)	Generates code that checks for and traps integer overflow.
R (Range Checking)	Generates code that checks for and traps out-of-range subscripts, pointers, and parameters.

Turning these options off makes object code smaller and faster, but they should be turned on while you are compiling code that might require debugging. Debugging operations are described below.

In addition, the compiler can be given directives by inserting special comments in the source code. Here are the most common *compiler directives* in THINK Pascal:

Directive	Default	Action
{$D+} or {$D-}	{$D+}	Enable/disable generation of code for debugger.
{$N+} or {$N-}	{$N+}	Enable/disable generation of names—symbol information—for the debugger. (Needed when debugging procedures and functions.)
{$N++}		Enables both tracing and Names generation.

{$V+} or {$V-}	{$V-}	Enable/disable overflow checking.
{$R+} or {$R-}	{$R-}	Enable/disable range checking.
{$I+} or {$I-}	{$I-}	Enable/disable autoinitialization in main prog.
{$J+} or {$J-}	{$J-}	Enable/disable external variable handling. (This is enabled in an interface file when using a library file, to prevent the error called "Link failed: multiply-defined symbols."
{$Z+} or {$Z-}	{$Z-}	Enable/disable external routine handling.

How THINK Pascal Differs from American National Standard Pascal (Partial list)

Identifiers can be no longer than 255 characters. As in the standard, all characters are significant and case is ignored.

All literal character-strings, even those of length 1, are of String type. String and character compatibility as the same as in ANS Pascal. String-types, packed-string-types, and char-types can be mixed where appropriate. The string functions Length, Pos, Concat, Copy, Delete, Omit, Insert, and Include are provided.

The requirement that a function assign a value to the function identifier is not enforced.

Functions can return not only simple types and pointers, but any type.

Changing the value of a FOR-loop control variable from inside the loop produces unpredictable results.

Only the standard file variables Input and Output are allowed as program parameters.

The following nonstandard keywords are reserved:
  Implementation, Inherited, InLine, Interface, Object, Otherwise, String, Uses, Unit.

Identifiers may contain underscores after the first character.

The CASE statement has an optional OTHERWISE clause.

The range of Integers is –32768... +32767.

The MOD operator performs a simple remainder, not a true modulo operation.

There is a LongInt type and there are additional real types called Double, Computational, and Extended. These are derived from the Macintosh Toolbox and SANE package.

Real arithmetic is performed as Extended, and produces an Extended result. Integer arithmetic involving LongInts is converted to LongInt, and produces a LongInt result.

The nonstandard @ operator can be used in place of ^ to extract the address of a variable, procedure, or function.

A file may be opened with Open to allow random read/write access to a file. An explicit Close procedure is provided. Seek is provided for random access; FilePos provides seek with the component-number of the current file position. Reset and Rewrite statements can be used to associate a filename with a file variable.

String-types and enumerated-types can be read with Read and ReadLn and written with Write and WriteLn.

"Lazy I/O" allows interactive and noninteractive I/O to be treated identically.

The Ord function converts pointers to integers; the Pointer function converts an integers to pointers. Ord4 converts an ordinal- or pointer-type to Longint.

Compilation units are supported. Each unit has an Interface part and Implementation part.

THINK supports the entire Macintosh Toolbox as described in Apple's manual, *Inside Macintosh.*

Data-Storage Representations in THINK Pascal

Boolean	8 bits, with value 0 or 1
Char	16 bits, with 0 in the high-order byte
Integer	16 bits, 2's-complement
LongInt	32 bits, 2's-complement
Enumerated	8 bits unsigned, ordinal values 0 thru 255
Real	32 bits, IEEE format
Double	64 bits, IEEE format
Extended	80 bits, IEEE format
Computational	64 bits, 2's-complement
Pointer	32 bits: lower 24 bits contain the address; the upper 8 bits depend on the Macintosh Memory Manager.
Set	A bit-vector consisting of an even number of words (exception: set of 8 or less elements is one byte)
String of *n* chars	1-byte length field, followed by *n* character bytes, followed, if needed, by an unused byte to ensure that the total number of bytes is even.

Lab 3.1:
Program Structure

Purpose: To create a program that converts angular degrees to radians.

Concepts: Interactive program design; incremental testing.

Lab Techniques: Use of a program skeleton; incremental testing.

Problem-Solving Techniques: Plan I/O first.

Prerequisites: Labs 1 and 2; Chapters 2 and 3 of text.

Now that you know how to run your Pascal system, it is time to try your hand at a simple program that uses real variables. In particular, let us design and build a program that displays a short table of angular degrees versus radians.

First plan the input and output, imagining how the program might look on the screen as it runs. As usual, the program should announce its purpose first, then do its work:

```
DEGREES VERSUS RADIANS
----------------------

   DEGREES      RADIANS
    30.00        0.52
    60.00        1.05
    90.00        1.57
```

Having planned the output in this detail—there is no input—you can imagine the steps followed by the program in accomplishing its task. There are four steps. Describe them below:

Step 1:   Display the purpose of the program.

Step 2: _____

Step 3: _____

Step 4: _____

What you've just written is an *algorithm*. When you have worked out the details and translated them into Pascal, you'll have a *program*.

Performing the conversion: To convert from degrees to radians, remember that a complete circle, 360 degrees, is defined to be 2π radians. Therefore, our program will use the conversion formula (fill in the blank)

$$\text{Radians} = \frac{1}{57.3} \cdot \text{Degrees}$$

(handwritten in left margin:)
$360° = 2\pi \; rad$

$1 \, rad = \dfrac{360}{2\pi}$

$rad = \dfrac{180}{\pi}$

$1 \, rad = 57.3°$

Only after planning the algorithm in this much detail do we start to write source code. We begin by writing a skeleton for the program:

```
PROGRAM DegreesToRadians ( Output );
VAR
    Degrees, Radians : Real;

BEGIN

    { Main program code will go here. }

END.
```

Key this skeleton into your editor *exactly* as shown (except for the comment), then compile it to check for syntax errors. If you check for syntax errors at this early stage, it will be easier to get your program running correctly when you complete it.

Learning to recognize syntax errors: The compiler is your best tool for learning to recognize syntax errors. You should experiment to see what error messages appear when known errors are introduced into the program. Try the following deliberate errors and report the error messages that result.

1. If the reserved word PROGRAM is misspelled, the resulting error message is

_____

2. If the semicolon is deleted from the end of the program header, the resulting error message is

_____

3. If the reserved word BEGIN is missing, the resulting error message is

_____

4. If the reserved word END is missing, the resulting error message is

_____

5. If the period is deleted from the end of the program, the resulting error message is

_____

Incremental testing: Once the skeleton has been successfully compiled, the rest of the code can be inserted into the skeleton. _Important tip:_ You will save a lot of time in debugging if you add a little code, then recompile and correct any errors before adding a little more code, recompiling, etc. This process of _incremental testing_ may seem like more work than adding a lot of code and compiling in one try, but beginners who work that way often see so many error messages that the errors are harder to recognize. When multiple syntax errors are present, spurious error messages will sometimes appear, making the debugging process more difficult.

Now add to the skeleton the code to display the purpose of the program and to display a header for the table itself. (Compare with the ConvertInchesToMillimeters program in Section 3.1 of the textbook.) Compile and test the program at this stage.

Once the first stages of the program are working correctly, add code to compute and display 30 degrees and the corresponding number of radians. Test this much before continuing. Even if you have done your part correctly, you will run afoul of one of Pascal's idiosyncrasies: Pascal normally prints real numbers in scientific notation. You are likely to see something like this:

```
DEGREES VERSUS RADIANS
----------------------


DEGREES      RADIANS
   3.00000000000000E+0001      5.23598775598657E-0001 rad
```

The exact appearance depends on the Pascal system you are using, but you will almost certainly see some kind of scientific notation. The "E" in the numbers means "exponent of ten," so the first number is

$$3.00000000000000 \times 10^1 \;=\; 30.0000000000000$$

which is the correct number of degrees. Similarly, the second number is

$$5.23598775598657 \times 10^{-1} \;=\; 0.523598775598657$$

Chapter 4 of the text explains how to control the formatting of displayed numbers, but we can deal with this now for the sake of nice output in this program. Just specify in the call to `WriteLn` the total number of characters and number of places that should appear to the right of the decimal point in the real-number output. For example, instead of a statement like `WriteLn( Radians )`, you would have

```
WriteLn( Radians:5:2 )
```

Number of digits to right of decimal point

Width of printed number, in characters, including the decimal point and sign (if any)

If you have designed the 30-degree code well, you will be able to repeat the same code almost exactly to print out the lines of the table for 60 and 90 degrees. (Later in the course, we will study how to make the repetition automatic.) Perform a final test on the program.

In addition to the lab pages containing your answers to questions, turn in a source code listing of your completed program and a printout of a run.

Credit: This lab benefited from comments by David Leasure, of the University of Kansas.

Lab 4.1:
Real Numbers, Roundoff Error, and I/O

Concepts: Real numbers; roundoff error; interactive programs; modularity.

Lab techniques: Use the computer system as a testbed; first write and test a skeleton.

Problem-solving techniques: Plan the I/O first, then divide until trivial.

Prerequisites: Labs 1 and 2; *Structures and Abstractions*, Chapter 4 (especially Section 4.2); college algebra.

Sections 1.3 and 4.2 of the textbook explain why real number arithmetic in a computer is not the same as the exact arithmetic we perform in our heads and on paper. In this lab, we will perform some experiments to check the seriousness of the problem. Along the way, we will design an interactive program and begin to modularize it.

We experiment with the problem shown in Section 4.2 of the textbook: finding the positive root x of the quadratic equation

$$x^2 + bx - 1 = 0$$

where b is a parameter to be specified by the user of the program. (This will allow us to try smaller and smaller values of b until we find the point at which roundoff error causes a serious error. This point will depend on the Pascal system being used.)

We begin by planning the I/O—a technique introduced in Section 2.2 of the textbook and reiterated in Section 4.5. We might, for example, design the program so that a run will look like this:

```
Seeking positive root of quadratic equation
x^2 + bx - 1 = 0.

Value of b: 1.0e10

Positive root = 0.00000000E+0000

Substituting back into the equation, we obtain
-1.00000000E+0000 = 0.0
```

In such a run, there are apparently five steps:

1. Announce the purpose of the program.
2. Prompt for, then read, a value for *b*.
3. Calculate the positive root.
4. Display the calculated root.
5. Display the equation with the calculated root substituted.

Ideally, the program should use procedures or functions for each of these five steps in the algorithm. But we don't yet know how to send data in and out of procedures and we don't know how to write functions. So we'll settle for the time being for a program that uses a procedure to announce its purpose, but performs the other steps in the main program unit. Then we can improve the modularity later, as we learn more about procedures.

We begin by writing and testing a skeleton. The program will read data from the keyboard and display data on the screen, so the program must (in Standard Pascal) declare Input and Output as program parameters. (Many compilers don't care about this.) We will need a variable to store the value of *b* read from the keyboard and a variable to store the positive root of the equation, so we will declare two Real variables:

```
PROGRAM QuadraticRoot ( Input, Output );
VAR
    B, Root : Real;

BEGIN

    { Step 1: Announce the purpose                       }
    { Step 2: Prompt for and read a value for b.         }
    { Step 3: Calculate the positive root.               }
    { Step 4: Display the root.                          }
    { Step 5: Display the equation with root substituted. }

END.
```

Key this skeleton into your Pascal system and compile it to make sure there are no syntax errors. Correct any errors before continuing.

Step 1

Next declare a ShowPurpose procedure and call it as Step 1 in the main program. Compile and test the program again.

> Use your Pascal system to print a source-code listing at this point, and turn it in as part of the lab report.

Step2

To prompt for a value for b, we call the built-in Write procedure, asking it to display the prompt we imagined earlier:

```
Write( 'Value of b: ' );
```

Unlike a WriteLn, this will leave the cursor on the same line, right after the message.

Then we call ReadLn to read a value from the keyboard into the B variable:

```
ReadLn( B );
```

Finally, for the sake of nice-looking I/O, we add a plain WriteLn to generate a blank line after the prompt and read:

```
WriteLn;
```

Key these three lines of code into your main program as Step 2. Then compile and test your program again.

Steps 3 and 4

Now, with a value stored in the B variable, we can compute the value of the positive root according to the quadratic formula. As you recall from algebra, the positive root of

$$x^2 + bx - 1 = 0$$

is

$$x = \left[-b + \sqrt{b^2 - 4ac} \right] / 2a$$

$x = -b + \sqrt{b^2 + 4} \big/ 2$

Convert this into a Pascal assignment statement, remembering that in our program, a is 1.0 and c is −1.0.

You will also need a WriteLn to display the resulting value of Root in the form shown earlier. Format the output to show scientific notation, with eight digits to the right of the decimal point.

Insert your assignment statement and `WriteLn` into the main program, and compile and test again. Again, correct any syntax errors before proceeding.

Step 5

All that's left is to display the resulting equation when our value of `Root` is substituted back in. An example was shown earlier in the imagined I/O. Write code that makes the output look as we imagined. Insert your code into the main program, then compile and test.

> Use your Pascal system to print a source-code listing at this point, and turn it in as part of the lab report.

Now use your program to see the effects of roundoff error

Your program will allow you to test the degree of roundoff error in your computer system. Make a number of runs, trying out the values of b shown below. In each case, report in the space provided the results reported by your program:

b	root	Left side of equation, which should be zero
1.0		
1.0×10^5		
1.0×10^{10}		
1.0×10^{20}		

From these results, as well as any others you might need, estimate the minimum value of b which results in loss of all significant digits in the root.

Finally, use a better formula

As a last embellishment to your program before we move on, replace the quadratic formula with the improved one developed in Section 4.2. Then perform your experiments again, reporting the program's output below:

b	root	Left side of equation, which should be zero
1.0	_____	_____
1.0×10^5	_____	_____
1.0×10^{10}	_____	_____
1.0×10^{20}	_____	_____

> Use your Pascal system to print a source-code listing at this point, and turn it in as part of the lab report. Also turn in the lab pages on which you wrote answers to questions.

Looking back, looking forward

As you finish these experiments, your `QuadraticRoot` program is not very modular because most of the code is in the main program. In Chapter 5 and 6 of the text and in the next few labs, you will learn to write more modular programs. Afterwards, we can return to the present program and improve it.

```
BEGIN

    WavyGravy

END.
```

A procedure like WavyGravy that calls itself is said to be *recursive*. Chapter 11 of *Structures and Abstractions* explains how to control recursion, but for now we are only interested in the bare fact that Pascal procedures can call themselves, something that is not allowed in some other languages.

Mutual recursion and forward declarations

Recursion can also be *indirect*: one procedure can call another, which in turn calls the first, which calls the second, and so on. Suppose a main program calls Here, which is declared as follows:

```
PROCEDURE Here;
BEGIN

    WriteLn('Over here . . .');
    There

END; { Here }

PROCEDURE There;
BEGIN

    WriteLn('                    . . . Over there');
    Here

END; { There }
```

The problem is that Here calls There, but There was not declared before it was called. However, if we declare There first, we will have the same problem again, because There calls Here. Obviously, Here and There can't *both* be declared first, so what do we do? Pascal provides a special compiler directive for just this purpose. It lets us insert a FORWARD declaration as a placeholder for a declaration that will be made later in the program. In the example below, the FORWARD declaration tells the compiler not to worry about the call to There before it is declared—it promises that the declaration will come later.

```
PROGRAM Lab4ForFun (Output);

PROCEDURE There;
FORWARD;

PROCEDURE Here;
BEGIN

   WriteLn('Over here . . .');
   There

END; { Here }

PROCEDURE There;
BEGIN

   WriteLn('                    . . . Over there');
   Here

END; { There }

BEGIN

   Here

END.
```

Try this program on your computer system without the code that is shown in boldface. What error message do you see when you try to compile the program?

_____

_____

Now add the boldface code and compile and run the program.

> Turn in the lab book pages on which you wrote answers to questions, plus the source-code listings for the programs you ran and printouts of test runs.

Lab 5.1:
Using the Turbo Pascal Integrated Debugger

Concepts: Source-code debugger; single-stepping; trace into; step over; watch window; breakpoint

Lab techniques: Interactive testing

Prerequisites: Labs 1–5; Chapters 1–5 in *Structures and Abstractions*

When you are having trouble finding a bug and you need to see what your program is doing in detail, nothing helps like an interactive *source-code debugger*. A source-code debugger is a testing program that lets you execute your Pascal source code slowly and interactively, executing one statement or a group of statements at a time, while watching the values change in the variables and evaluating any expressions you want to check. In this laboratory session, we will try out some of the features of the debugger in the Turbo Integrated Development Environment.

From the floppy disk accompanying this manual, copy the files called BUG5A.PAS, BUG5B.PAS, and BUG5C.PAS into the subdirectory where you work on your source code files. Then start up Turbo Pascal, loading BUG5A.PAS:

```
C:\TP>TURBO BUG5A.PAS
```

Here is a source listing of the program you should see on your screen:

```
PROGRAM Bug5A ( Input, Output );
{
  This program contains a common error
  in using a procedure.
}
VAR
   Angle : Real;

PROCEDURE GetAngle( Angle : Real );
BEGIN

   Write( 'Angle in radians? ' );
   ReadLn( Angle )

END; { GetAngle }
```

```
BEGIN { main program }

   GetAngle( Angle );

   WriteLn;
   WriteLn( 'Main has angle = ', Angle:6:2, ' radians' )

END.
```

This program contains a common error in using a procedure, as mentioned in Section 5.9 of the textbook. When the program has been loaded under Turbo Pascal, press Control-F9 to compile, link, and run. When the program prompts for an angle in radians, key in whatever you like and press return. At the end of the run, the main program will say that it has some garbage angle. Somehow, the main program has failed to receive the parameter value sent to it by GetAngle.

If we were debugging by simply watching output, we could insert a WriteLn at the end of the GetAngle procedure to help see what's happening:

```
PROCEDURE GetAngle( Angle : Real );
BEGIN

   Write( 'Angle in radians? ' );
   ReadLn( Angle );
   WriteLn( 'GetAngle procedure has Angle = ', Angle:6:2 )


END; { GetAngle }
```

Try this, make a run, and report the output you see on the screen:

_____

_____

_____

_____

_____

_____

_____

_____

What conclusion, if any, do you draw about the nature of the error?

_____

_____

Once again—this time with the debugger

Now let's explore the same error with the help of Turbo's interactive debugger. The debugger allows us to *trace* the execution of the program—single-step through it—while *watching* the variables change. In version 5.x of Turbo Pascal, a special Watch window is automatically opened at the bottom of the screen. In version 6.0, open the Watch window by pulling down the *Window* menu and selecting *Watch*. The Watch window will appear at the bottom of the screen, covering up part of the editing window, and along with it, some of your source code. This is shown in Figure 6.1.

```
≡  File  Edit  Search  Run  Compile  Debug   Options  Window  Help
════════════════════════════ BUG5A.PAS ═══════════════════════════1═
PROGRAM Bug5A ( Input, Output );
{
  From Sec. 5.9.
  This program contains a common error in using a procedure.
}
VAR
    Angle : Real;


PROCEDURE GetAngle( Angle : Real );
BEGIN

    Write( 'Angle in radians? ' );
    ReadLn( Angle )
╞═══════════════════════════ Watches ══════════════════════════2═╡
▲



▼
◄                                                                 ►
F1 Help  F7 Trace  F8 Step  ◄──┘ Edit   Ins Add   Del Delete  F10 Menu
```

FIGURE 1. *The Watch window has been opened and is now the active window, as indicated by its visible scroll bars and the new command list at the bottom of the screen. This is version 6.0 of Turbo Pascal, in which the Watch window initially covers up the bottom of the Edit window. In version 5.x, the Watch window appears automatically and does not cover up any source code.*

To prevent your source code from being covered up, pull down the *Window* menu and select *Tile*, which will treat the two windows as separate "tiles" of the screen, preventing them from overlapping.

Whichever version of Turbo you are using, add to the Watch window the names of the variables whose values you want to observe during execution. In the present program, there is only one variable name—Angle—but it names both a global variable and a local variable of the procedure. (Hmm . . . why is that?) Press Control-F7 to add a watch variable to the Watch window. You will see a dialog box in which you key in the Angle identifier. Key K for *OK* or click on the *OK* button or press Enter, and Angle will be added to the Watch window, as shown in Figure 6.2.

The Unknown identifier message appears because the program is not yet running, and the variable does not yet exist in memory. To start single-stepping through the program, press the F7 function key, which is equivalent to the *Trace into* command on the *Run* menu. The main program's BEGIN will be highlighted by an *execution bar*, marking the next statement to be executed. With the

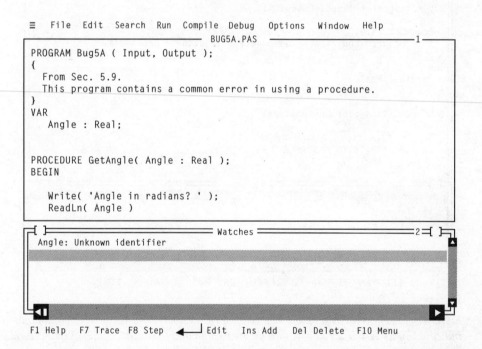

FIGURE 2. The Watch window has now been tiled, so that it does not cover any of the Edit window. The Angle variable has been added to the Watch window, but is still unknown to the debugger because the program is not yet running, and therefore the memory cell has not yet been allocated.

execution bar on BEGIN, you will see a garbage value in the main program's Angle variable. Why is there garbage in the variable?

_____

_____

Press F7 again. The execution bar indicates that GetAngle is about to be called. Press F7 again, and execution passes to the GetAngle procedure, in which the BEGIN is highlighted. Now the Watch window is showing us the contents of the procedure's local Angle variable—a different memory cell than before. Why does this Angle variable have the same value as the one in the main program?

_____

_____

Press F7 twice more. Now the ReadLn is executing, waiting for you to key in an angle in radians. Enter a value that is easy to remember, then press Enter. The output screen goes away automatically, and you can see your value stored in the procedure's Angle variable. The execution bar indicates that the procedure will terminate the next time you press F7.

Press F7 again, and execution returns to the main program, as shown in Figure 6.3. But now you see that the main program's Angle variable still contains garbage! Obviously, the procedure's value of Angle is not being copied back into the main program's Angle. That is the error we have been looking for—the correct value was in the formal parameter, but it wasn't copied into the actual parameter. The error is—what?

_____

_____

Switching between windows

To make a different window active on the screen—for example, to switch activities from the editing window to the Watch window or vice versa—press the **F6** key. To go back to the previous window, press **Shift-F6**.

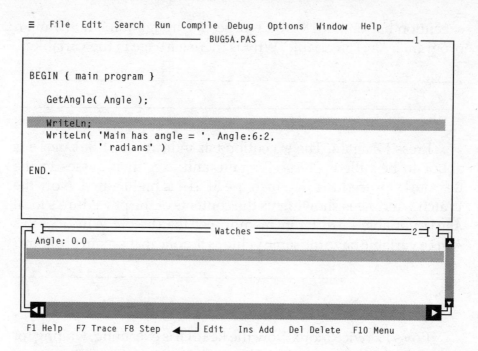

FIGURE 3. *After tracing the program to the point marked by the execution bar, we see that the main program's Angle variable does not contain the value entered by the user. In this run, the user had entered 1.0.*

Stepping over

So far, the only single-stepping mode we have used is the one called *Trace into*, which traces not only through the main program, but through all subprograms as well. There is another mode as well, called *Step over*. This mode single-steps through the main program, but executes a subprogram in one swoop, without single-stepping through the subprogram's internal code.

Step into is associated with the F8 function key. To see how it works, start at the beginning of the Bug5A program again. (If necessary, select *Program Reset* from the *Run* menu, or key Control-F2.) Press F8 twice, so that the call to GetAngle will be the next statement to execute. Then, when you press F8 again, the procedure will execute completely. After responding to the procedure's prompt for data, you will find yourself back in the main program, at the WriteLn following the call to GetAngle.

In our present example, stepping over the procedure is not as informative as tracing into the procedure, but in a program with many subprograms, stepping over them could speed up debugging of the main program. Use it when you need it.

Go to a breakpoint

Press Control-F2 to reset the program again. Suppose that you want to execute Bug5A normally and continuously down to the main program's first WriteLn statement, where you want the program to stop so that you can examine the value in the Angle variable. To make it do this, you set a *breakpoint* at the WriteLn statement—that is, you erect a conceptual "stop sign" there. Use the arrow keys or mouse to place the cursor in the line containing the WriteLn; then select *Toggle breakpoint* from the *Debug* menu, as in Figure 6.4, or key Control-F8. The WriteLn lights up, indicating that a breakpoint has been set. (On color screens, it is "stop sign red.") Then press Control-F9 to run the program. The program will execute automatically all the way to the breakpoint, then will halt, with the WriteLn the next statement to execute when you give the command. From there, you can execute with another Control-F9 or you can single-step with F7 or F8.

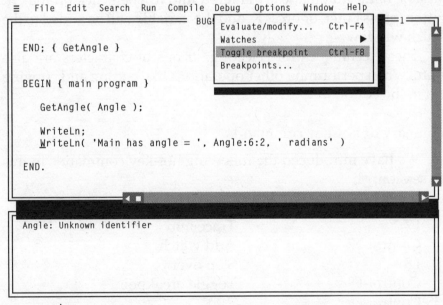

FIGURE 4. Using the Debug menu to set a breakpoint on the line containing the cursor. After selecting Toggle breakpoint from the menu, the END statement will "light up," indicating that a breakpoint has been set there. If Toggle breakpoint is selected again with the cursor on that line, the breakpoint will be turned off.

A shortcut when adding watches

You can avoid keying variable names into the *Add watch* dialog box if you *select* (highlight) the variable name in the editing window before you give the *Add watch* command. There are four ways to select the variable name; use whichever is most convenient:

- Drag the mouse pointer through the variable name.

- Move the cursor to one end of the word, then hold the shift key down while moving through the word by means of the arrow keys *in the numeric keypad*.

- Move the cursor to one end of the word, then with the NumLock key down, move through the word by means of the arrow keys *in the arrow pad*.

- Move the cursor into the word, then key Control-K-T. (Hold the Control key down while pressing K, then T.)

After selecting the variable name in one of these ways, key Control-F7 (for *Add watch*). A dialog box will appear with the variable name automatically entered into it. Then click on the OK button, press Enter, or press K, and the variable will be added to the Watch window.

These techniques for selecting strings of characters are also useful when performing other operations like cutting and copying text in the editor.

Summary of hot-key commands

We have introduced the following hot-key commands in this lab session:

Control-F2	Add watch
F7	Trace into
Control-F7	Add watch
F8	Step over
Control-F8	Toggle breakpoint
Control-F9	Run
Control-K-T	Select word at cursor
Shift-NumArrows	Select characters

Now for some practice . . .

For further practice in using these techniques, load into Turbo the Bug5B.PAS file you copied earlier. Here is the program:

```
PROGRAM Bug5B ( Input, Output );
{
  This program contains a common error
  in using a procedure.

  Note that the Pi constant is predefined in Turbo Pascal.
}
VAR
    Degrees, Radians : Real;

PROCEDURE GetAngle( VAR Rads, Degs : Real );
BEGIN

    Write( 'Angle in radians? ' );
    ReadLn( Rads );

    {--Convert to degrees }
    Degs := ( 360.0 / ( 2.0 * Pi ) ) * Rads

END; { GetAngle }

BEGIN { main program }

    GetAngle( Degrees, Radians );

    WriteLn;
    WriteLn( 'Main has angle = ', Radians:6:2,
            ' radians' );
    WriteLn;
    WriteLn

END.
```

If you are using version 6.0, open the Watch window and tile it as we did before. First run the program to see the symptom of the bug. How does the output indicate a bug?

_____

_____

Now add the variables Degrees, Radians, Degs, Rads to the Watch window and trace the execution until the execution bar lies on the GetAngle procedure's END statement. Study the contents of the Watch window, which now contains enough clues to identify the bug. What is the bug?

_____

_____

Fix the bug and test the program. When you are satisfied that the program is running correctly, add whatever output you need to fill in these blanks:

　　　1.00 radians　　= _____ degrees

　　　6.2832 radians　= _____ degrees

Practice with breakpoints

For your last exercise in this lab session, load the BUG5C.PAS program into Turbo Pascal. This program was intended to add up the weights of our good friends, Larry, Moe, and Curly. The I/O was supposed to look like this:

```
This program displays the total weights
of Larry, Moe, and Curly,
and incidentally shows how to achieve
repetition by nested procedure calls.

Larry's weight (lbs)? 100
Total so far is 100.0 lbs

Moe's weight (lbs)? 200
Total so far is 300.0 lbs

Curly's weight (lbs)? 300
Total so far is 600.0 lbs

Press enter to terminate...
```

Unfortunately, this is not what happens when you run the program. The source code is shown below. Run it and report the actual I/O.

```
PROGRAM Bug5C ( Output );
{
  From Lab 6.
  Contains deliberate errors for debugging practice.
}

PROCEDURE Curly( VAR Total : Real );
VAR
    CurlysWeight : Real;

BEGIN

    WriteLn;
    Write( 'Curly''s weight (lbs)? ' );
    ReadLn( CurlysWeight );
    Total := Total + CurlysWeight;

    WriteLn( 'Total so far is ', Total:6:2, ' lbs' )

END; { Curly }


PROCEDURE Moe( VAR Total : Real );
VAR
    MoesWeight : Real;

BEGIN

    WriteLn;
    Write( 'Moe''s weight (lbs)? ' );
    ReadLn( MoesWeight );
    Total := Total + MoesWeight;

    Curly( Total );

    WriteLn( 'Total so far is ', Total:6:2, ' lbs' )

END; { Moe }
```

```
PROCEDURE Larry;
VAR
    LarrysWeight, Total : Real;

BEGIN

    WriteLn;
    Write( 'Larry''s weight (lbs)? ' );
    ReadLn( LarrysWeight );
    Total := LarrysWeight;

    Moe( Total );

    WriteLn( 'Total so far is ', Total:6:2, ' lbs' )

END; { Larry }



PROCEDURE ShowPurpose;
BEGIN

    WriteLn;
    WriteLn;
    WriteLn( 'This program displays the total weights' );
    WriteLn( 'of Larry, Moe, and Curly,' );
    WriteLn( 'and incidentally shows how to achieve' );
    WriteLn( 'repetition by nested procedure calls.' );
    WriteLn

END; { ShowPurpose }



PROCEDURE SayGoodbye;
BEGIN

    WriteLn;
    WriteLn( 'Press Enter to continue...' );
    ReadLn;
    WriteLn

END; { SayGoodbye }
```

```
BEGIN { main program }

    ShowPurpose;
    Larry;
    SayGoodbye

END.
```

Show in the space below what happens when you run the program:

_____

_____

_____

_____

_____

_____

_____

_____

_____

_____

_____

_____

_____

Next, follow the debugging instructions on the next page.

What's wrong with Larry, Moe, and Curly?

Insert breakpoints where the `Larry` procedure calls `Moe`, where `Moe` calls `Curly`, and where `Larry` displays its value of `Total`. Run the program to each breakpoint in turn and see if you can tell what's wrong. If not, reset the program and run to the first breakpoint, then trace the rest of the way with the F7 key. Notice the sequence of execution and watch the values change in the variables.

When you have identified the problem(s), fix what you can and then test the program again. Don't expect to fix everything in one try. Fix as much as you can, then test, then fix some more, and test.

When you are satisfied with your program, print out a source listing and turn it in along with the rest of your lab report.

Lab 5.2:
Using the THINK Pascal Integrated Debugger

Concepts: Source-code debugger; single-stepping; step into; step over; Observe window; breakpoint.

Lab techniques: Interactive testing.

Prerequisites: Labs 1–5; Chapters 1–5 in *Structures and Abstractions.*

When you are having trouble finding a bug and you need to see what your program is doing in detail, nothing helps like an interactive *source-code debugger*. A source-code debugger is a testing program that lets you execute your Pascal source code slowly and interactively, executing one statement or a group of statements at a time, while watching the values change in the variables and evaluating any expressions you want to check. In this laboratory session, we will try out some of the features of the debugger in the THINK Pascal environment.

From the floppy disk accompanying this manual, copy the files called BUG5A.PAS, BUG5B.PAS, and BUG5C.PAS into the subdirectory where you work on your source code files. Then start up THINK Pascal, adding BUG5A.PAS to your project. Here is a source listing of the program you should see on your screen:

```
PROGRAM Bug5A ( Input, Output );

{ This program contains a common error }
{ in using a procedure. }

VAR
   Angle : Real;

PROCEDURE GetAngle( Angle : Real );
BEGIN

   Write( 'Angle in radians? ' );
   ReadLn( Angle )

END; { GetAngle }
```

```
BEGIN { main program }

   GetAngle( Angle );

   WriteLn;
   WriteLn( 'Main has angle = ', Angle:6:2, ' radians' )
END.
```

This program contains a common error in using a procedure, as mentioned in Section 5.9 of the textbook. When the program has been loaded under THINK Pascal, press Command-G to compile, link, and run. When the program prompts for an angle in radians, key in whatever you like and press return. At the end of the run, the main program will say that it has some garbage angle. Somehow, the main program has failed to receive the parameter value sent to it by GetAngle.

If we were debugging by simply watching output, we could insert a WriteLn at the end of the GetAngle procedure to help see what's happening:

```
PROCEDURE GetAngle( Angle : Real );
BEGIN

   Write( 'Angle in radians? ' );
   ReadLn( Angle );
   WriteLn( 'GetAngle procedure has Angle = ', Angle:6:2 )


END; { GetAngle }
```

Try this, make a run, and report the output you see on the screen:

_____

_____

_____

_____

_____

_____

What conclusion, if any, do you draw about the nature of the error?

_____

_____

Once again—this time with the debugger

Now let's explore the same error with the help of THINK's interactive debugger. The debugger allows us to *trace* the execution of the program—single-step through it—while *observing* the variables change. Open the Observe window by pulling down the *Debug* menu and selecting *Observe*. The Observe window will appear on the the screen, covering up part of the editing window, and along with it, some of your source code. Drag the window to a convenient position on the screen, resizing the windows as necessary. An example is shown in Figure 1.

Add to the Observe window the names of the variables whose values you want to observe during execution. In the present program, there is only one variable name—Angle—but it names both

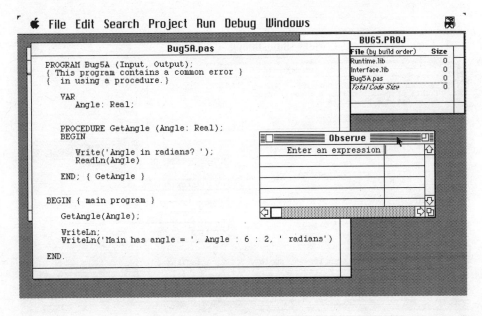

FIGURE 1. *The Observe window has been opened and is now the active window, as indicated by its visible scroll bars and the new command list at the bottom of the screen. The Observe window has been dragged to a convenient position and the Edit window has been resized.*

a global variable and a local variable of the procedure. (Hmm . . . why is that?) Enter the Angle identifier into the Observe window, and press Return. The screen will look as shown in Figure 2.

The program is not yet running, so the variable does not yet exist in memory. To start single-stepping through the program, press Command-I, which is equivalent to the *StepInto* command on the *Run* menu. The program will compile and link if necessary, then a "hand" icon will appear in your source code, with its finger pointing at the main program's BEGIN. This marks the next statement to be executed. With the finger pointing at BEGIN, you will see a garbage value in the main program's Angle variable. Why is there garbage in the variable?

Press Command-I again. The finger indicates that GetAngle is about to be called. Press Command-I again, and execution passes to the GetAngle procedure, in which the BEGIN is highlighted. Now the Observe window is showing us the contents of the procedure's

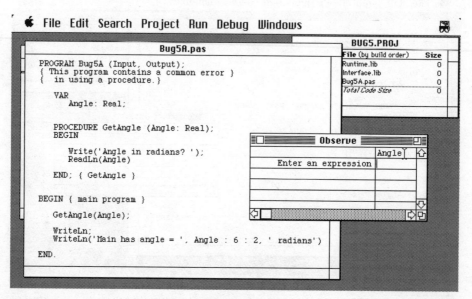

FIGURE 2.   *The Angle variable has been added to the Observe window, but is still unknown to the debugger because the program is not yet running, and therefore the memory cell has not yet been allocated.*

local `Angle` variable—a different memory cell than before. Why does this `Angle` variable have the same value as the one in the main program?

_____

_____

Press Command-I three more times. Now the `ReadLn` is executing, waiting for you to key in an angle in radians. Enter some value that is easy to remember, then press Return. Now you see your value stored in the procedure's `Angle` variable. (You may have to click on the Observe window to see all of it, if it overlaps the Edit window.) The finger indicates that the procedure will terminate the next time you press Command-I.

Press Command-I again, and execution returns to the main program, as shown in Figure 3. But now you see that the main program's `Angle` variable still contains garbage! Obviously, the procedure's value of `Angle` is not being copied back into the main program's `Angle`. That is the error we have been looking for—the correct value was in the formal parameter, but it wasn't copied into the actual parameter. The error is—what?

_____

_____

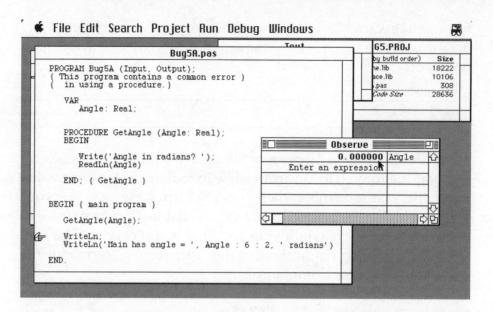

FIGURE 3. *After tracing the program to the point marked by the pointing finger, we see that the main program's Angle variable does not contain the value entered by the user. In this run, the user had entered 1.0.*

Stepping over

So far, the only single-stepping mode we have used is the one called *Step Into,* which traces not only through the main program, but through all subprograms as well. There is another mode as well, called *Step Over.* This mode single-steps through the main program, but executes a subprogram in one swoop, without single-stepping through the subprogram's internal code.

Step Over is activated by Command-J. To see how it works, start at the beginning of the Bug5A program again. (If necessary, select *Reset* from the *Run* menu.) Press Command-J twice, so that the call to GetAngle will be the next statement to execute. Then, when you press Command-J again, the procedure will execute completely. After responding to the procedure's prompt for data, you will find yourself back in the main program, at the WriteLn following the call to GetAngle.

In our present example, stepping over the procedure is not as informative as stepping into the procedure, but in a program with many subprograms, stepping over them could speed up debugging of the main program. Use it when you need it.

Go to a breakpoint

Reset the program again. Suppose that you want to execute Bug5A normally and continuously down to the main program's first WriteLn statement, where you want the program to stop so that you can examine the value in the Angle variable. To make it do this, you set a *breakpoint* at the WriteLn statement—that is, you erect a conceptual "stop sign" there. On the *Debug* menu, select *Stops In*. A margin will appear down the left side of your Edit window. Then click in this margin beside the first WriteLn in the main program. A stop sign appears, indicating that a breakpoint has been set at that point. (Figure 4.) Now press Command-G to run the program. Execution will proceed automatically all the way to the stop sign, then will halt, with the WriteLn the next statement to execute when you give the command. While execution is halted, you can inspect the Observe window. Then you can resume execution with another Command-G or single-step with Command-I or Command-J.

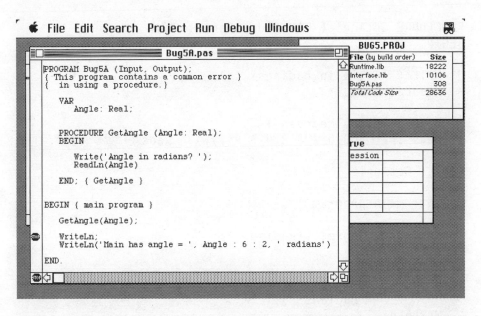

FIGURE 4. Placing a stop sign in the left margin of the Edit window after selecting Stops In from the Debug menu. When the Go command is given, the code will execute down to the stop sign, then halt, allowing inspection of the Observe window. The statement on which the stop sign is placed will be the next to excute when another Go or Step command is given.

Summary of hot-key commands

We have introduced the following hot-key commands in this lab session:

Command-G	Go
Command-I	Step Into
Command-J	Step Over

Now for some practice . . .

For further practice in using these techniques, load into THINK the Bug5B.PAS file you copied earlier. Here is the program:

```pascal
PROGRAM Bug5B ( Input, Output );
{
  This program contains a common error
  in using a procedure.
}
CONST
  Pi = 3.14159265;

VAR
    Degrees, Radians : Real;

PROCEDURE GetAngle( VAR Rads, Degs : Real );
BEGIN

    Write( 'Angle in radians? ' );
    ReadLn( Rads );

    {--Convert to degrees }
    Degs := ( 360.0 / ( 2.0 * Pi ) ) * Rads

END; { GetAngle }

BEGIN { main program }

    GetAngle( Degrees, Radians );

    WriteLn;
    WriteLn( 'Main has angle = ', Radians:6:2,
            ' radians' );
    WriteLn;
    WriteLn

END.
```

First run the program to see the symptom of the bug. How does the output indicate a bug?

_____

_____

Now watch the variables Degrees, Radians, Degs, Rads in the Observe window and single-step until the execution finger lies on the GetAngle procedure's END statement. Study the contents of the Observe window, which now contains enough clues to identify the bug. What is the bug?

_____

_____

Fix the bug and test the program. When you are satisfied that the program is running correctly, add whatever output you need to fill in these blanks:

   1.00 radians   = _____ degrees

   6.2832 radians   = _____ degrees

Practice with breakpoints

For your last exercise in this lab session, load the BUG5C.PAS program into THINK. This program was intended to add up the weights of our good friends, Larry, Moe, and Curly. The I/O was supposed to look as shown on the next page:

```
This program displays the total weights
of Larry, Moe, and Curly,
and incidentally shows how to achieve
repetition by nested procedure calls.

Larry's weight (lbs)? 100
Total so far is 100.0 lbs

Moe's weight (lbs)? 200
Total so far is 300.0 lbs

Curly's weight (lbs)? 300
Total so far is 600.0 lbs

Press enter to terminate...
```

Unfortunately, this is not what happens when you run the program. The source code is shown below. Run it and report the actual I/O.

```
PROGRAM Bug5C ( Output );
{
  From Lab 6.
  Contains deliberate errors for debugging practice.
}

PROCEDURE Curly( VAR Total : Real );
VAR
    CurlysWeight : Real;

BEGIN

    WriteLn;
    Write( 'Curly''s weight (lbs)? ' );
    ReadLn( CurlysWeight );
    Total := Total + CurlysWeight;

    WriteLn( 'Total so far is ', Total:6:2, ' lbs' )

END; { Curly }
```

```
PROCEDURE Moe( VAR Total : Real );
VAR
   MoesWeight : Real;

BEGIN

   WriteLn;
   Write( 'Moe''s weight (lbs)? ' );
   ReadLn( MoesWeight );
   Total := Total + MoesWeight;

   Curly( Total );

   WriteLn( 'Total so far is ', Total:6:2, ' lbs' )

END; { Moe }


PROCEDURE Larry;
VAR
   LarrysWeight, Total : Real;

BEGIN

   WriteLn;
   Write( 'Larry''s weight (lbs)? ' );
   ReadLn( LarrysWeight );
   Total := LarrysWeight;

   Moe( Total );

   WriteLn( 'Total so far is ', Total:6:2, ' lbs' )

END; { Larry }


PROCEDURE ShowPurpose;
BEGIN

   WriteLn;
   WriteLn;
   WriteLn( 'This program displays the total weights' );
   WriteLn( 'of Larry, Moe, and Curly,' );
   WriteLn( 'and incidentally shows how to achieve' );
   WriteLn( 'repetition by nested procedure calls.' );
   WriteLn

END; { ShowPurpose }
```

```
PROCEDURE SayGoodbye;
BEGIN

   WriteLn;
   WriteLn( 'Press Enter to continue...' );
   ReadLn;
   WriteLn

END; { SayGoodbye }


BEGIN { main program }

   ShowPurpose;
   Larry;
   SayGoodbye

END.
```

Show in the space below what happens when you run the program:

_____

_____

_____

_____

_____

_____

_____

_____

_____

_____

_____

_____

Next, follow the debugging instructions on the next page.

What's wrong with Larry, Moe, and Curly?

Insert breakpoints where the Larry procedure calls Moe, where Moe calls Curly, and where Larry displays its value of Total. Run the program to each breakpoint in turn and see if you can tell what's wrong. If not, reset the program and run to the first breakpoint, then step the rest of the way with Command-I. Notice the sequence of execution and watch the values change in the variables.

When you have identified the problem(s), fix what you can and then test the program again. Don't expect to fix everything in one try. Fix as much as you can, then test, then fix some more, and test.

> When you are satisfied with your program, print out a source listing and turn it in along with the rest of your lab report.

Lab 6.1
Animating a Function

Concepts: Function.

Lab techniques: Watching the sequence of execution and checking the scopes of identifiers with the help of a debugger.

Prerequisites: Chapters 5 and 6 of *Structures and Abstractions*.

Section 6.2 of the textbook presents a version of the FahrenheitToCelsius program in which a function is used to perform the unit conversion. There, a sequence of diagrams is used to show how the CelsiusConversion function receives its parameter value, how it performs the conversion, and how it returns a value to the main program. In this lab, we will do better: we will literally *watch* the execution and program state, step by step, with our own eyes, with the help of an interactive debugger.

The program

Here is the source code for the program, as described in Section 6.2 of the text and provided in the file FTOC5.PAS accompanying this lab manual. The call to the function, and the function itself, are highlightedbelow.

```
PROGRAM FahrenheitToCelsius5 ( Input, Output );
{
  Fully modular version, using a conversion function
}
VAR
   Fahrenheit, Celsius : Real;

PROCEDURE ShowPurpose;
{
  POSTCONDITION:
  The purpose of the program is displayed
  on the screen.
}
BEGIN

   WriteLn( 'CONVERTING FAHRENHEIT TO CELSIUS' );
   WriteLn

END; { ShowPurpose }
```

6.1–2   Animating a Function

```
PROCEDURE GetFahrenheit( VAR F : Real );
{
  POSTCONDITION:
  The parameter contains a Fahrenheit temperature.
}
BEGIN

  Write( 'Fahrenheit temperature? ' );
  ReadLn( F )

END; { GetFahrenheit }


FUNCTION CelsiusConversion( F : Real ) : Real;
{
  PRECONDITION:
  F has a value.

  POSTCONDITION:
  Returns the Celsius temperature corresponding
  to the Fahrenheit temperature F.
}
BEGIN

  CelsiusConversion := ( 5.0 / 9.0 ) * ( F - 32.0 )

END; { CelsiusConversion }


PROCEDURE ShowTemperature( F, C : Real );
{
  PRECONDITION:
  F and C contain corresponding Fahrenheit and
  Celsius temperatures.

  POSTCONDITION:
  The values of F and C are displayed on the screen.
}
BEGIN

  WriteLn;
  WriteLn( F:6:1, ' deg. F. = ', C:6:1, ' deg. C.' )

END; { ShowTemperature }
```

```
BEGIN { main program }

    ShowPurpose;
    GetFahrenheit( Fahrenheit );
    Celsius := CelsiusConversion( Fahrenheit );
    ShowTemperature( Fahrenheit, Celsius )

END.
```

Using the debugger

To begin with, we need a clear picture of what we want to watch. Here's a list, written in the order in which things should occur as we run the program:

1. Observe the value of Fahrenheit and Celsius just before the function is called.

2. Just as the function begins to execute, what is the value of the local variable F? What is the value of Celsius-Conversion?

3. As the function executes its assignment statement, what value appears in CelsiusConversion?

4. Just before the function returns execution to the main program, what is the value of the main program's Celsius variable?

5. Just after execution returns to the main program what value is assigned to Celsius? Is the value of Fahrenheit the same as it was before the function was called?

To watch these changes occur step by step in the variables, we will need to single-step through the calling of the function, the execution of the function, and the return to the main program from the function. We can use the Watch window to see the values in the variables. (It's called the Observe window by some debuggers.)

The plan

We will insert a breakpoint at the point where the main program calls the function, so that execution will proceed normally down to there, then stop. We will add Fahrenheit, Celsius, F, and CelsiusConversion to the Watch/Observe window. Then we will execute to the breakpoint and Trace Into/Step Into from there.

Report your results

Carry out the steps described above. When prompted for a Fahrenheit temperature, enter 68 and report your observations and conclusions below.

1. After entering 68 at the prompt for a Fahrenheit temperature, execute the program to the breakpoint where the main program calls the CelsiusConversion function. What are the values of Fahrenheit and Celsius just before the function is called?

Fahrenheit = _____

Celsius = _____

At this point, what does the debugger say about the value of F, and why does it say this?

_____

_____

2. Single-step into the function. Just as the function begins to execute, what is the value of the local variable F? What is the value of CelsiusConversion?

F = _____

CelsiusConversion = _____

At this point, how does the debugger know the values of Fahrenheit and Celsius—aren't they declared outside the function?

_____

_____

3. Single-step to the function's END statement. As the function executes its assignment statement, what value appears in CelsiusConversion?

_____

4. At this point, just before the function returns execution to the main program, what is the value of the main program's `Celsius` variable?

_____

Why does it have this value and not the value of `CelsiusConversion`?

_____

_____

5. Take another step, so that execution returns to the main program, then another step to execute the main program's assignment statement. What value is assigned to `Celsius`?

_____

Is the value of `Fahrenheit` the same as it was before the function was called?

_____

At this point, what does the debugger say about the value of `F`?

_____

6. From your observations during the execution of this function, answer these questions:

How does the information supplied by the debugger reflect the scope of the `F` variable?

_____

_____

What is the scope of `CelsiusConversion`?

_____

_____

What is the scope of `Fahrenheit` and `Celsius`?

_____

_____

Credit: This lab has benefited from suggestions by Matthew Dickerson, of Middlebury College.

Lab 7.1
Experimenting with Integers

Concepts: The integer data type.

Lab techniques: Learning by experimentation.

Prerequisites: Chapter 7 of *Structures and Abstractions*.

Ordinal data are discrete and enumerable. That is, we can list the values for any ordinal type in order, from the first to the last. Pascal has three fundamental ordinal types: `Integer`, `Char`, and `Boolean`. Later on, we will see that Pascal also allows us to build new ordinal types.

This lab is concerned with Pascal's `Integer` type; the following labs deal with characters and booleans. In each case, we will use the computer to experiment with the properties of these ordinal types.

Properties of integers

Pascal defines a maximum integer value, called `MaxInt`. The value of `MaxInt` depends on your Pascal system, including the hardware, but is constant for a given system. In becoming familiar with integers in your Pascal system, one of the first things to do is to determine `MaxInt` experimentally. (Yes, you can look it up in the system reference manual, but sometimes manuals are wrong.) Run the following program and report the output:

```
PROGRAM TestMaxInt ( Output );
BEGIN

   WriteLn( 'In this system, MaxInt = ', MaxInt )

END.
```

Show the output of this program:

`In this system, MaxInt =` _____

In Standard Pascal, the allowed integer values are

```
( -MaxInt, -MaxInt+1, -MaxInt+2, ...,
          0, 1, 2, 3, ..., MaxInt-2, MaxInt-1, MaxInt )
```

but in some Pascal systems, the minimum integer is -MaxInt-1 rather than -MaxInt. To determine the limits in your Pascal system, you will need to perform a test. The test relies on the fact that there are upper and lower limits to integers, beyond which we go outside the storable range, which is an error condition. *Make sure that range checking and overflow checking are turned on in your Pascal system, so that out-of-range values will be reported as errors.* (See the material on compiler directives and compiler options in Labs 1.3 and 1.4.) Then run the following program:

```
PROGRAM TestIntRange (Output);
{ From Lab 7.1. }
VAR
    IntNum: Integer;

BEGIN

    IntNum := MaxInt;
    WriteLn('TESTING UPPER LIMIT:');
    WriteLn('MaxInt + 1 = ', Succ(IntNum));
    WriteLn;

    IntNum := -MaxInt;
    WriteLn('TESTING LOWER LIMIT:');
    WriteLn('-MaxInt - 1 = ', Pred(IntNum));
    WriteLn('-MaxInt - 2 = ', Pred(Pred(IntNum)))

END.
```

Report the output below. (*Be sure range and overflow checking are turned on!*)

_____

_____

_____

_____

_____

_____

Now turn *off* the range and overflow checking, recompile, and run the program again. Report the output below; it may or may not be different from the previous run. Look carefully at the output; do the numbers "wrap around" when you go beyond the upper or lower limit?

_____

_____

_____

_____

_____

_____

Judging from the output from these two runs, what are the upper and lower limits to integer values in your Pascal system?

Maximum integer = _____

Minimum integer = _____

Investigating DIV and MOD

Next we investigate the properties of Pascal's two integer-division operators, DIV and MOD. DIV gives the quotient of integer division, while MOD gives—for nonnegative integers—the remainder. Run this program and report the results:

```
PROGRAM TestDivMod ( Output );
BEGIN

    WriteLn( '7 DIV 2   = ', 7 DIV 2,
             '    7 MOD 2   = ', 7 MOD 2 );
    WriteLn( '6 DIV 2   = ', 6 DIV 2,
             '    6 MOD 2   = ', 6 MOD 2 );
    WriteLn( '5 DIV 2   = ', 5 DIV 2,
             '    5 MOD 2   = ', 5 MOD 2 );
    WriteLn( '(-7) DIV 2 = ', (-7) DIV 2,
             '    (-7) MOD 2 = ', (-7) MOD 2 )

END.
```

Output from run:

_____

_____

_____

_____

Now remove the parentheses from the expressions (-7) DIV 2 and (-7) MOD 2. Recompile the program and run it again. Does the last line of output change? What does this tell you about the relative order of precedence of unary minus and DIV and MOD? (The results may differ in different Pascal systems.)

_____

_____

_____

_____

Next, modify the program to show that, for any *positive* integers I and J,

```
I DIV J  =  Trunc( I / J )
```

> Turn in your source code and printout from a test run, together with these lab pages.

The difference between MOD and the remainder

The text explains that I MOD J yields the remainder of the integer division I DIV J when I and J are both nonnegative, but that

1. The result is *not* the same as the remainder when I is negative, and

2. The operation is *illegal* when J is negative.

According to the definition in Standard Pascal, MOD should yield the following sample results:

```
 3 MOD 3  =  0
 2 MOD 3  =  2
 1 MOD 3  =  1
 0 MOD 3  =  0
-1 MOD 3  =  2
-2 MOD 3  =  1
-3 MOD 3  =  0
```

What does your Pascal system give when the dividend goes negative? Write a program to test this.

> Turn in your source code and printout from a run that tests the cases shown above.

Effect of delimiters when reading integer data

Section 7.2 of the text explains that integer data must be delimited (terminated or separated) by whitespace—by spaces, tabs, or end-of-line signals. Some examples are given there.

Write a small program to test the actions of the following prompt-and-read pair when Larry, Moe, and Curly are integer variables:

```
WriteLn( 'Give me three integers:' );
ReadLn( Larry, Moe, Curly );
```

Run the program with the following sets of input data and report the resulting values stored in Larry, Moe, and Curly. Also explain *why* the variables have these values. (In the runs shown, the symbol Δ is used to indicate a space, <Tab> is used to indicate a horizontal tab, and <EOLn> is used to indicate end-of-line, where the user pressed the Return or Enter key.)

Run 1:

```
Give me three integers:
1ΔΔ3<Tab>5<EOLn>
```

Resulting values in the variables:

Larry contains _____

Moe contains _____

Curly contains _____

Explanation:

_____

_____

_____

Run 2:

```
Give me three integers:
1ΔΔ3<EOLn>5<Tab>
```

Resulting values in the variables:

Larry contains _____

Moe contains _____

Curly contains _____

Explanation:

_____

_____

_____

Lab 7.2
Experimenting with Characters

Concepts: Character data.

Lab techniques: Learning by experimentation.

Prerequisites: Chapter 7 of *Structures and Abstractions*.

A Char (character) variable stores just one character at a time and typically occupies just one byte of main memory. Individual character variables have only limited uses; their main importance lies in the way we can build an entire array of them, for storing a string of characters. Until Chapter 14, we don't have the tools for doing this, however. For now, we will confine ourselves to the properties of single characters.

Ordinal properties of characters

Being an ordinal data type, Char is a kind of storage for which the allowed values can be enumerated (listed) in order, from first to last. The allowed values, however, and even the first and last allowed values, depend on the computer system being used. Standard Pascal uses the International Standards Organization (ISO) character set, of which the American variant is called the American Standard Code for Information Interchange. This is listed in Appendix C.

Even within the ASCII character set, there is a lack of standardization. ASCII is nominally a seven-bit character code, in which the most significant bit of a storage byte is not used. This allows ordinal values from 0 through 127. Many actual computer systems, however, use this extra bit to define nonstandard characters, because eight bits of storage allow ordinal values from 0 through 255. In all cases, though, ordinal values 0 through 127 represent the characters defined by the ASCII standard; only the ordinal values 128–255 represent nonstandard characters.

It helps if you have some knowledge of the ordinal values of the most commonly used characters, because we will encounter them from time to time. So let's try out the following little test program:

```
PROGRAM CharCodes ( Input, Output );
VAR
    Ch : Char;

BEGIN

    Write( 'Give me a character: ' );
    ReadLn( Ch );
    WriteLn;

    WriteLn( 'The character code for ', Ch,
            ' is ', Ord( Ch ):3 )

END.
```

Run this program with the characters '0', '9', 'A', 'Z', 'a', 'z', ' ' (space), and carriage return (<CR>), and report the corresponding character codes for your computer system below:

The character code for 0 is _____

The character code for 9 is _____

The character code for A is _____

The character code for Z is _____

The character code for a is _____

The character code for z is _____

The character code for <space> is _____

The character code for <CR> is   _____

In the last example, you are likely to encounter a weird property of Standard Pascal (but not Turbo Pascal): when a Read or ReadLn reads a carriage-return into a character variable, it is translated to a space before being stored!

It is also interesting to go the other way, from ordinal values to characters. Here is a small program that does the conversion, displaying the results:

```
PROGRAM CharsFromCodes ( Input, Output );
VAR
    Code : Integer;
BEGIN

    Write( 'Give me a character code (0-127): ' );
    ReadLn( Code );
    WriteLn;

    WriteLn( 'The character with ordinal value ', Code:3,
            ' is .', Chr( Code ), '.' )
END.
```

The program prints a period before and after the character, as an aid in seeing how "invisible" characters show up on the screen.

You have to be careful when running this program, though: the ordinal values 0–31 correspond to the so-called *control characters*, which are used to control various things in the computer system. Many of these control characters are not displayable in the normal sense, and attempting to display them may cause funny things to happen on your screen. (Of course, if you *like* excitement . . . .) Run the cases listed below, and report what happens. (On some computer systems, nothing will happen in some cases.)

```
The character with ordinal value   0 is _____
The character with ordinal value   7 is _____
The character with ordinal value  13 is _____
The character with ordinal value  32 is _____
The character with ordinal value  48 is _____
The character with ordinal value  65 is _____
The character with ordinal value  96 is _____
The character with ordinal value 126 is _____
The character with ordinal value 127 is _____
```

Predecessors and successors

Since characters are ordinal values, each character but the first has a predecessor, and each but the last has a successor. Try out the following little program:

```
PROGRAM PredAndSuccChars ( Input, Output );
VAR
   Ch : Char;

BEGIN

   Write( 'Give me a character: ' );
   ReadLn( Ch );
   WriteLn;

   WriteLn( 'The predecessor of ', Ch, ' is ', Pred(Ch) );
   WriteLn( 'The successor of   ', Ch, ' is ', Succ(Ch) )
END.
```

Report the results in the following cases:

The predecessor of 0 is _____

The successor of   0 is _____

The predecessor of 1 is _____

The successor of   2 is _____

The predecessor of Y is _____

The successor of   Y is _____

The predecessor of a is _____

The successor of   a is _____

The predecessor of b is _____

The successor of   b is _____

Check these results against the ASCII chart in Appendix C, and see if your results agree with the chart. Do they?

_____

Going out of range

As with integers, there's a question about what happens if we try to compute the predecessor of the first ASCII character, or the successor of the last one. In either case, we go outside the range of legal character values. Let's see what happens. Key in the little program shown below and then *compile it and run it with range checking turned on.*

```
PROGRAM CharacterRange ( Output );
VAR
    Ch : Char;

BEGIN

    {--Try the first allowed character }
    Ch := Chr( 0 );
    WriteLn( 'The predecessor of character 0 is ',
            Pred( Ch ) );

    {--Try the last standard character }
    Ch := Chr( 127 );
    WriteLn( 'The successor of character 127 is ',
            Succ( Ch ) );

    {--Try the last character of extended ASCII set }
    Ch := Chr( 255 );
    WriteLn( 'The successor of character 255 is ',
            Succ( Ch ) )

END.
```

Be sure that range checking is turned on when you compile and run this program. Then show your results below. (You may get an error message!)

_____

_____

_____

Now compile the program again with range checking turned *off*. Do you get different results? If so, show them below:

_____

_____

_____

If you performed these tests on a computer system other than the one assigned for your class, please report what system you used:

_____

_____

Credit: This lab was improved by comments from Phillip Tomovitch, of SUNY at Stony Brook, and George Novacky, of the University of Pittsburgh.

Lab 8.1:
Booleans and Conditionals

Concepts: Boolean expressions; decision structures; conditional execution

Lab techniques: Tracing with the debugger.

Prerequisites: Sections 7.6–7.8 and Chapter 8 of *Structures and Abstractions*

A boolean expression is an expression having a boolean value—a value that is either True or False. Two kinds of operators produce boolean values. Relational operators perform comparisons among reals, among ordinal values of the same type, or among string arrays of the same type. There are six relational operators:

=	equality
<>	inequality
<	less than
<=	less than or equal to
>	greater than
>=	greater than or equal to

In addition, there are three boolean operators that act on boolean operands and produce boolean values:

NOT	negation
AND	conjunction
OR	disjunction

All nine of these operators are discussed in detail in Section 7.6 of *Structures and Abstractions*.

Experimenting with boolean expressions

The best way to become comfortable with boolean expressions and truth tables is to build them into little programs and try them out. Seeing is believing. For example, try the following program, which is found on the accompanying floppy disk:

```
PROGRAM Lab8A ( Output );
BEGIN

    WriteLn( 'True AND True   = ', True AND True );
    WriteLn( 'True AND False  = ', True AND False );
    WriteLn( 'False AND True  = ', False AND True );
    WriteLn( 'False AND False = ', False AND False )

END.
```

What does this program display when you run it?

_____

_____

_____

_____

Similarly, try the next program from the disk:

```
PROGRAM Lab8B ( Output );
BEGIN

    WriteLn( 'True OR True   = ', True OR True );
    WriteLn( 'True OR False  = ', True OR False );
    WriteLn( 'False OR True  = ', False OR True );
    WriteLn( 'False OR False = ', False OR False )

END.
```

What does this program display when you run it?

_____

_____

_____

_____

Finally, try this one:

```
PROGRAM Lab8C ( Output );
BEGIN

    WriteLn( 'NOT False = ', NOT False );
    WriteLn( 'NOT True  = ', NOT True );
    WriteLn( 'True AND (NOT False)  = ',
             True AND (NOT False) );
    WriteLn( '(NOT True) OR False   = ',
             (NOT True) OR False );
    WriteLn( 'NOT( True AND False ) = ',
             NOT( True AND False ) );
    WriteLn( '(NOT True) OR (NOT False)  = ',
             (NOT True) OR (NOT False) );
    WriteLn( '(NOT True) AND (NOT False) = ',
             (NOT True) AND (NOT False) )

END.
```

What does this program display when you run it?

_____

_____

_____

_____

_____

_____

In which of these boolean expressions will the results change drastically if the parentheses are removed? In these cases, explain why the parentheses are required for correct results.

_____

_____

_____

_____

_____

_____

The meanings of boolean expressions

In order to use boolean expressions fluently, you must be clear on what they mean. The best way to do this is to practice relating them to everyday English sentences. Here are some examples:

```
(Angle >= Pi) OR (Direction < 0.0)
```

In English, this might be worded in several ways, all of which are equivalent:

"Either the angle is at least π or the direction is negative, or both."

"Either the angle is greater than or equal to π, or the direction is negative, or both."

"The angle is at least π or the direction is negative."

(Note that the Pascal OR is an *inclusive OR*: it means "either this or that, *or both*." It might be helpful for the class to discuss the use of inclusive and exclusive ORs in everyday language. We often don't distinguish carefully between them in casual speech, but a programming language must be unambiguous.

For a second example of translating a Pascal boolean expression into everyday speech, consider this conjunction:

```
(NOT(Angle >= Pi)) AND (Direction < 0.0)
```

In English, this might be worded in these ways, among others:

"It is not true that the angle is greater than or equal to π, and furthermore, the direction is negative."

"The angle is less than π and the direction is negative."

"It is not true that the angle is greater than or equal to π, but the direction is negative."

Note that *and* is sometimes represented by *but* in English sentences. This might be worth some discussion in class, too.

Finally, consider this one:

```
NOT( (Angle >= Pi) AND (Direction < 0.0) )
```

In English, this might be worded

"It is not true that the angle is greater than or equal to π and the direction is negative."

"It is false to say that the angle is greater than or equal to π and the direction is negative."

You can even word it this way: (Think about it!)

"Either the angle is not greater than or equal to π or the direction is not negative, or both."

Or this way:

"Either the angle is less than π or the direction is nonnegative, or both."

The equivalence of this last pair of sentences to the first pair follows from DeMorgan's Laws of logic, which are spelled out in Project 6 of Chapter 8, in the textbook. Discuss this in class also; discussing the meanings of English propositions will help to clarify some of the issues, which are quite important in the work ahead. Also, it may help to read the sections on negation, conjunction, and disjunction in a good logic textbook like the ones listed below:

Irving M. Copi. *Symbolic Logic*, third edition (MacMillan, 1967)

Samuel D. Guttenplan and Martin Tamny. *Logic: A Comprehensive Introduction* (Basic Books, 1971).

Virginia Klenk. *Understanding Symbolic Logic* (Prentice-Hall, 1983).

Bangs L. Tapscott. *Elementary Applied Symbolic Logic* (University Press of America, 1985).

Exercises with English translations of boolean expressions

Write an English sentence that conveys the meaning of each of these boolean expressions:

```
(Year - 1989) <> 3
```

English:_____

_____

_____

```
NOT( (Ch = 'a') OR (Ch = 'A') )
```

English:_____

_____

_____

```
( (Ch = 'a') AND ( NOT (Ch = 'A') )
```

English:_____

_____

_____

Translate each of the following sentences into a Pascal boolean expression:

"My exam score is at least 80 but no more than 90."

Pascal:_____

_____

_____

"My exam score is neither less than 80 nor more than 90."

Pascal:_____

_____

_____

"My speed is more than 65 but I haven't been arrested."

Pascal:_____

_____

_____

"The temperature is either less than 30 or greater than 40, but not both."

Pascal:_____

_____

_____

The primary use of booleans is to control the execution of a program—to automate decisions about the actions to be taken. Chapter 8 of the textbook introduces this concept, and explains how *decision structures* are used to control which statements are executed. Let's review this concept.

Controlling execution by means of boolean values

The primary use of booleans is to control the execution of a program—to automate decisions about the actions to be taken. Chapter 8 of the textbook introduces this concept, and explains how *decision structures* are used to control which statements are executed. Let's review this concept.

The IF . . THEN structure

```
IF BooleanExpression THEN
    Statement
```

The IF..THEN performs what is called *conditional execution*: if *BooleanExpression* is True, *Statement* is executed; otherwise, it is skipped. This is discussed in the textbook in Section 8.2. One way to visualize the IF..THEN is shown below. It's called a *flowchart*.

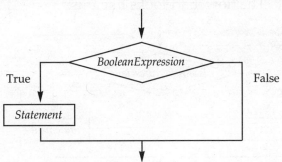

Another way to visualize the action is to picture the flow through the structure as it is written. When *BooleanExpression* is True, *Statement* is executed, followed by the next statement after the IF..THEN structure:

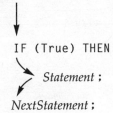

On the other hand, if *BooleanExpression* is False, *Statement* is skipped and execution passes immediately to the statement after the IF..THEN structure:

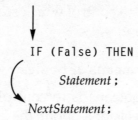

```
IF (False) THEN
       Statement;

   NextStatement;
```

The IF .. THEN .. ELSE structure

The IF..THEN is actually a special case of a two-way decision structure called IF..THEN..ELSE:

```
IF BooleanExpression THEN
    Statement1
ELSE
    Statement2
```

In this decision structure, if *BooleanExpression* is True, *Statement1* is executed and *Statement2* is skipped; otherwise, *Statement2* is executed and *Statement1* is skipped. This is discussed in Section 8.3 of the textbook. The flowchart looks like this:

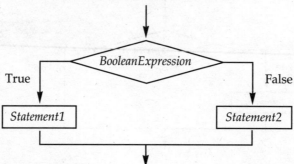

You might prefer to visualize the action in the code itself. When *BooleanExpression* is True, we have

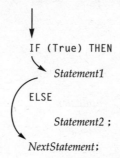

```
IF (True) THEN
       Statement1
   ELSE
       Statement2;

   NextStatement;
```

On the other hand, when *BooleanExpression* is False, we have the following flow:

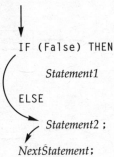

```
IF (False) THEN
        Statement1
ELSE
        Statement2 ;
NextStatement;
```

The CASE structure

The IF..THEN and IF..THEN..ELSE structures are the work-horse decision structures in Pascal, but there is one more decision structure that is useful in special circumstances:

```
CASE Selector OF
    ConstantList1 : Statement1;
    ConstantList2 : Statement2;

          .

          .

    ConstantListN : StatementN
END
```

The CASE structure has significant limitations: the *Selector* must take on ordinal values and in Standard Pascal, the *Selector* is required to have one of the ordinal values listed in the *ConstantList*s. If the *Selector* has a value in *ConstantList1*, the CASE structure executes *Statement1* but not *Statement2* through *StatementN*; if the *Selector* has a value in *ConstantList2*, the CASE structure executes *Statement2* but skips *Statement1* and *Statement3* through *StatementN*; and so on. This is explained in Section 8.6. The CASE structure can be thought of as a ready-made nested IF..THEN..ELSE structure of the form shown on the next page.

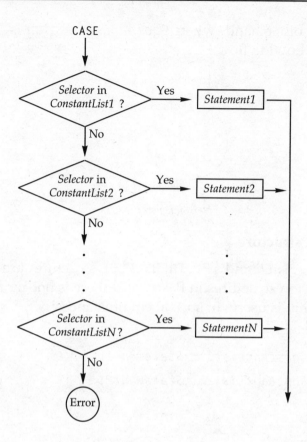

As a result, if *Selector* has a value contained in `ConstantList2`, the flow through the code is as shown below: `Statement2` is executed, then execution passes immediately to the next statement after the CASE structure.

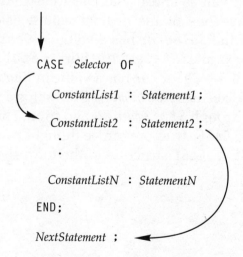

A CASE structure is equivalent to a nested IF.THEN..ELSE

The flowchart for a CASE structure indicates that it is equivalent to a sequence of two-way decisions. Therefore, it can be written as a nested sequence of IF..THEN..ELSE structures. For example, if Choice is a Char variable and Result, X, and Y are Real, the CASE structure

```
CASE Choice OF
    'A' : Result := X + Y;
    'S' : Result := X - Y;
    'M' : Result := X * Y
END;
```

is equivalent to the following nested IF..THEN..ELSE structure:

```
IF Choice = 'A' THEN
    Result := X + Y
ELSE
    IF Choice = 'S' THEN
        Result := X - Y
    ELSE
        IF Choice = 'M' THEN
            Result := X * Y;
```

Clearly, the CASE structure is easier to read and check, and is therefore better style in such a situation.

To fully appreciate them, you have to play with them...

As you can see, decision structures execute some code statements while skipping others. An interactive source-code debugger is especially helpful in animating decision structures so you can see which statements are executed under given conditions. We will use this technique through the rest of the lab session.

Trying out conditional execution

The IF..THEN structure is the textbook's first example of a *control structure*. Control structures simply control the flow of execution through the code. To appreciate them, you must develop a feeling for the flow associated with each structure. When you get good at it, each structure will evoke a mental picture of the flow of execution: *you'll see moving pictures in your code.*

If your Pascal system provides an interactive source-code debugger, you have in your hands the perfect tool for *seeing* the flow of execution with your own eyes as it occurs. Study our earlier description of IF..THEN structures, then single-step (trace) through the following subprograms with your debugger. Answer the questions about each program. (The programs are provided on the accompanying floppy disk.)

From program Lab8D.pas:

```
FUNCTION UpperCase( Ch : Char ) : Char;
BEGIN

   UpperCase := Ch;
   IF (Ch >= 'a') AND (Ch <= 'z') THEN
      UpperCase := Chr( Ord(Ch) - Ord('a') + Ord('A') )

END; { UpperCase }
```

If Ch = 'B', what is the value of the boolean expression in the IF..THEN structure?

_____

If Ch = 'B', how many times does this function assign a value to UpperCase?

_____

If Ch = 'h', what is the value of the boolean expression in the IF..THEN structure?

_____

If Ch = 'h', how many times does this function assign a value to UpperCase?

_____

From program Lab8E.pas:

```
PROCEDURE ShowIfVisible( Ch : Char );
{ Assumes ASCII }
BEGIN

   IF ( Ch >= ' ' ) AND ( Ch <= '~' ) THEN
      Write( Ch );

   WriteLn

END; { ShowIfVisible }
```

If `Ch = '!'`, what is the value of the boolean expression in the `IF..THEN` structure? (See the ASCII chart in Appendix C.)

_____

If `Ch = '!'`, what is the first output statement executed?

_____

If `Ch =` Control-A (ordinal value 1), what is the value of the boolean expression in the `IF..THEN` structure?

_____

If `Ch =` Control-A (ordinal value 1), what is the first output statement executed?

_____

From program Lab8F.pas:

```
FUNCTION AbsoluteValue( X : Real ) : Real;
BEGIN

   IF X < 0.0 THEN
      AbsoluteValue := -X
   ELSE
      AbsoluteValue := X

END; { AbsoluteValue }
```

If `X = -1.23`, what is the value of the boolean expression in the `IF..THEN..ELSE` structure?

_____

If X = 4.321, what is assigned to AbsoluteValue?

_____

If X = 4.321, what is the value of the boolean expression in the IF..THEN..ELSE structure?

_____

If X = -4.321, what is assigned to AbsoluteValue?

_____

From program Lab8G.pas:

```
FUNCTION IsLeapYear( Yr : Integer ) : Boolean;
{
  PRECONDITION: Yr > 0.

  NOTE THIS CODE CAN BE WRITTEN MORE SIMPLY AS A
  BOOLEAN EXPRESSION! SEE PROJECT 4, CHAPTER 7.
}
BEGIN

  IF (Yr MOD 4) = 0 THEN
     IF (Yr MOD 100) = 0 THEN
        IF (Yr MOD 400) = 0 THEN
           IsLeapYear := True      { #1 }
        ELSE
           IsLeapYear := False     { #2 }
     ELSE
        IsLeapYear := True         { #3 }
  ELSE
     IsLeapYear := False           { #4 }

END; { IsLeapYear }
```

If Yr = 1900, which (if any) assignment statement is executed? (They are numbered 1, 2, 3, 4.)

_____

If Yr = 2000, which (if any) assignment statement is executed? (They are numbered 1, 2, 3, 4.)

_____

If Yr = 1995, which (if any) assignment statement is executed? (They are numbered 1, 2, 3, 4.)

_____

If Yr = 1996, which (if any) assignment statement is executed? (They are numbered 1, 2, 3, 4.)

_____

From program Lab8H.pas:

```
PROCEDURE ShowDaysInMonth( Month, Yr : Integer );
BEGIN

   CASE Month OF

      1, 3, 5, 7, 8, 10, 12 :
         WriteLn( '31 days' );

      4, 6, 9, 11 :
         WriteLn( '30 days' );

      2 :
         IF IsLeapYear( Yr ) THEN
            WriteLn( '29 days' )
         ELSE
            WriteLn( '28 days' )

   END

END; { ShowDaysInMonth }
```

In Standard Pascal, the selector *must* have one of the values listed in the constant lists appearing in the structure. Many Pascal systems relax this rule, however, adding to the CASE syntax an ELSE or OTHERWISE clause to handle the possibility that the selector has none of the values in the constant lists. Check with your reference manual or instructor to see whether your Pascal system makes such a provision.

Run program Lab8H.pas and trace through it with your source-code debugger, if you have one. Then answer the following questions. Turn in all the lab pages containing your answers.

If Month = 9 and Yr = 1994, what is displayed by the procedure?

_____

If Month = 2 and Yr = 1994, what is displayed by the procedure?

_____

If Month = 2 and Yr = 1996, what is displayed by the procedure?

_____

Credit: This lab has benefited from suggestions made by David E. Leasure, of the University of Kansas, and by Jack Mostow and Lou Steinberg, of Rutgers, The State University of New Jersey.

Lab Project 8.2:
Top-Down Design of a Calendar Function

Concepts: Decision structures; top-down design.

Lab Techniques: Top-down design; incremental testing; stepwise refinement.

Prerequisites: Chapter 8 of *Structures and Abstractions*.

Business applications involving investments and deprecia-tions often require calendar calculations—how many days have passed since a given date, the day of the week corresponding to a given date, and so on. In this lab and in Lab 9.2, we develop a pair of utility subprograms that illustrate the kinds of computations involved, ending up with a perpetual calendar program.

The ultimate goal

After we finish both labs, we hope to have a program that will print the calendar for any desired month in the calculable range. As usual, we begin the process by imagining how the I/O might look in a typical run:

```
CALENDAR PRINTING
-----------------


Month <Number from 1 to 12> ? 8
Year <1961 or later> ? 1994


            AUGUST

     S   M   T   W   T   F   S
     ------------------------
         1   2   3   4   5   6
     7   8   9  10  11  12  13
    14  15  16  17  18  19  20
    21  22  23  24  25  26  27
    28  29  30  31
```

There are many pitfalls here. First of all, the program will have to determine automatically how many days are in the requested month. Not only must the program know that April, June, September, and November have 30 days, but it must know that the number of days in February depend on whether the current year is a leap year. (Leap year determination was discussed in the textbook in Project 4 at the end of Chapter 7 and mentioned again in Exercise 7 in Section 8.4.)

More difficult than this, the program needs to determine automatically the day of the week on which the given month begins, so that the calendar can be printed with the correct offset. In fact, the present lab session is devoted entirely to the solution of this problem. The subprogram we construct will be used in Lab 9.2 to complete the perpetual calendar program.

The immediate problem

For the time being, then, we focus our attention on computing the day of the week on which a given month begins in a given year. In particular, we need a subprogram that does this. Should it be a procedure or function? The subprogram should receive a month (an integer from 1 through 12) and a year as input data, then return, let us say, an integer representing a day of the week. Because the subprogram will return only a single integer and will do no I/O, we should make it a function rather than a procedure.

To test the function, we will need a driver, which we can imagine running like this:

```
Month (Number from 1 to 12) ? 8
Year (1961 or later) ? 1994

 8/1994 begins on day 1
```

This much planning provides a picture of how the main program should run. There will be two main steps:

1. Prompt for and read both a month and a year.

2. Calculate and display the first day of the given month in the given year.

The first task performs I/O and returns two values; for both of these reasons, it should be performed by a procedure. The second task, as we've said, can be performed by a function whose returned value can then be displayed by the main program. This thinking leads to a main program like the following one:

```
BEGIN

    GetMonthAndYear( Month, Year );

    Write( Month:2, '/', Year:4, ' begins on day ',
           FirstDayOfMonth( Month, Year ):1 )

END.
```

This is the top level of our top-down design. Seeing how the main program should run tells us what needs to happen in the subprograms. We'll need a GetMonthAndYear procedure with two VAR parameters—one for the month and another for the year. Then we'll need to send copies of these two values to a FirstDayOfMonth function, which will return an integer representing the day of the week on which the month begins. The resulting two-level design is found on the accompanying floppy disk as the file FIRSTDAY.PAS:

```
PROGRAM FindFirstDayOfMonth ( Input, Output );

VAR
    Month, Year : Integer;


PROCEDURE GetMonthAndYear( VAR Month, Year : Integer );
BEGIN

    Write( 'Month (Number from 1 thru 12) ? ' );
    ReadLn( Month );

    Write( 'Year (1961 or later) ? ' );
    ReadLn( Year );

    WriteLn

END; { GetMonthAndYear }
```

```
FUNCTION FirstDayOfMonth( Mnth, Yr : Integer ) : Integer;
{
   PRECONDITIONS:
   1 <= Mnth <= 12; Yr >= 1961.

   POSTCONDITIONS:
   Returns integer code for day of week on which month
   begins. 0 = Sunday, 1 = Monday, ..., 6 = Saturday.
}
BEGIN

   {--Function is only a stub }
   FirstDayOfMonth := 0

END; { FirstDayOfMonth }


BEGIN

   GetMonthAndYear( Month, Year );

   Write( Month:2, '/', Year:4, ' begins on day ',
          FirstDayOfMonth( Month, Year ):1 )

END.
```

Now (and only now) we are ready to design the inner workings of the FirstDayOfMonth function.

Finding an algorithm

We know what we are trying to calculate, but where are we starting? We begin with the facts about calendars:

1. Years that are not leap years have 365 days, with 28 in February.

2. Leap years have 366 days, with 29 in February.

3. A year is a leap year if it is exactly divisible by 4, unless it is a century year—that is, divisible by 100. A century year is a leap year only if it is exactly divisible by 400. Thus 1600 and 2000 are leap years, but 1700, 1800, and 1900 are not. (This is all intended to bring the length of the average year close to the astronomical value of 365.2422 days.)

4. The months have 31 days, except for April, June, September, and November, which have 30, and February, which has 28 or 29, as explained above.

These are all the facts we need for the algorithm, so let's dive in by working some examples.

Consider 1961. It was the year after a leap year, so February had only 28 days in 1961. It happens that January 1 was a Sunday. (I looked it up.) From these few pieces of information, we can easily figure out the days on which the months began in that year. For the sake of numerical calculations, we use the following code for days of the week: 0 = Sunday, 1 = Monday, . . ., 6 = Saturday. Then we calculate

1/1/1961 fell on day 0 = Sunday.
2/1/1961 was 31 days after the first of the year,
    so it fell on day (31 MOD 7) = 3 = Wednesday.
3/1/1961 was 31 + 28 = 59 days after the first of the year,
    so it fell on day (59 MOD 7) = 3 = Wednesday.
4/1/1961 was 31 + 28 + 31 = 90 days after the first of the year,
    so it fell on day (90 MOD 7) = 6 = Saturday.
⋮

12/1/1961 was 334 days after the first of the year,
    so it fell on day (334 MOD 7) = 5 = Friday.

The year 1962 began one non-leap year after January 1, 1961, which is to say, 365 days later. 1962 was another non-leap year, so February had 28 days. Thus

1/1/1962 was 365 days after 1/1/1961,
    so it fell on day (365 MOD 7) = 1 = Monday.
2/1/1962 was (365 + 31) = 396 days after 1/1/1961,
    so it fell on day (396 MOD 7) = 4 = Thursday.
3/1/1962 was (365 + 31 + 28) = 424 days after 1/1/1961,
    so it fell on day (424 MOD 7) = 4 = Thursday.
⋮

In successive years, the calculation continues in the same way until we reach the next leap year, 1964. As 1964 began, three non-leap years had passed since the beginning of 1961, so

1/1/1964 was (3*365) = 1095 days after 1/1/1961,
    so it fell on day (1095 MOD 7) = 3 = Wednesday.

2/1/1964 was (3*365 + 31) = 1126 days after 1/1/1961,
    so it fell on day (1126 MOD 7) = 6 = Saturday.

But then, because 1964 was a leap year, February had 29 days, so there was an extra day before March begins:

3/1/1964 was (3*365 + 31 + *29*) = 1155 days after 1/1/1961,
    so it fell on day (1155 MOD 7) = 0 = Sunday.

Question: How would this algorithm differ if January 1, 1961 had been a Thursday instead of a Sunday? For example, how would we compute the day of the week for 3/1/1964?

Notice that the first three years considered by the program—1961, 1962, 1963—are not leap years, but the fourth one is. This pattern continues, with every fourth year a leap year. Consider, too, that the year 2000 is also a leap year. Only one-fourth of the century years are leap years, but 2000 is one of them. By starting our algorithm in 1961—the year after a leap year—we achieve an easy algorithm for counting leap years as we move forward through time. The number of years that pass, DIV 4, is the number of leap years we pass through on the way to the given year.

The pattern is now apparent. If we let NumDays be the number of days from 1/1/1961 up to, but not including, the first day of the given Month in the given Year, we have a calculation in three parts:

NumDays = [365 * (Year - 1961)]

  + [One extra day for every
      leap year among the years
      1962, 1963, ..., (Year - 1)]

    + [Number of days in the given Year
        before the given Month]

The third term in this sum can be calculated conveniently by means of a CASE structure. The second term can be done by a simple DIV. I leave the rest to you. Complete the FirstDayOfMonth function, along with any other subprograms you need.

When you test the completed program, you will find it useful to know that

August 1, 1991 = Thursday;
January 1, 1992 = Wednesday;
March 1, 1996   = Friday;
January 1, 2000 = Saturday;
January 1, 2001 = Monday.

How to test your program

Start with January 1, 1961, and check to see that your program reports that day to be a Sunday. If so, move on to March 1, 1961, to see if the program computes the length of February correctly for this nonleap year. If your program reports that March 1 was a Wednesday, move on to the beginning of the following year. Everything still okay? Then keep coming forward in time. Be sure to check whether March 1, 1964 was a Sunday, because 1964 was the first leap year after 1961. Keep moving forward in time until you confirm the days shown at the top of this page. If your program makes an incorrect prediction at any stage, correct the error before going on with the testing.

Overflow errors!

Many Pascal systems store integers in two bytes, so that `MaxInt` = 32,767. In such systems, the algorithm described here will be able to move forward in time only 32,767 days, or 89.8 years. If your system is like this, your calendar function will work over the years from 1961 through 2049 and part of 2050. If you try to enter later dates, you may see the integers "wrap around" into negative values, producing weird results. In some Pascal systems, you can use a nonstandard "long integer" type, usually called `LongInt`, to get around this limitation. Otherwise, you'll have to settle for the range of integers or find a clever modification of the algorithm that avoids such early overflow. **Hint:** Can you use a decision structure to protect your program from inputs that would cause it to overflow?

Have courage!

This project is harder than earlier ones, so expect to make mistakes. Remember that no one ever succeeds at creative work without making lots of mistakes!

When you are finished, turn in your source code and printouts of test runs for the sample dates provided.

Lab 9.1
Studying Loops with the Debugger

Concepts: Iteration; WHILE, FOR, and REPEAT..UNTIL structures; pre- and posttest loops; preinitialization.

Lab techniques: Single-stepping.

Prerequisites: Chapter 9 of *Structures and Abstractions*.

Chapter 9 of the textbook introduces Pascal's three iterative control structures: the WHILE, FOR, and REPEAT..UNTIL loops. For each of these structures, the text explained the order of execution. Now we examine the order of execution for ourselves, with the help of a source-code debugger and its ability to single-step through the code. In this way, we can watch a slow-motion animation of each of these loop types.

The WHILE loop

A WHILE loop is a pretest loop: that is, the looping condition is tested at the beginning (the "top") of the loop, before the loop body is next executed. Here is the general structure:

```
WHILE BooleanExpression DO
    LoopBody
```

If BooleanExpression is True, LoopBody is executed and BooleanExpression is tested again, and so on. Thus, BooleanExpression is tested before each execution of Loopbody. If BooleanExpression is False, there are no more executions of LoopBody.

An important result of this structure is that the loop body is *never* executed if BooleanExpression is False when execution first reaches the loop. Therefore, a WHILE loop is appropriate in situations in which we may need to skip the loop.

Animating an example of a WHILE loop

Suppose we want to compute the average of a sequence of numbers read from the keyboard. We will use a loop to read the sequence of numbers, but there is a possibility that the user will have no numbers to key in, in which case we want to skip the loop. One student in the class proposes the loop shown in procedure GetAverage of the file TSTWHILE.PAS and shown below:

```
PROCEDURE GetAverage( VAR Average : Real );
VAR
    ThereIsMore : Boolean;
    Answer      : Char;
    Count       : Integer;
    Number, Sum : Real;

BEGIN

    Count   := 0;
    Sum     := 0.0;
    Average := 0.0;

    Write( 'Are there numbers to average? <y/n> ' );
    ReadLn( Answer );
    WriteLn;
    ThereIsMore := ( Answer = 'y' ) OR ( Answer = 'Y' );

    WHILE ThereIsMore DO
    BEGIN

        Write( 'Number? ' );
        ReadLn( Number );

        Sum     := Sum + Number;
        Count   := Count + 1;
        Average := Sum / Count;

        Write( 'Are there more? <y/n> ' );
        ReadLn( Answer );
        WriteLn;

        ThereIsMore := ( Answer = 'y' ) OR ( Answer = 'Y' )

    END

END; { GetAverage }
```

Run this procedure and answer "N" to the prompt asking if there are numbers to average. You will see no I/O from the body of the loop, indicating that the loop body is never executed. To see in more detail how this happens, single-step through another run, using your debugger's Step Into or Trace Into command. While

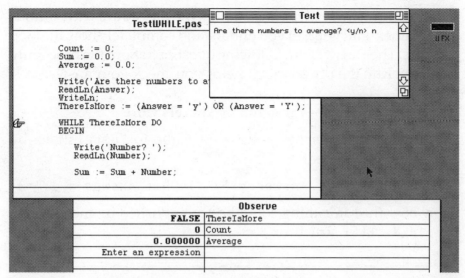

FIGURE 1. *A snapshot while single-stepping through the GetAverage procedure in THINK Pascal on a Macintosh computer. The user told the procedure that no numbers will be entered, and execution has arrived at the beginning of the WHILE loop with ThereIsMore = False. (The finger points at the next statement to execute.) Because of this, the loop condition is False, and one more single-step will take us immediately to the end of the procedure with Average = 0.0.*

single-stepping, use the Watch or Observe window to see how the values in `ThereIsMore`, `Count`, and `Average` change during the run. Examples are shown in Figures 1 and 2.

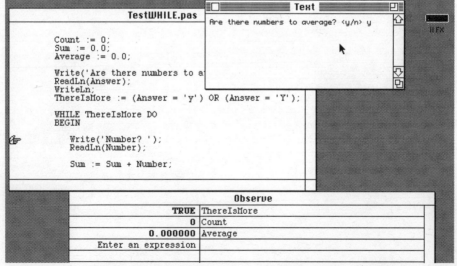

FIGURE 2. *In this run, the user told the procedure that numbers will be entered, and execution arrived at the beginning of the WHILE loop with ThereIsMore = True. Because of this, the loop condition is True and the body of the loop is beginning to execute.*

Continue single-stepping through the procedure with various input values until you feel you understand completely how the loop operates. Then answer the following questions about the procedure and loop. Run the program if it helps you check your answers.

Questions about the evaluation of ThereIsMore

The programmer has assigned a value to ThereIsMore by means of the statement

```
ThereIsMore := ( Answer = 'y' ) OR ( Answer = 'Y' )
```

Show how the same thing could be accomplished by means of an IF..THEN..ELSE structure:

_____

_____

_____

_____

Which method is preferable? Why?

_____

_____

_____

_____

Calculating the average

The programmer has chosen to recalculate the average every time a number is read from the keyboard. This isn't necessary, however, because the loop could be rewritten as shown below:

```
Count    := 0;
Sum      := 0.0;

Write( 'Are there numbers to average? <y/n> ' );
ReadLn( Answer );
WriteLn;
ThereIsMore := ( Answer = 'y' ) OR ( Answer = 'Y' );

WHILE ThereIsMore DO
BEGIN

    Write( 'Number? ' );
    ReadLn( Number );

    Sum      := Sum + Number;
    Count    := Count + 1;

    Write( 'Are there more? <y/n> ' );
    ReadLn( Answer );
    WriteLn;

    ThereIsMore := ( Answer = 'y' ) OR ( Answer = 'Y' )

END;

Average := Sum / Count
```

However, this version of the program will crash in a special situation mentioned earlier. What situation will cause the crash, and what will be the nature of the error?

_____

_____

_____

_____

Show what extra code would have to be added in order to prevent the error that can occur in the second version of the procedure:

_____

_____

_____

_____

Event-driven WHILE structures

The loop shown above is controlled by the test on the value of `ThereIsMore`, which switches from `True` to `False` when the user announces that no more data will be entered. Such a loop iterates a number of times that cannot be predicted ahead of time, and is said to be *event-controlled* or *event-driven*. Contrast this to another kind of `WHILE` loop, in which a predetermined number of iterations are performed under control of a counter variable, as described next.

Counter-driven WHILE structures

A `WHILE` loop can count out the iterations when we know ahead of time how many are needed. Consider, for example, the problem of computing the value of *e* (Napier's number and the base of natural logarithms). It is shown in calculus that

$$e = 1 + (1 / 1!) + (1 / 2!) + (1 / 3!) + \ldots$$

This is called an infinite series. Naturally, we cannot add up the whole series in a finite length of time, even on a computer. Furthermore, we don't need to, because the terms in the sum eventually become negligibly small, and we need the result to only a finite number of digits. It turns out that we can get enough significant figures by adding only a few terms. (We'll determine how many by actual experiment; the significant figures at any given point in the summation will consist of those digits that have "stttled down" and are no longer changing as we add smaller and smaller terms.)

A program to carry out the summation is given in the file `CDWHILE.PAS`, the central procedure of which is shown on the next page.

```
FUNCTION ESeries( NumberOfTerms : Integer ) : Real;
{
  PRECONDITION:
  1 <= NumberOfTerms.

  POSTCONDITION:
  Returns an estimate of e, obtained by summing the
  specified number of terms of the series.
}
VAR
    Index      : Integer;
    Term, Sum : Real;

BEGIN

    Term := 1.0;
    Sum  := 1.0;

    Index := 1;
    WHILE Index <= NumberOfTerms DO
    BEGIN

       Term := Term / Index;
       Sum  := Sum + Term;

       Index := Index + 1

    END;

    ESeries := Sum

END; { ESeries }
```

In this example, the WHILE loop is controlled by the value of Index because the loop continues iterating until Index exceeds NumberOfTerms. Index is initially 1, then the loop increments it, so Index must eventually exceed NumberOfTerms. Thus we know that the loop will terminate if the precondition is satisfied.

Single-step through the function, observing the Index, Term, and Sum variables in the Watch/Observe window, until you are sure you understand the following key features:

1. Index receives an initial value before the loop begins: we say it has been *preinitialize*d.

2. Index is tested at the top of the loop: that is, before each iteration. We say that the WHILE is a *pretest loop*.

3. Index is incremented at the bottom of the loop, just before execution loops back to the top. We say that Index undergoes *postincrementation*.

What if the precondition is violated?

There is no guarantee that the function will actually be called with NumberOfTerms ≥ 1, as the precondition demands. What will happen if NumberOfTerms is less than 1? What value will be returned by ESeries?

_____

_____

_____

_____

Test the procedure

Run the program to add five terms, then seven, nine, eleven and thirteen terms, and report the results below:

With 5 terms: e = _____

With 7 terms: e = _____

With 9 terms: e = _____

With 11 terms: e = _____

With 13 terms: e = _____

How many terms must be added to yield eight significant figures? (That is, how many terms must be added before eight digits of the Sum become stable?)

_____

For nine significant figures?

_____

Pascal provides a built-in `Exp( X )` function, as described in Section 6.4 of the textbook. Alter the program to print out `Exp( 1 )` as well as `ESeries( 11 )`. Do these two results differ in value in the first eight decimal places? If so, report the observed difference below:

_____

_____

_____

The FOR structure

A `FOR` structure is a convenient shorthand for a counter-driven `WHILE` loop. In particular, the upward-counting structure

```
Index := StartingValue;
WHILE Index <= FinalValue DO
BEGIN
   { Calculation }
   Index := Index + 1
END;
```

is equivalent to the `FOR` structure

```
FOR Index := StartingValue TO FinalValue DO
   { Calculation };
```

The `FOR` structure implicitly contains the preinitialization, the pre-test, and the postincrementation of the `WHILE`. This is discussed in detail in Section 9.5 of the text.

Similarly, the downward-counting

```
Index := StartingValue;
WHILE Index >= FinalValue DO
BEGIN
   { Calculation }
   Index := Index - 1
END;
```

is equivalent to the `FOR` structure

```
FOR Index := StartingValue DOWNTO FinalValue DO
   { Calculation };
```

This `FOR..DOWNTO` structure implicitly contains the preinitialization, the pretest, and the postdecrementation of the `WHILE`.

But there's a difference!

There *is* a difference between the FOR loop and the corresponding counter-driven WHILE loop, though. It has to do with the fact that a FOR loop's index becomes undefined as the loop terminates. Consider the following loop, which is contained in the program FORWHILE.PAS:

```
PROGRAM ForWhile ( Output );
VAR
   Index : Integer;
BEGIN

   FOR Index := (MaxInt - 2) TO MaxInt DO
      WriteLn( Index )
END.
```

Load this program into your Pascal system and *turn on overflow checking* before compiling it. Then run the program and report the output below:

_____

_____

_____

Now replace the FOR structure by the corresponding WHILE structure, so that the code reads

```
PROGRAM ForWhile ( Output );
VAR
   Index : Integer;

BEGIN

   Index := (MaxInt - 2);
   WHILE Index <= MaxInt DO
   BEGIN
      WriteLn( Index );
      Index := Index + 1
   END

END.
```

With overflow checking turned on, compile and run this version of the program. Describe what happens and explain *why* it happens:

_____

_____

_____

_____

As you can see, the FOR loop suppresses the last incrementation of its index but the WHILE loop doesn't.

Adding terms in a series

In order to fully appreciate what the FOR structure does, you should single-step through the following procedure, which uses a FOR loop to accomplish the same thing as the WHILE shown in the previous program. Use the Watch/Observe window to watch the values in Index, Term, and Sum as you execute the code one step at a time. The code is found in the file called FORLOOP.PAS.

```
FUNCTION ESeries( NumberOfTerms : Integer ) : Real;
{
  PRECONDITION:
  1 <= NumberOfTerms.

  POSTCONDITION:
  Returns an estimate of e, obtained by summing the
  specified number of terms of the series.
}
VAR
   Index      : Integer;
   Term, Sum : Real;

BEGIN

   Term := 1.0;
   Sum  := 1.0;

   FOR Index := 1 TO NumberOfTerms DO
   BEGIN

      Term := Term / Index;
      Sum  := Sum + Term

   END;

   ESeries := Sum

END; { ESeries }
```

Embellishing the ESeries function

As it is shown here, ESeries must be told the number of terms to sum. It is always a bad idea to ask the user of a function to set its computational parameters, so it would be nice if ESeries determined automatically how many terms to sum. In fact, this is not difficult. Mathematically, no finite number of terms will yield e exactly. But in a computer, arithmetic has only a finite number of digits to work with, so eventually the terms in the infinite series become so small that they make no further contribution to the sum. (The terms underflow, as explained in Section 1.3 of the textbook.) We can make use of this in the function. All we have to do is add terms until the latest term added makes no change in the sum. Add this embellishment, remove the parameter from the function, and turn in your resulting source code listing together with output from a run showing how your function's result compares with Exp(1).

You are now fully prepared to attack Projects 3 and 4 at the end of Chapter 9 in the textbook. The code you have just created will carry over directly, requiring only slight embellishment to complete Project 3. Project 4 then illustrates a fundamental fact of numerical summation: addition is not commutative in a computer!

The REPEAT . . UNTIL structure

Pascal provides one last looping structure—a posttest loop of the form

```
REPEAT

    Statement1;
    Statement2;
    ...
    StatementN

UNTIL BooleanExpression
```

Note that the loop body in this structure does not need to be bracketed by BEGIN and END as it does in a WHILE structure; instead, the words REPEAT and UNTIL do the bracketing.

The body of a REPEAT..UNTIL loop is always executed at least once, because the looping test is not performed until execution reaches the bottom of the loop structure. In this kind of loop, the loop test is an exit test: if BooleanExpression is True, looping is terminated and execution passes on to the next statement after the loop structure.

Clearly, a REPEAT..UNTIL loop is appropriate only when we know ahead of time that at least one trip must be made through the loop body. One of the most common applications of the REPEAT..UNTIL is in processing input data from the keyboard, refusing to accept it until it is in the legal range.

Guarding against out-of-range inputs

Examples of this are shown in Section 9.2 of the textbook. Another example occurs in FORLOOP.PAS., where the number of terms to be summed are obtained from the keyboard by means of the following procedure:

```
PROCEDURE GetNumTerms( VAR HowMany : Integer );
BEGIN

   Write( 'How many terms from the series? ' );
   ReadLn( HowMany )

END; { GetNumTerms }
```

In order to protect the ESeries function from unreasonable values of HowMany, the GetNumTerms procedure should read a value of HowMany, check to see if it is greater than or equal to 1, then loop back and prompt again if it is not. Show in the space below how to make it do this, using a REPEAT..UNTIL structure. You may want to clarify the prompt so that user understands what is required.

Other uses of REPEAT..UNTIL

Guarding against out-of-range inputs is not the only good use for REPEAT..UNTIL structures: they are useful whenever we need a loop that will always make at least one trip. We had another kind of example in the ESeries function itself, where a REPEAT..UNTIL would be appropriate for the summation of terms. In the space provided on the next page, write a new version of ESeries that does this:

```
FUNCTION ESeries( NumberOfTerms : Integer ) : Real;
{
  PRECONDITION:
  1 <= NumberOfTerms.

  POSTCONDITION:
  Returns an estimate of e, obtained by summing the
  specified number of terms of the series.
}
VAR
   Index      : Integer;
   Term, Sum : Real;

BEGIN

   Term  := 1.0;
   Sum   := 1.0;
```

```
   ESeries := Sum

END; { ESeries }
```

As before, you should single-step through this function, watching the values of Index, Term, and Sum, until you are thoroughly familiar with the sequence of execution and the way in which the loop terminates.

> Turn in the lab pages on which you have answered questions, plus source-code listings for the completed programs and printouts of test runs.

Lab Project 9.2:
Completing the Calendar Program

Concepts: Loops; top-down design.

Lab Techniques: Top-down design; incremental testing; stepwise refinement; don't be satisfied with your first idea.

Prerequisites: Chapter 9 of *Structures and Abstractions*.

Now, with the help of loops, we are ready to finish the perpetual calendar program we began in Lab 8.2. Our goal is to build a program that prints the calendar for any desired month in a given year. We previously agreed that a typical run might look like this:

```
CALENDAR PRINTING
-----------------


Month <Number from 1 to 12> ? 8
Year <1961 or later> ? 1994


          AUGUST

    S   M   T   W   T   F   S
   --------------------------
        1   2   3   4   5   6
    7   8   9  10  11  12  13
   14  15  16  17  18  19  20
   21  22  23  24  25  26  27
   28  29  30  31
```

We previously wrote code to read the desired month and year from the keyboard, and to compute the day of the week on which the month begins. (The day of the week is expressed as a numerical code—0 for Sunday, 1 for Monday, . . ., 6 for Saturday.) Now all we need is a procedure that displays the calendar for the given month in the given year. Looking at the program from the top down, we begin with driver that will eventually produce output like that shown above. The driver needs to show the program's purpose, get the inputs, then print the calendar for the requested month. It is called CALENDAR.PAS on the accompanying floppy disk, and the code is shown on the next page.

```
PROGRAM Calendar (Input, Output);

{ Perpetual Gregorian calendar for years after 1960. }
{ Labs 8.2 and 9.2. }

CONST
   FirstYear = 1961;     { Earliest year handled = 1961 }
   FirstDayOffset = 0;   { Day of week for Jan. 1, 1961 }

VAR
   Month, Year : Integer;


PROCEDURE ShowPurpose;
BEGIN

   WriteLn( 'CALENDAR PRINTING' );
   WriteLn( '-----------------' );
   WriteLn

END; { ShowPurpose }


PROCEDURE GetMonthAndYear( VAR Month, Year : Integer );
BEGIN

   REPEAT
     WriteLn( 'Month <Number from 1 to 12> ? ' );
     ReadLn( Month )
   UNTIL ( Month >= 1 ) AND ( Month <= 12 );

   REPEAT
     WriteLn( 'Year <', FirstYear:4, '-',
              (FirstYear+88):4, '> ? ' );
     ReadLn( Year )
   UNTIL (Year >= FirstYear) AND (Year <= (FirstYear+88));

   WriteLn;
   WriteLn

END;  { GetMonthAndYear }
```

```
PROCEDURE PrintHeader( Month : Integer );
BEGIN

   CASE Month OF

      1:  WriteLn( '              JANUARY' );

      2:  WriteLn( '             FEBRUARY' );

      3:  WriteLn( '               MARCH' );

      4:  WriteLn( '               APRIL' );

      5:  WriteLn( '                 MAY' );

      6:  WriteLn('               JUNE');

      7:  WriteLn('               JULY');

      8:  WriteLn('              AUGUST');

      9:  WriteLn('           SEPTEMBER');

      10: WriteLn('             OCTOBER');

      11: WriteLn('            NOVEMBER');

      12: WriteLn('            DECEMBER')

   END;

   WriteLn;
   WriteLn( '  S   M   T   W   T   F   S' );
   WriteLn( '  -------------------------' )

END; { PrintHeader }


FUNCTION IsLeapYear( Year : Integer ) : Boolean;
BEGIN

   {-- This is only a stub -- you finish it! }
   IsLeapYear := False

END; { IsLeapYear }
```

```
FUNCTION FirstDayOfMonth(Month, Year: Integer) : Integer;
BEGIN

    {-- Stub only: Your code from Lab 8.2 goes here. }
    FirstDayOfMonth := 0

END; { FirstDayOfMonth }



FUNCTION DaysInMonth( Month, Year : Integer ) : Integer;
VAR
    NumDays : Integer;

BEGIN

    CASE Month OF

        1:  DaysInMonth := 31;

        2:  IF IsLeapYear(Year) THEN
                DaysInMonth := 29
            ELSE
                DaysInMonth := 28;

        3:  DaysInMonth := 31;

        4:  DaysInMonth := 30;

        5:  DaysInMonth := 31;

        6:  DaysInMonth := 30;

        7:  DaysInMonth := 31;

        8:  DaysInMonth := 31;

        9:  DaysInMonth := 30;

        10: DaysInMonth := 31;

        11: DaysInMonth := 30;

        12: DaysInMonth := 31

    END

END; { DaysInMonth }
```

```
PROCEDURE PrintCalendar( Month, Offset : Integer );
BEGIN

   PrintHeader( Month );
   {--You supply the code }

END; { PrintCalendar }


BEGIN

   ShowPurpose;

   GetMonthAndYear( Month, Year );

   PrintCalendar( Month, Year )

END.
```

Note the use of REPEAT..UNTIL loops to protect the program from out-of-range input data in the GetMonthAndYear procedure. (Recall the discussion of overflow error in Lab 8.2.)

Note also the use of CASE structures in PrintHeader and DaysInMonth. These two subprograms are on the third level of the hierarchy, because they will be called by PrintCalendar.

How to display the calendar . . .

The main problem remaining is to implement the PrintCalendar procedure—that is, to equip it with code. One approach is to imagine the calendar as a series of up to six rows, with each row representing a successive week. Then PrintCalendar would be something like this:

```
PROCEDURE PrintCalendar( Month, Year : Integer );
VAR
   Week : Integer;

BEGIN

   PrintHeader( Month );
   FOR Week := 1 TO 6 DO
      PrintWeek( Week )

END; { PrintCalendar }
```

Stepwise refinement

The real work is concealed in `PrintWeek`. When we print the first week, there will be an offset of some number of days before the month begins. For example, if the month starts on a Thursday, the offset will be four: that is, four blank days must be printed before the first of the month:

```
               JUNE

     S    M    T    W    T    F    S
    -------------------------------
                         1    2    3
     4    5    6    7    8    9   10
    11   12   13   14   15   16   17
    18   19   20   21   22   23   24
    25   26   27   28   29   30
```

So one lesson is that `PrintWeek` must be provided with the offset. This changes our `PrintCalendar` code a little, making use of the `FirstDayOfMonth` function from Lab 8.2:

```
PrintHeader( Month );
Offset := FirstDayOfMonth( Month, Year );
FOR Week := 1 TO 6 DO
   PrintWeek( Offset, Week )
```

Furthermore, our loop will sometimes print a blank row or two in the calendar. If a February starts on a Sunday, it will occupy only four rows. Many months will occupy only five rows, as in the example above. Only occasionally will we need six rows for a month, so let's have the program calculate the number of weeks really needed. It's easiest if we start with some examples:

Number of days in month	Offset	Number of weeks
28	0	4
28	1–6	5
29	0–6	5
30	0–5	5
30	6	6
31	0–4	5
31	5–6	6

You can see that the number of weeks is roughly (#days DIV 7), but it tends to increase also with the offset. After a little trial and error, we discover that

$$(\# \text{ weeks}) = [\,(\#\text{days} + \text{offset} - 1)\ \ DIV\ 7\,] + 1$$

Exercise: Complete the following table in order to verify the formula for number of weeks:

#days	Offset	#weeks	[(#days + offset − 1) DIV 7] + 1
28	0	4	_____
28	1–6	5	_____
29	0–6	5	_____
30	0–5	5	_____
30	6	6	_____
31	0–4	5	_____
31	5–6	6	_____

This result gives us a further refinement in the PrintCalendar code:

```
PROCEDURE PrintCalendar( Month, Year : Integer );
VAR
    Week, NumWeeks, Offset : Integer;

BEGIN

    PrintHeader( Month );
    Offset   := FirstDayOfMonth( Month, Year );
    NumWeeks :=
      ((DaysInMonth(Month, Year) + Offset - 1) DIV 7) + 1;
    FOR Week := 1 TO NumWeeks DO
       PrintWeek( Offset, Week )

END; { PrintCalendar }
```

Next comes the fun part, as we implement the PrintWeek procedure. To print a week—a row—of the calendar, we sweep out seven day-positions. We can imagine these day positions as being numbered from zero upward, through the month:

```
Day positions
in month printouts

 0   1   2   3   4   5   6
 7   8   9  10  11  12  13
14  15  16  17  18  19  20
21  22  23  24  25  26  27
28  29  30  31  32  33  34
35  36  37  38  39  40  41
```

These are all the "slots" that can possibly be occupied by dates in all possible calendars. In a given calendar, only some of these slots will be filled. Notice first that the slot numbers can be calculated from the corresponding week numbers. If Week begins with FirstDay and ends with LastDay, then

```
FirstDay := ( Week - 1 ) * 7
```

and   `LastDay  := FirstDay + 6`

Then if we let a Day variable sweep through the week from FirstDay to LastDay, we can easily compute what to print. Consider a month that starts on a Thursday and has 30 days. We show both the Day values (not highlighted) and the dates (highlighted).

```
 0   1   2   3   4   5   6
                 1   2   3
 7   8   9  10  11  12  13
 4   5   6   7   8   9  10
14  15  16  17  18  19  20
11  12  13  14  15  16  17
21  22  23  24  25  26  27
18  19  20  21  22  23  24
28  29  30  31  32  33  34
25  26  27  28  29  30
35  36  37  38  39  40  41
```

As you can see, the date is always (Day − Offset + 1). This gives us the following implementations of PrintWeek and PrintCalendar:

```
PROCEDURE PrintWeek( Offset, MaxDay, Week : Integer );
VAR
    FirstDay, LastDay, Day, Date : Integer;

BEGIN

    FirstDay := ( Week - 1 ) * 7;
    LastDay  := FirstDay + 6;
    FOR Day := FirstDay TO LastDay DO
    BEGIN

        Date := ( Day - Offset + 1 );
        IF ( Date < 1 ) OR ( Date > MaxDay ) THEN
            Write( ' ':4 )
        ELSE
            Write( Date:4 )

    END;
    WriteLn

END; { PrintWeek }


PROCEDURE PrintCalendar( Month, Year : Integer );
VAR
    TotalDays, Week, NumWeeks, Offset : Integer;

BEGIN

    PrintHeader( Month );

    TotalDays := DaysInMonth(Month, Year);
    Offset    := FirstDayOfMonth( Month, Year );
    NumWeeks  := ( ( TotalDays + Offset - 1 ) DIV 7 ) + 1;

    FOR Week := 1 TO NumWeeks DO
        PrintWeek( Offset, TotalDays, Week )

END; { PrintCalendar }
```

Don't be satisfied with your first idea!

You should use this code to complete the Calendar program and try it out. It does work correctly, but it seems excessively complicated for what it needs to do; it isn't elegant. Whenever you have this feeling, it is a good idea to sit back, distance yourself from your new creation, and rethink the solution from the beginning.

Remember the immortal words of Frank Lloyd Wright:

"The architect's most important tool is his trash can."

In fact, it is easy to think of another approach to printing a calendar. *Instead of looping over weeks of the month and computing the dates and slots for the dates, we can loop over all the days of the month and compute where to print the offset and where to put ends of lines.* That is, we first print four spaces for each day of initial offset, then execute

```
Write( Date:4 )
```

for every date in the month, from 1 to DaysInMonth(Month, Year). But whenever we've printed enough offset and dates to reach the end of a week, we print a WriteLn.

A skeleton for this approach is shown below. You supply what's missing. Insert the resulting procedure in your calendar program, complete the other parts, and test it thoroughly. (Some example data were given in Lab 8.2, and more can be found in an almanac.) When you are satisfied that your program runs correctly, turn in a complete source code listing along with printouts of sample runs.

```
PROCEDURE PrintCalendar( Month, Year : Integer );
{
   PRECONDITIONS:
   1 <= Month <= 12; 0 <= Offset <= 6.

   POSTCONDITIONS:
   Calendar for month has been printed with correct offset.
}
VAR
   Date : Integer;

BEGIN

   PrintHeader( Month );
   Offset := FirstDayOfMonth( Month, Year );

   {--Initial offset: skip days before month starts }
   FOR Date := 1 TO Offset DO
      Write( ' ':4 );

   FOR Date := 1 TO DaysInMonth( Month, Year ) DO
   BEGIN
      { YOU SUPPLY WHAT'S MISSING! }
   END

END; { PrintCalendar }
```

Lab 10.1
Testing Loop Invariants

Concepts: Pre- and postconditions, loop invariants, loop bounds.

Lab techniques: Using the debugger's Watch or Observe window to check the validity of loop invariants.

Prerequisites: Sections 10.1–10.4 of *Structures and Abstractions*.

The purpose of a loop is to perform the same actions repeatedly. A loop builds a desired result by repeatedly making the same kind of contribution to the result. The essence of a loop consists of what the loop does over and over again, and how many times the loop does it.

Notice that a loop does not make the same contribution to the result during every trip, but merely the same *kind* of contribution. In other words, there is a constant pattern in the actions of the loop. This constant pattern is what we call a *loop invariant*. Specifically, a loop invariant is a property of a loop that is valid at the beginning and end of each trip through the loop. The invariant can be stated by the programmer as an assertion inserted as a comment in the code, and is useful in designing the loop and in checking for correct behavior after writing it. This is discussed in Section 10.1 of *Structures and Abstractions*.

In this lab session, we first use the source-code debugger to check the invariant discussed in Section 10.1 of the text. Then we go on to other examples and other methods to check invariants.

Summing whole numbers up to N

As described in the text, our loop calculates

```
Sum  =  0 + 1 + 2 + 3 + . . . + N
```

A function that performs this calculation is provided in the disk file SUMN.PAS and shown on the next page.

```
PROGRAM SumN ( Input, Output );
{ From Lab 10.1. }

VAR
    Num : Integer;


PROCEDURE ShowPurpose;
BEGIN

    WriteLn( 'Summing 0 + 1 + 2 + ... + N' );
    WriteLn( '----------------------------' );
    WriteLn

END; { ShowPurpose }


PROCEDURE GetN( VAR N : Integer );
BEGIN

    REPEAT

        Write( 'Give me a nonnegative N: ' );
        ReadLn( N )

    UNTIL N >= 0;

    WriteLn

END; { GetN }


FUNCTION SumOfWholesUpTo( N : Integer ) : Integer;
{
  PRECONDITION:
  N >= 0.

  POSTCONDITION:
  Returns the sum 0 + 1 + 2 + 3 + .. . + N.
}

VAR
    I, Sum : Integer;

BEGIN
```

```
{ ASSERTION: N >= 0 }
I    := 0;
Sum := 0;

{
  PRECONDITIONS: I := 0
  and Sum = ( 0 + 1 + 2 + .. . + I ) = 0.
}
WHILE I < N DO
BEGIN

   I    := I + 1;
   Sum := Sum + I

END;
{
  POSTCONDITIONS: I := N
  and Sum = ( 0 + 1 + 2 + .. . + I )
          = ( 0 + 1 + 2 + .. . + N ).
}

SumOfWholesUpTo := Sum

END; { SumOfWholesUpTo }


BEGIN

ShowPurpose;
GetN( Num );

WriteLn( '1 + 2 + 3 + ... + N = ',
         SumOfWholesUpTo( Num ):3 )
END.
```

We are interested in proving the correct operation of the loop in the SumOfWholesUpTo function, shown at the top of this page. Before the loop begins, the program state is given by the preconditions:

```
{
  PRECONDITIONS: I := 0
  and Sum = ( 0 + 1 + 2 + .. . + I ) = 0.
}
```

After the loop has done its work, the program should be in the following state:

```
{
  POSTCONDITIONS: I := N
  and Sum = ( 0 + 1 + 2 + .. . + I )
          = ( 0 + 1 + 2 + .. . + N ).
}
```

The purpose of the loop is to carry the program state from the preconditions to the postconditions. Let's think about this for a moment. Before the loop begins, I is initialized to 0. Then the loop continues as long as I < N, incrementing I during each trip and adding the latest value of I to the Sum. When the loop terminates, I is necessarily equal to N. This last statement is necessarily true because (you give the reasons):

(1)_____

(2)_____

(3)_____

We quickly see one of the invariant properties of the loop:

```
{
  LOOP INVARIANT:
  0 <= I <= N.
}
```

This is fine as far as it goes, but it doesn't yet capture the purpose of the loop, which is to build up a sum. The central actions of the loop are to increment I and *to add the latest value of I to the sum.* Both of these actions should be reflected in the loop invariant. Thus we are led to assert

```
{
  LOOP INVARIANT:
  0 <= I <= N
  and Sum = (0 + 1 + 2 + ... + I).
}
```

If it is true that Sum = (0 + 1 + 2 + ... + I) and that I sweeps from 0 up to N, then Sum must equal (0 + 1 + 2 + ... + N) when the loop terminates. Perhaps a diagram would best show how the preconditions are carried into the postconditions:

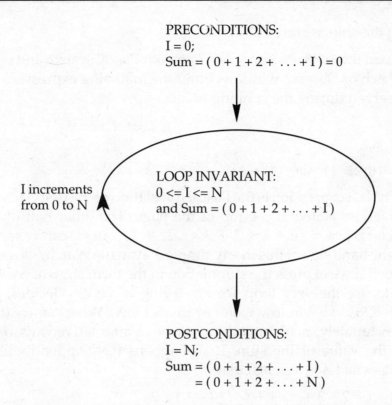

PRECONDITIONS:
I = 0;
Sum = (0 + 1 + 2 + ... + I) = 0

LOOP INVARIANT:
0 <= I <= N
and Sum = (0 + 1 + 2 + ... + I)

I increments
from 0 to N

POSTCONDITIONS:
I = N;
Sum = (0 + 1 + 2 + ... + I)
    = (0 + 1 + 2 + ... + N)

This is the desired result. But are we *sure* that the loop actually satisfies the invariant at the beginning and end of every trip? With the help of the computer, we can get the program to confirm this.

In addition to making sure that the body of the loop makes the correct contribution to the result on each trip, it is important to verify that the loop makes the correct number of trips. In making the latter check, programmers often assert an algebraic expression for the number of trips remaining before the loop terminates. This is called a *loop bound*. In the present example, I increases from 0, approaching N as the loop runs and reaching N as the loop terminates. Therefore, the expression (N - I) measures the number of trips remaining at any given time. It is the loop bound for this loop.

The example loop is simple enough that you can check the invariant and bound assertions in your head. Later on, however, you will encounter trickier loops, and for those, you need systematic ways to check loop assertions. You can do it either with a source-code debugger or by means of extra output statements inserted manually into the loop code. We will consider both methods in this lab.

Using the source-code debugger

Load the SUMN.PAS program into your Pascal system and open the Watch or Observe window. Enter the following expressions to be observed during the running of the loop:

```
I

Sum

(0 <= I) AND (I <= N)
```

The last expression is the Pascal translation of the first clause of the invariant stated at the top of the page. The other half of the invariant is Sum = (0 + 1 + 2 + 3 + ... + I), but we can't express the right-hand side of this in any simple way in the Watch/Observe window. If we express the summation in the form shown, we will need to use the very loop we are trying to verify. Besides, the Watch/Observe window won't evaluate loops. What can we do?

Fortunately, mathematics provides an alternative way to express the value of the sum. It so happens (see Appendix G of *Structures and Abstractions*) that

$$0 + 1 + 2 + 3 + \ldots + I = I(I+1)/2$$

We can therefore enter the second half of the loop invariant into the Watch/Observe window in simplified form:

```
Sum = ( I * ( I + 1 ) ) DIV 2
```

Now we have four items in the Watch/Observe window, and we want to see if the third and fourth are True before and after each trip through the loop. To do this, insert a breakpoint on the WHILE statement itself and another on the SumOfWholesUpTo assignment statement after the loop. Then run the program with N = 3, checking the Watch/Observe expressions at each break. Record your observations below:

Expression	Value of Expression
(At start of first trip)	
I	_____
Sum	_____
(0 <= I) AND (I <= N)	_____
Sum = (I * (I + 1)) DIV 2	_____

(At start of second trip)

I   _____

Sum   _____

(0 <= I) AND (I <= N)   _____

Sum = (I * (I + 1)) DIV 2   _____

(At start of third trip)

I   _____

Sum   _____

(0 <= I) AND (I <= N)   _____

Sum = (I * (I + 1)) DIV 2   _____

(At start of fourth trip)

I   _____

Sum   _____

(0 <= I) AND (I <= N)   _____

Sum = (I * (I + 1)) DIV 2   _____

(After loop terminates)

I   _____

Sum   _____

(0 <= I) AND (I <= N)   _____

Sum = (I * (I + 1)) DIV 2   _____

Is an invariant true everywhere in the loop?

Now place a breakpoint on the statement that assigns a value to Sum inside the loop. Run your program again and record the values of the four expressions at the first three breaks:

Expression	Value of Expression
(At start of first trip)	
I	_____
Sum	_____
(0 <= I) AND (I <= N)	_____
Sum = (I * (I + 1)) DIV 2	_____
(In middle of first trip)	
I	_____
Sum	_____
(0 <= I) AND (I <= N)	_____
Sum = (I * (I + 1)) DIV 2	_____
(At end of first trip, start of second trip)	
I	_____
Sum	_____
(0 <= I) AND (I <= N)	_____
Sum = (I * (I + 1)) DIV 2	_____

Explain in your own words why the invariant doesn't seem to be valid when execution is in the middle of the loop body.

_____

_____

_____

A trickier way to use some debuggers

In the work above, we used mathematics to cast the invariant

    Sum = (0 + 1 + 2 + ... + I)

into the equivalent form

    Sum = (I * (I + 1)) DIV 2

because that form could be entered directly in the Watch/Observe window. However, some debuggers allow another intriguing approach. Because the sum (0 + 1 + 2 + ... + I) is the same as SumOfWholesUpTo(I), we can enter the expression

```
Sum  = SumOfWholesUpTo(I)
```

in the Watch/Observe window. This constitutes a debugger call to the SumWholesUpTo function from within the function itself, sending it I instead on N. In other words, the function calls itself, a process called *recursion*. The Turbo Pascal debugger does not allow this, which is why we originally used the other approach. But other debuggers, like the one in THINK Pascal, allow recursion.

The recursive approach is open to the criticism we made earlier, however. We are trying to check the correctness of the loop. How can we do that by comparing it to shorter loops of the same form? You might want to discuss this in class with your instructor.

Shortcomings of the debugger method

There is a severe limitation in using debugger methods to check loop invariants: the Watch/Observe window allows us to evaluate only closed-form expressions. For example, we cannot directly check that

```
Sum = ( sum of integers from 0 through (I-1) )
```

We got around this limitation by finding a closed-form expression that had the same value as the sum. But that raises the question of why we bother to use a loop to perform the sum in the first place, if we already know a shorter way to compute the sum. Of course, we used the loop summation because it provides a simple example of how loop invariants can be used to guarantee the correct operation of a loop.

In doing this, we have seen that debugger techniques for checking loops are quite limited. When we encounter a loop invariant that is not expressible in closed form, it is better to use extra output statements to check the validity of the invariant. So let's try that method on a problem that doesn't lend itself to debugger methods.

Using output statements to check an invariant and bound

If you don't have a debugger with a Watch/Observe window, or if you are checking a loop invariant not expressible as a closed-form expression, you can use output statements to check the validity of the invariant. Consider the following program, which is supposed to find the maximum of five real numbers read from the keyboard. It is called MAXOF5.PAS on the disk:

```
PROGRAM TestMaxOfFive ( Input, Output );
{ From Lab 10.1 }

VAR
    Maximum : Real;


PROCEDURE MaxOfFive( VAR Maximum : Real );
VAR
    Num    : Real;
    Count : Integer;

BEGIN

    WriteLn( 'Enter five real numbers, one per line:' );

    Count := 0;
    REPEAT

        ReadLn( Num );
        Count := Count + 1;

        IF Count = 1 THEN
            Maximum := Num
        ELSE IF Num > Maximum THEN
            Maximum := Num

    UNTIL Count = 5

END; { MaxOfFive }


PROCEDURE ShowResult( Result : Real );
BEGIN

    WriteLn;
    WriteLn( 'Maximum is ', Maximum:10:2 )

END; { ShowResult }
```

```
BEGIN

    MaxOfFive( Maximum );
    ShowResult( Maximum )

END.
```

The loop of interest is the one in the MaxOfFive procedure. It has three preconditions. Very informally,

```
{
    PRECONDITIONS: Count = 0,
    no numbers have been read,
    and Maximum contains garbage.
}
```

After the loop has done its work, we should have the following postconditions:

```
{
    POSTCONDITIONS: Count = 5
    and Maximum = ( largest of the 5 values entered )
}
```

The purpose of the loop is to carry the program state from the preconditions to the postconditions. Before the loop begins, Count = 0, no numbers have been read from the keyboard, and Maximum has an unknown value. After the loop ends, Count = 5, five numbers have been read from the keyboard, and Maximum is the largest of the five. It follows that the loop invariant to carry the preconditions into the postconditions is

```
{
    LOOP INVARIANT:
    Count numbers have been read so far
    and Maximum >= ( numbers read so far )
}
```

Again, it helps to have a picture of how and why the loop works. This is shown on the next page.

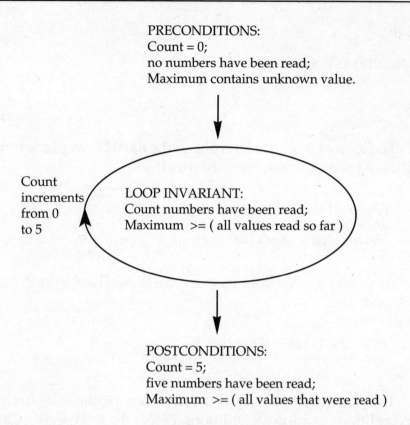

PRECONDITIONS:
Count = 0;
no numbers have been read;
Maximum contains unknown value.

Count
increments
from 0
to 5

LOOP INVARIANT:
Count numbers have been read;
Maximum >= (all values read so far)

POSTCONDITIONS:
Count = 5;
five numbers have been read;
Maximum >= (all values that were read)

Now we can insert into the source code output statements that allow us to check by eye the operation of the loop invariant, as it sweeps the program state from preconditions to postconditions:

```
Count := 0;
WriteLn( 'Initially, Count = ', Count );
WriteLn( 'and no numbers have been read.' );
WriteLn;

REPEAT

   WriteLn( 'ASSERTION: (numbers so far) <=',
            Maximum:6:2);

   ReadLn( Num );
   Count := Count + 1;

   IF Count = 1 THEN
      Maximum := Num
   ELSE IF Num > Maximum THEN
      Maximum := Num;
```

```
    WriteLn( 'ASSERTION: (numbers so far) <=',
             Maximum:6:2 );
    WriteLn

UNTIL Count = 5;

WriteLn( 'Finally, Count = ', Count, '.' );
WriteLn( 'five numbers have been read, ' );
WriteLn( 'and (all numbers read) <= ', Maximum )
```

Insert such output statements into the program and run it with various sets of data. Does all the output make sense? Does the output show how Maximum always contains the maximum number read so far, whenever execution is at the top or bottom of the loop?

_____

_____

_____

Suppose that the statement

```
    WriteLn( 'ASSERTION: (numbers so far) <=',
             Maximum:6:2 );
```

is inserted in the middle of the loop, between the incrementation of Count and the IF..THEN..ELSE structure. Will it output a true statement? Why?

_____

_____

_____

Remove this last output statement from the middle of the loop, leaving output statements at the top and bottom of the loop. Then add an output statement that will test the loop bound.

┌───┐
│ Turn in your resulting source code listing, together │
│ with a printout of a test run, along with the pages │
│ from this lab on which you wrote answers to ques- │
│ tions. │
└───┘

Now here's one for you

After you have used output statements to confirm the invariant in the MaxOfFive example, you should apply the same method to the SumN problem. Insert the appropriate output statements in SumN and use them to confirm both the invariant and the loop bound.

> Turn in your resulting source code listing, together with a printout of a test run, along with the pages from this lab on which you wrote answers to questions.

Credits: This lab has benefited greatly from conversations with Jack Mostow and Lou Steinberg, of Rutgers, The State University of New Jersey.

Lab Project 10.2:
Checking Text for Readability

Concepts: Iteration, program states, text file I/O.

Lab techniques: Top-down design.

Prerequisites: Chapter 9 and Sections 10.6 and 10.7 of *Structures and Abstractions*.

In Section 9.2, the textbook develops a procedure for counting the number of characters in the Input text file. We now build on this material as we design a program to estimate the "readability" of text.

Reading level of text

One of the common measures of readability is the estimation of the "grade level" of text, using methods suggested by Rudolph Flesch and Robert Gunning. (See the references at the end of this lab.) The grade level is a function of two simple measures:

1. The average number of syllables per word.

2. The average number of words per sentence.

Obviously, text with long words and long sentences is harder to read. Here, for example, is some first-grade text. You'll probably remember reading it in school:

Look, look, said Jane. See Spot run. See the big dog run.
Oh, darn, cried Dick. Spot ate my Spam.

By contrast, here is some typical text written by a college professor at grade level 16:

It is immediately apparent that rudimentary processes
of assimilation are at work when I masticate the substance
known as Spam.

Most writing experts recommend writing at grade levels between these two extremes. Grade 8 writing is recommended for magazines and newspapers:

According to a usually reliable source, Spot ate the Spam.

Gunning has proposed a so-called "Fog Index" to measure the difficulty of reading text:

Fog Index = Grade Level =

0.4 * (AvWordsPerSentence + PercentHardWords)

Here AvWordsPerSentence is the average number of words per sentence and PercentHardWords is the percentage of words that have three or more syllables, not counting proper names, three-syllable words that are combinations of one- and two-syllable words (like "bookkeeper"), or three-syllable words ending in "ed" or "es." Gunning's Fog Index correlates roughly with school grade level—text with a Fog Index of 7 or 8 should be readable by junior high school students, while text with a Fog Index of 13 should be readable by college freshpersons.

Flesch, on the other hand, proposed a measure of the ease of reading:

Reading Ease =

207 – [(1.02 * AvWordsPerSentence)

+ (84.6 * AvSyllablesPerWord)]

Here, AvSyllablesPerWord is, of course, the average number of syllables per word. The Flesch Reading Ease formula produces a rather arbitrary number. According to the formula, empty text with no words and no syllables would have Reading Ease = 207, which is the maximum possible.

Designing the program

Suppose that we want a program that prompts for the name of a text file, then reads and displays the file, and finally estimates the grade level and readability of the text it reads. A sample run might look like this:

```
GRADE LEVEL AND READABILITY OF TEXT
-------------------------------------

Name of file to read?  ESSAY.TXT

Reading the file...
```

```
The text in this file has

   Grade Level  = 11
   Reading Ease = 74
```

The sequence of events is apparent from the I/O:

1. Show the purpose of the program.

2. Prompt for and read the name of the text file to be processed.

3. Estimate the grade level and reading ease.

4. Display the results.

The skeleton of the program then follows directly from this outline. The code is available on the accompanying floppy disk as the file READABIL.PAS.

```
PROGRAM Readability( Input, Output );
{
  Computes grade level and Flesch reading ease
  for requested text file.
}

VAR
   InFile : Text;
   AvLettersPerWord, AvWordsPerSentence : Integer;
   PercentHardWords : Real;

PROCEDURE ShowPurpose;
BEGIN

   WriteLn( 'GRADE LEVEL AND READABILITY OF TEXT' );
   WriteLn( '-----------------------------------' );
   WriteLn

END; { ShowPurpose }
```

```
PROCEDURE OpenFile( VAR InFile : Text );
{
  POSTCONDITION:
  InFile is open for reading.
}
VAR
   FileName : String;

BEGIN

   Write( 'Text file to read? ' );
   ReadLn( FileName );

   Reset( InFile, FileName )

END; { OpenFile }



PROCEDURE GetStats( VAR InFile            : Text;
                    VAR AvSylsPerWord      : Integer;
                    VAR AvWordsPerSentence : Integer;
                    VAR PercentHardWords   : Real );
{
  PRECONDITIONS:
  InFile is open for reading.

  POSTCONDITIONS:
  AvSylsPerWord, AvWordsPerSentence, PercentHardWords
  have values that reflect the text in InFile.
}
BEGIN

   {--This is only a stub }
   AvSylsPerWord      := 0;
   AvWordsPerSentence := 0;
   PercentHardWords   := 0.0

END; { GetStats }
```

```
PROCEDURE ShowReadability( SyllablesPerWord : Integer;
                           WordsPerSentence : Integer;
                           PcntHardWords    : Real );
{
  PRECONDITIONS:
  SyllablesPerWord, WordsPerSentence, PcntHardWords
  have values.

  POSTCONDITIONS:
  Grade level and reading ease of text have been
  estimated and displayed.
}
VAR
   GradeLevel, ReadingEase : Real;

BEGIN

   GradeLevel :=
           0.4 * ( WordsPerSentence + PcntHardWords );

   ReadingEase :=
           207 - ( 1.02 * WordsPerSentence )
               - ( 84.6 * SyllablesPerWord );
   IF ReadingEase < 0.0 THEN
      ReadingEase := 0.0;

   WriteLn;
   WriteLn( 'Grade level  = ', GradeLevel:5:1 );
   WriteLn( 'Reading Ease = ', ReadingEase:5:1 );
   WriteLn

END; { ShowReadability }


BEGIN

   ShowPurpose;

   {--Prompt for and open the text file to be tested }
   OpenFile( InFile );

   {--Measure statistics for the given text file }
   GetStats( InFile, AvLettersPerWord,
          AvWordsPerSentence, PercentHardWords );

   {--Display calculated grade level and reading ease }
   ShowReadability( AvLettersPerWord, AvWordsPerSentence,
                 PercentHardWords )

END.
```

Sketching the algorithm

The `GetStats` procedure needs to compute three quantities:

`AvSyllablesPerWord =`
Total number of syllables / Total number of words

`AvWordsPerSentence =`
Total number of words / Total number of sentences

`PercentHardWords =`
Number of hard words / Total number of words

As you can see, the procedure will first need to count the numbers of syllables, words, hard words, and sentences in the text file. Let's approach this in stages, taking the easy parts first.

A loop to read characters from the text file

Because the text file is a stream of characters, we read the file with a `WHILE` loop that reads characters one by one until encountering the end-of-file signal. As shown in Section 10.7 of the textbook, the loop must check for `<EOF>` before reading each character, to avoid the possibility of trying to read past the last character:

```
VAR
   Ch : Char;

BEGIN
   WHILE NOT EOF( InFile ) DO
   BEGIN

      Read( Ch );

   END;
```

Put this code into your `GetStats` procedure and test it. In the next several steps, you will gradually add the counting features to this loop.

Counting words and sentences

It's pretty easy to tell when the loop has encountered the end of a word because the end is marked by whitespace, punctuation, or the end of the file. But not every single whitespace character that comes along—tab, space, carriage return, form feed—marks the end of a word. A pair of words might be separated by a couple of

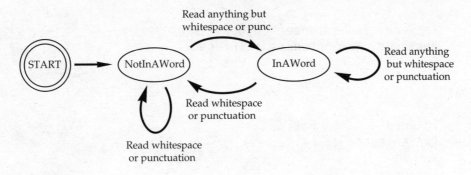

Figure 1. Program state transitions while counting words in text.

spaces, or a period followed by a space. Furthermore, the whole file might start with a space or tab before the first word. Our procedure will have to allow for these exceptional cases.

It helps to think of the states of the algorithm as it reads through the text. On encountering the first character that is not whitespace or punctuation, the algorithm "knows" that it is entering a word. It stays in that word until it reads a character that is either whitespace or punctuation. At that point, it counts one word completed and "knows" that it is no longer in the midst of a word. Thus we've considered two parameters of the algorithm state: the state of being in a word, and the state of not being in a word. The state transitions are shown in Figure 1.

Counting sentences works the same way, with the state parameters being `InASentence` and `NotInASentence`. The state transitions are shown in Figure 2.

Next, we add code to the `GetStats` procedure, to implement the state transitions indicated in Figures 1 and 2. The code is shown on the next page.

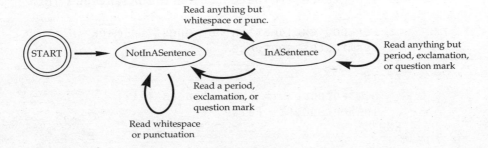

Figure 2. Program state transitions while counting sentences.

```
VAR
    InAWord, InASentence   : Boolean;
    NumWords, NumSentences : Integer;
    Ch                     : Char;

BEGIN

    InAWord      := False;
    InASentence  := False;

    NumWords      := 0;
    NumSentences := 0;

    WHILE NOT EOF( InFile ) DO
    BEGIN

        Read( InFile, Ch );

        IF IsWhitespace( Ch ) THEN

            IF InAWord THEN
            {--Whitespace terminates word }
            BEGIN
                NumWords := NumWords + 1;
                InAWord  := False
            END

        ELSE IF IsPunctuation(Ch) THEN
        BEGIN

            IF InAWord THEN
            {--Punctuation terminates word }
            BEGIN
                NumWords := NumWords + 1;
                InAWord := False;
            END;

            IF IsSentenceTerminator(Ch) AND InASentence THEN
            {
             --Period, exclamation, or question mark
               terminates sentence
            }
            BEGIN
                NumSentences := NumSentences + 1;
                InASentence := False
            END

        END { ELSE IF }
```

```
        ELSE { Ch is considered to be a letter }
        BEGIN

            InAWord      := True;
            InASentence := True

        END

    END; { WHILE }

    {
      ASSERTION: There are no more characters in the file.
    }

    IF InASentence THEN
        {--<EOF> terminates sentence }
        NumSentences := NumSentences + 1;

    IF InAWord THEN
        {--<EOF> terminates word }
        NumWords := NumWords + 1;

    IF NumSentences > 0 THEN
        AvWordsPerSentence :=
                        Round( NumWords / NumSentences )
    ELSE
        AvWordsPerSentence := NumWords;
```

The program states in this code are specified by boolean state variables, InAWord and InASentence, which mirror Figures 1 and 2, respectively. The state transitions are implemented by means of structures like the following, which carries the program state from InAWord = True to InAWord = False:

```
        IF IsWhitespace( Ch ) THEN

            IF InAWord THEN
            {--Whitespace terminates word }
            BEGIN
                NumWords := NumWords + 1;
                InAWord  := False
            END
```

Note also that the code assumes that we will have appropriate functions called IsWhitespace, IsPunctuation, and IsSentenceTerminator.

Question: In the code, the transitions to InAWord = True and InASentence = True are accomplished by the code

```
ELSE { Ch is considered to be a letter }
BEGIN

    InAWord     := True;
    InASentence := True

END
```

Would it be better to write the following?

```
ELSE { Ch is considered to be a letter }
BEGIN

    IF NOT InAWord THEN
        InAWord     := True;

    IF NOT InASentence THEN
        InASentence := True

END
```

Argue the pros and cons.

> Before going on to the next stage of the lab, use the debugger or extra output statements to trace the execution of the program as it exists so far, making sure that you thoroughly understand the operation of the state variables.

Counting syllables

The last task is to count syllables so that we can count the "hard words" with three or more syllables and compute the average number of syllables per word. This task is very much like counting words or sentences. It is easiest to use a boolean state variable, InASyllable, to keep track of whether we are currently in the midst of a syllable. Simplistically, we can consider that a new syllable has begun when we read a vowel, and can consider that the syllable ends when we encounter the next nonvowel.

Question: We said that a syllable ends when we encounter the first nonvowel after a vowel. Is this the same as saying that it ends when we encounter the first consonant after a vowel? Why or why not?

Now you finish it . . .

We've gone most of the way into the program design. Now you complete the program by inserting all of the state transition code and its needed procedures and functions. Test your program with the text provided in the files GRADE1.TXT, GRADE9.TXT, and GRADE13.TXT. The reading ease indices for these files can be found within the files themselves. Turn in your source-code listing and printouts from the test runs.

Wait, there's more!

After you get the whole program working (and not before), it's time to look back over what you've built. Notice that the program does not take into account that

- Two successive vowels may belong to different syllables, as in the word "coop."

- A terminal "e" does not begin a new syllable in words like "stagnate" and "state."

- Three-syllable words that are combinations of one- and two-syllable words are not considered to be hard words. Examples: "coffeepot"; "anyway."

- Proper names and three-syllable words ending in "es" or "ed" are not considered to be hard words.

Such issues can be the focus of a project to follow this lab.

References

Rudolph Flesch. *The Art of Readable Writing* (Harper & Row, 1974).
Robert Gunning. *The Technique of Clear Writing* (McGraw-Hill, 1968).

Credits: David E. Leasure, of the University of Kansas, made several suggestions that improved this lab.

Lab 10.3
Profiling Nested Loops in Turbo Pascal

Concepts: Nested loops.

Lab techniques: Using a profiler.

Prerequisites: Section 10.5 of *Structures and Abstractions*.

Section 10.5 of the textbook analyzes the running times of nested loops, giving some feel for the time consumed by a loop within another loop. But there's nothing like hands-on testing, and Turbo Pascal provides a special tool for this purpose. It's called a *profiler*, and it analyzes the executions times of each statement in a program while the program is running. Profilers are used by advanced programmers trying to improve the speed and efficiency of their programs.

How to compile for profiling

The Turbo Profiler is a separate program that controls the running of your program while measuring the time spent in each statement. To do this, it requires that your program be compiled to generate special debugging object code, and that the object code be linked to produce an executable machine-code program saved as a .EXE disk file. For these reasons, the following steps must be taken when compiling and linking your program before profiling it:

1. In the Compile menu, select **Destination Disk**.
    (This makes the linker save a .EXE file.)

2. In the **Options** menu, select **Compiler**. In the Compiler Options submenu, make sure the **Debug** Information box is selected.

3. In the **Options** menu, select **Debugger**. In the Debugger submenu, make sure that the **Standalone** box is selected.

4. In the **File** menu, select **Save as . . .**, and give your file a name.

5. In the **Compile** menu, select **Make** (or press F9). This will create your executable file.

For practice, carry out these steps with the RUNTIME1.PAS program supplied on the accompanying disk and shown on the next page.

```
PROGRAM RunTime1 ( Output );
VAR
   N, Row, Col: Integer;

BEGIN

   { -- Code segment 10.5.1 }
   N := 4;
   FOR Row := 1 TO N DO
   BEGIN

      FOR Col := 1 TO ( N - 1 ) DO
         Write('*');

      WriteLn

   END

END.
```

Running the profiler

With RUNTIME1.PAS compiled with the debugger switches turned on and linked to produce a RUNTIME1.EXE file, you can invoke the profiler to run your program. If the profiler and RUNTIME1 program are both in the current subdirectory, the command is

```
TPROF RUNTIME1
```

If either is in a different subdirectory, you will have to give the appropriate pathnames.

Once the profiler has loaded your program, your screen should look approximately like that shown in Figure 1. If you get an error message like "Program has no symbol table" or you see a lot of hexadecimal numbers and assembly-language gibberish on your screen instead of a Pascal program, it means that you failed to perform steps 2 and 3 listed above, and your program does not contain the debugging code needed by the profiler. If you get the error message "Program not found," it means that there is no .EXE file for your program in the subdirectory you specified.

```
 ≡    File  View  Run  Statistics  Print  Options  Window  Help      Ready
┌[ ]═ Module: RUNTIME1  File: D:\TP\RUNTIME1.PAS 7 ══════════════1═[↑H↓]┐
│                                                                      ▲
│     PROGRAM Runtime1 ( Output );                                     
│     VAR                                                              
│        N, Row, Col : Integer;                                        
│                                                                      
│=>> BEGIN                                                             
│                                                                      
│        { -- Code segment 10.5.1 }                                    
│=>      N := 4;                                                       
│=>      FOR Row := 1 TO N DO                                          ▼
└◄▌██████████████████████████████████████████████████████████▐►┘
┌─ Execution Profile ──────────────────────────────────────────2─┐
│                                                                 │
│  Total time: 0 sec           Display: Time                      │
│  % of total: 100%             Filter: All                       │
│        Runs: 0 of 1             Sort: Frequency                 │
│                                                                 │
├─────────────────────────────────────────────────────────────────┤
│                                                                 │
│                                                                 │
│                                                                 │
│                                                                 │
└─────────────────────────────────────────────────────────────────┘

   F1-Help  F2-Area  F3-Mod  F5-Zoom  F6-Next  F9-Run  F10-Menu
```

FIGURE 1. *This is how your screen should look after starting the profiler, telling it to run the RUNTIME1 program. The upper window, called the Module window, shows the program's source code. The lower window, called the Execution Profile window, shows runtime statistics. So far, we have no statistics because we haven't run the program.*

Running a profile of your program

With the Module (upper) window active, give the command **Alt-F10** in order to call up a local menu for that window. Select **Add areas** and then, in the resulting submenu, select **Every line in module**. This tells the profiler to collect statistics on every line of code in your program. Then press **F9** to run the program. After the program runs, you will see the program's running statistics in the Execution Profile window, as shown in Figure 2.

The Execution Profile window has two panes. The upper pane shows the program's total running time, plus some of the display parameters. It says that

- It is displaying running times rather than counts of executions.

- Its "filter" is set to show statistics for all modules loaded.

- Its display shows running times sorted from longest time downward.

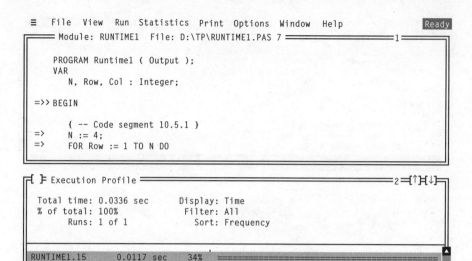

```
  ≡   File  View  Run  Statistics  Print  Options  Window  Help          [Ready]
  ═══ Module: RUNTIME1  File: D:\TP\RUNTIME1.PAS 7 ═══════════════1═══

      PROGRAM Runtime1 ( Output );
      VAR
         N, Row, Col : Integer;

  =>> BEGIN

        { -- Code segment 10.5.1 }
  =>      N := 4;
  =>      FOR Row := 1 TO N DO


  ⌐ ⊢ Execution Profile ════════════════════════════2═[↑H↓]⌐
     Total time: 0.0336 sec      Display: Time
     % of total: 100%            Filter: All
          Runs: 1 of 1             Sort: Frequency


     RUNTIME1.15      0.0117 sec    34%  ══════════════════════════════
     RUNTIME1.21      0.0098 sec    29%  ═══════════════════════════
     RUNTIME1.7       0.0075 sec    22%  ═════════════════════
     RUNTIME1.17      0.0039 sec    11%  ══════════════

  F1-Help  F2-Area  F3-Mod  F5-Zoom  F6-Next  F9-Run  F10-Menu
```

FIGURE 2. After giving the F9 Run command, the statistics of your program appear in the Execution Profile window. The profiler shows that line 15 of the program consumes 34% of the program's running time, followed by 29% for line 21, 22% for line 7, and 11% for line 17. The other statements in the program take negigible time.

If you "zoom" the Execution Profile window by pressing F5, you will be able to see the whole statistics display.

What the statistics mean

Each line in the lower pane of the Execution Profile window represents the running time consumed by a single line of source code. For example, the line

```
RUNTIME1.15  0.0117 sec  34%  |══════════════════════════════════════
```

indicates that line 15 of RUNTIME1 executed for a total of 0.0117 seconds during the run, consuming 34% of the total excution time for all statements marked with arrows. (In this case, all the statements in the program.) The bar on the right is a graph indicating the relative time spent executing line 15.

If you prefer, you can press Alt-F10 now, while the Execution Profile window is active, and see its local menu. Select **Display ...** and then, in the display submenu, select **Counts**. Then the Execution Profile window will look as shown in Figure 3, displaying the

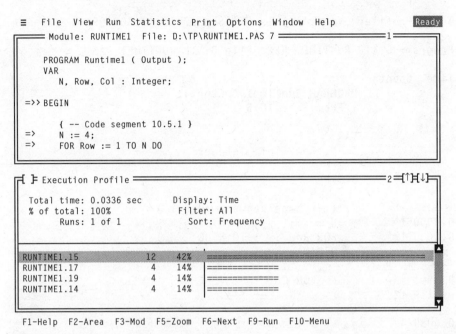

FIGURE 3. *Displaying execution counts—the number of times each statement was executed—instead of execution times.*

number of times each statement was executed during the run, and the percentage of total statement executions that corresponded to each statement. Or you can select **Both** from the display submenu, and see both times and counts. Try it.

Printing the results

The Turbo Profiler provides two kinds of printed reports. A Module report shows your source code, with the running time of each statement marked beside the line of code. To get this kind of report, select the **Options** in the **Print** menu, then in the submenu, choose whether you want output to go to the printer or to a file. (If you choose a file, you will have to name the file.) Then select **Module** from the **Print** menu, and your report will be printed. Here's a sample of a Module report for RUNTIME1.PAS:

```
Turbo Profiler  Version 1.1  Fri Sep 27 15:40:50 1991

Program: D:\TP\RUNTIME1.EXE  File D:\TP\RUNTIME1.PAS

Time   Counts
                PROGRAM RunTime1 (Output);
                { From Sec. 10.5 }

                VAR
                  N, Row, Col: Integer;

0.0074 1        BEGIN

                { -- Code segment 10.5.1 }
0.0000 1        N := 4;
0.0000 1        FOR Row := 1 TO N DO
                BEGIN

0.0001 4          FOR Col := 1 TO ( N - 1 ) DO
0.0115 12           Write('*');

0.0039 4          WriteLn

0.0001 4        END

0.0098 1        END.
```

There are some interesting results here. Notice that the FOR statement, the WriteLn, and the END statement were each executed four times, but the WriteLn consumed enormously more time than the other two. This is because output is a lot slower than computation in the CPU. Notice too that the program's BEGIN statement consumed 0.0074 seconds all by itself. That's because the program first allocates storage for variables and for the output buffer. Then notice that the Write statement was executed $N(N-1) = 12$ times, or three times as often as the WriteLn. However, it consumed more than three times as muchtime as the WriteLn, showing that printing an asterisk is a little slower than going to a new line. (On this system, at least.)

Another perspective can be gained by selecting **Statistics** from the **Print** menu. When this is done, we get the following report:

```
Turbo Profiler  Version 1.1  Fri Sep 27 15:41:15 1991

Program: D:\TP\RUNTIME1.EXE

Execution Profile
Total time: 0.0332 sec
% of total: 100%
       Run: 1 of 1

    Filter: All
      Show: Time
      Sort: Frequency

RUNTIME1.15      0.0115 sec   34%  |******************************************
RUNTIME1.21      0.0098 sec   29%  |*************************************
RUNTIME1.7       0.0074 sec   22%  |****************************
RUNTIME1.17      0.0039 sec   11%  |**************
RUNTIME1.19      0.0001 sec   <1%  |
RUNTIME1.14      0.0001 sec   <1%  |
RUNTIME1.10      0.0000 sec   <1%  |
RUNTIME1.11      0.0000 sec   <1%  |
```

This, of course, is the same information that appeared in the Execution Profile window.

Now you do it!

Run the profiler on your own copy of RUNTIME1. You won't get the same results exactly because your machine isn't the same as mine. But you should get similar results.

> Run the five RUNTIME programs under your profiler and report your observations and conclusions. What do you learn about the execution of the various statements and loops by using the profiler? Try changing a FOR loop into the corresponding counter-driven WHILE loop; are the running times the same? Turn in a lab report together with both Module and Statistics printouts from the profiler.

Note: This has been a brief introduction to only a few of the Turbo Profiler's capabilities. For further information, see the *Turbo Profiler User's Guide* that comes with the software.

Lab 11.1
Animating Recursion

Concepts: Recursion.

Lab techniques: Using intermediate output to clarify the sequence of execution and evaluation.

Prerequisites: Chapter 11 of *Structures and Abstractions*.

In programming, it is always necessary to be able to picture what's happening in a program, but it's never more necessary than it is with recursion. With recursion, a beginner will get lost completely without good mental pictures. Chapter 11 of the textbook provides examples of such pictures, but you should practice making your own. With only slight effort, you can even get your programs to draw their own pictures! That's our goal in this lab.

Rewriting the Strange procedure

Chapter 11 begins with a procedure that reverses input text. It's a good example of a very simple recursive procedure that would be much more difficult to write iteratively. In this lab, we will use a slightly revised version of the procedure, designed to avoid some problems with I/O buffering that might otherwise arise as we animate the program. The new code is found in the file called STRANGE0.PAS:. Here's the procedure:

```
PROCEDURE Strange;
VAR
   Ch : Char;

BEGIN

   IF NOT EOF THEN
   BEGIN

      ReadLn( Ch );
      Strange;
      WriteLn( Ch )

   END

END; { Strange }
```

This version of the procedure, unlike the one in the textbook, requires the user to press Return or Enter after every character entered. A typical run might look like this. First the user enters characters, one per line. An end-of-file signal is used to signal the end of the inputs to the program:

```
a
b
c
<EOF>
```

Immediately after pressing <EOF> and then Return, more output appears in a gush:

```
c
b
a
```

The end-of-file signal keyed by the user will, of course, depend on the Pascal system being used. In Turbo Pascal running under MS-DOS, <EOF> is Control-Z; on a Macintosh in THINK Pascal, it is Control-C with some keyboards, and Enter with others; in the Unix operating system, it is Control-D.

The final gush of output gives the impression that the program does almost nothing until seeing the end-of-file signal, but in fact, this is not the case. The best way to see what's going on is to have the program show us. In fact, this is an important laboratory technique in general:

> When in doubt, print it out!
> That is, whenever you aren't sure what's going on, add enough intermediate output statements to your program that you can SEE what's going on.

Suppose, for example, we add WriteLns to show every call to Strange and every return from Strange. With the simplest choice of printouts, our program would look as shown on the next page and contained in the file STRANGE1.PAS. You should run this program with the same data we used before.

```
PROGRAM Surprise ( Input, Output );


PROCEDURE Strange;
VAR
   Ch : Char;

BEGIN

   IF NOT EOF THEN
   BEGIN

      ReadLn( Ch );

      WriteLn( 'Strange calls Strange...' );
      Strange;
      WriteLn( 'Returned to Strange.' );

      WriteLn( Ch )

   END

END; { Strange }


BEGIN { main program }

   WriteLn('Main program calls Strange...');

   Strange;

   WriteLn('Execution returned to main program;');
   WriteLn('program ends.');

END.
```

Now the same inputs produce the I/O shown on the next page:

```
Main program calls Strange...
a
Strange calls Strange...
b
Strange calls Strange...
c
Strange calls Strange...
<EOF>
Returned to Strange.
c
Returned to Strange.
b
Returned to Strange.
a
Execution returned to main program;
program ends.
```

The new output indicates correctly that a new call is made to Strange for every character that is read, and that, after <EOF> is signalled by the user, execution returns up the chain of recursion level by level, printing one stored character at each level. The visual quality of the output is not very good however. It would be better if we could get the program to suggest the depth of recursion at each stage.

Stepwise refinement

Suppose we redesign the output to look more like the diagrams in the book, with deeper recursion moving toward the right, and the final return up the chain moving back toward the left. We can also separate inputs from outputs, showing the inputs on the left of the screen and outputs on the right. Can we get the output to look as shown on the next page?

```
INPUT              ACTION                            OUTPUT
----------------------------------------------------------
         Main program calls Strange...
a
             Strange calls Strange...
b
                 Strange calls Strange...
c
                     Strange calls Strange...
<EOF>
                 Returned to Strange.
                                                      c
             Returned to Strange.
                                                      b
         Returned to Strange.
                                                      a
         Execution returned to main program;
         program ends.
```

The problem here is to get each copy of Strange to indent its output by an amount proportional to the depth of recursion. To help us, Pascal provides a useful trick. A Write or WriteLn can print out a single space character, formatted to be in a field of any computed width. For example,

```
Width := 8;
WriteLn( ' ':Width, 'Strange calls Strange...' );
```

prints

```
        Strange calls Strange...
```

while

```
Width := 11;
WriteLn( ' ':Width, 'Strange calls Strange...' );
```

indents three spaces more:

```
           Strange calls Strange...
```

This trick will solve our problem if we can get each copy of Strange to know how deep it is in the recursive chain. To do that, all we need is to send a count to Strange each time it is called, telling it how deep it is. That is, the main program could call Strange(1), sending 1 to Strange. Then that Strange could call Strange(2), which in turn could call Strange(3), and so on. Within a given Strange, the printout could indent 3 * Count spaces in addition to the initial indentation, which is eight spaces in the output shown above. A sample WriteLn would then read

```
WriteLn( ' ':( 3 * Count + 8 );
        'Strange calls Strange...' );
```

where Count is the formal parameter of the current copy of Strange.

Another refinement

As a matter of fact, if each copy of Strange has its own value of Count, showing the depth of recursion, it would be a good idea to display these numbers. Let's make the I/O look like this:

```
INPUT           ACTION                              OUTPUT
------------------------------------------------------------
        Main program calls Strange(1)...
a
        Strange(1) calls Strange(2)...
b
            Strange(2) calls Strange(3)...
c
                Strange(3) calls Strange(4)...
<EOF>
        Returned to Strange(3).
                                                    c
        Returned to Strange(2).
                                                    b
        Returned to Strange(1).
                                                    a
    Execution returned to main program;
    program ends.
```

This version of the I/O design makes it clearer who calls whom and who returns to whom during execution. Now the level of recursion shows at each stage during the run.

Now you finish it

Your job now is to modify STRANGE1.PAS along the suggested lines, making the I/O look as shown above. When you finish, you will have a program that animates its own recursion!

> Turn in a source code listing of your completed program together with printouts of sample runs. Be sure to test your program for correct operation even when <EOF> is the first input.

Lab Project 11.2
How Many Ways to Make Change?

Concepts: Modularity, hierarchy, iteration.

Lab techniques: Top-down design; incremental testing; stepwise refinement.

Prerequisites: Chapter 9 of *Structures and Abstractions*.

Recently, I was paying for a purchase at a gas station when things went haywire. The clerk rang up the sale on the cash register, entered the amount I had paid him, and then tried to give me more change than the amount I had originally given him. I explained that the change could not be more than the amount paid, which confused him a little. He kept looking back and forth, between me and the result displayed on the cash register. Then he rang up the whole thing again, and got a different result, which was still more than the amount I gave him. Again he tried to pay me; again I corrected him. He agreed that I was right, but he couldn't believe that his cash register was mistaken! So he entered the whole calculation a third time and got a third result, even worse than the first two. (Do you believe that $20.00 – $11.67 = $33,197.98?) We finally had to settle the business on paper—he couldn't do the calculation by hand, so I had to do it.

I found this whole experience thought-provoking. It was a good example of our increasing dependence on machines and our increasing helplessness when the machines fail. It was also a good example of how dependence on automatic machines tempts people to stop thinking for themselves.

It also got me thinking about how even a well-behaved cash register doesn't do everything for the salesperson. A human still has to figure out what bills and coins to use in making change. This isn't a trivial task because there are usually many different ways to give the same amount of change.

In this way, I arrive at the problem for today's lab: How many distinct ways are there to give a certain amount of change, using only quarters, dimes, nickels, and pennies? This is an example of what mathematicians call a **combinatoric** problem—a problem in which we must count the ways to do something. The present problem was popularized by George Polya, the author of *How to Solve It*, in a famous paper. (See references at the end of the lab.)

First imagine how the I/O should look

To define the problem a little more precisely, it helps to state what the I/O should look like in a typical calculation:

```
NUMBER OF WAYS TO MAKE CHANGE
-----------------------------

How much change (dollars and cents)? 0.12
There are 4 ways to make change.
```

There are, in fact, four ways to make twelve cents in change:

> **1.** A dime and two pennies.
>
> **2.** Two nickels and two pennies.
>
> **3.** One nickel and seven pennies.
>
> **4.** Twelve pennies.

(These four choices of coins make no distinctions between the *orderings* of coins, so they are **combinations** rather than **permutations**.)

The four choices are listed above in decreasing order of the largest coin. We can use at most one dime, because only one dime will "fit" into twelve cents. After using a dime or not, whatever change remains must be paid out as nickels and pennies. Whatever change remains after the nickels' contribution must be distributed as pennies.

Larger amounts of change can be doled out in surprisingly many ways:

```
NUMBER OF WAYS TO MAKE CHANGE
-----------------------------

How much change (dollars and cents)? 0.50
There are 49 ways to make change.
```

Next write a skeleton with stubs

After imagining the I/O, we write a skeleton for the program. At this point, we do not worry about how we will accomplish the calculation; instead, we act on faith that designing the skeleton will make the solution of the problem a little clearer. All we are concerned with at this point is that there are four main tasks to be accomplished:

1. Show the purpose of the program.

2. Get the user to tell the program how much change is needed.

3. Compute the number of distinct ways to make change.

4. Display the results.

Thus we can use a skeleton like the following. Steps 1, 2, and 4 are simple enough that we can implement them immediately.

```
PROGRAM MakingChange ( Input, Output );
{
   Counts the number of ways to make a given amount
   of change using quarters, dimes, nickels, and pennies.
}

VAR
    TotalCents : Integer;


PROCEDURE ShowPurpose;
BEGIN

    WriteLn( 'NUMBER OF WAYS TO MAKE CHANGE' );
    WriteLn( '-----------------------------' );
    WriteLn

END; { ShowPurpose }


PROCEDURE GetAmount( VAR TotalCents : Integer );
VAR
    DollarsAndCents : Real;

BEGIN

    REPEAT
       Write( 'How much change (dollars and cents)? ' );
       ReadLn( DollarsAndCents )
    UNTIL DollarsAndCents > 0.0;

    TotalCents := Round( 100.0 * DollarsAndCents )

END; { GetAmount }
```

```
FUNCTION NumWaysToGiveChange( Amount : Integer )
                             : Integer;
BEGIN

   {--This is just a stub right now }
   NumWaysToGiveChange := 0

END; { NumWaysToGiveChange }


BEGIN { main program }

   ShowPurpose;
   GetAmount( TotalCents );

   WriteLn;
   WriteLn( 'There are ',
           NumWaysToGiveChange( TotalCents ),
           ' ways to make change.' );
   WriteLn

END.
```

This leaves only the `NumWaysToGiveChange` function to be implemented. Before working on that function, compile and run the skeleton (which is called `CHANGE.PAS` on the accompanying floppy disks) to make sure everything is correct so far.

How do I make change? Let me count the ways...

Now we get to the heart of the problem—counting the number of distinct ways to make a given amount of change. Let

Q_C = The number of ways to pay out C cents, using coins of all denominations up through quarters.

D_C = The number of ways to pay out C cents, using coins of all denominations up through dimes.

N_C = The number of ways to pay out C cents, using coins of all denominations up through nickels.

P_C = The number of ways to pay out C cents, using only pennies.

However, there is only one way to pay out C cents in pennies, so $P_C = 1$ for all $C \geq 0$.

Now consider the number of ways to pay out C cents using pennies, nickels, dimes, and quarters. These ways of making change can be divided into two classes: ways that do not use quarters, and those that use at least one quarter. In other words,

Q_C = (The number of ways to pay out C cents,
        using only dimes, nickels, and pennies)

    + (The number of ways to pay out C cents, using
        dimes, nickels, and pennies, and at least one
        quarter)

But the first term is just D_C, and the second term is the same as the number of ways to pay out $C - 25$ cents, using quarters, dimes, nickels, and pennies. (Think about it.) Therefore,

$$Q_C = D_C + Q_{C-25} \qquad (1)$$

Similarly,

$$D_C = N_C + D_{C-10} \qquad (2)$$

and

$$N_C = P_C + N_{C-5} = 1 + N_{C-5} \qquad (3)$$

These are *recurrence relations* (see Section 11.2 of the text), in which the number of ways of making C cents in change is expressed in terms of the numbers of ways to make lesser amounts of change. In solving these equations, we work our way downward from C through terms that involve $C - 25$, $C - 10$, and so on. Eventually the subscripts reach zero or go negative. When the subscript reaches zero, we make use of the fact that there is only one way to pay out zero cents:

$$Q_0 = D_0 = N_0 = 1 \qquad (4)$$

Furthermore, there is *no* way to pay out a negative amount of money:

$$Q_C = D_C = N_C = 0 \text{ when } C < 0. \qquad (5)$$

With these conventions, we can solve the equations in specific cases. Consider the number of ways to pay out 12 cents, using coins up to quarters. According to equation (1),

$$Q_{12} = D_{12} + Q_{-13} = D_{12}$$

But according to equation (2),

$$D_{12} = N_{12} + D_2 = N_{12} + (N_2 + D_{-8}) = N_{12} + N_2$$

Applying equation (3), we end up with

$$Q_{12} = D_{12} = N_{12} + N_2 = (1 + N_7) + (1 + N_{-3})$$
$$= (1 + 1 + N_2) + (1)$$
$$= (1 + 1 + 1) + (1)$$
$$= 4$$

This result is correct because the following are the only distinct ways to make 12 cents in change:

1.   One dime and two pennies.

2.   Two nickels and two pennies.

3.   One nickel and seven pennies.

4.   Twelve pennies.

Expressing the recurrence relations in Pascal

The recurrence relations express how the original calculation of Q_C can be broken down into simpler and simpler calculations until we reach trivial cases. The trivial, nonrecursive cases are expressed by the equations

$$Q_C = D_C = N_C = P_C = \begin{cases} 0 \text{ when } C < 0 \\ \\ 1 \text{ when } C = 0 \end{cases}$$

A single stage of the recursive calculation of Q_C can therefore be pictured as shown below:

$$Q_C = D_C + Q_{C-25}$$

If $C - 25 < 0$, then $Q_{C-25} = 0$;
otherwise, if $C = 25$, then $Q_{C-25} = 1$;
otherwise, $Q_{C-25} = D_{C-25} + Q_{C-50}$

If $C < 0$, then $D_C = 0$;
otherwise, if $C = 0$, then $D_C = 1$;
otherwise, $D_C = N_C + D_{C-10}$

The obvious way to implement this in Pascal is to express each recurrence relation as a distinct function:

```
FUNCTION P( Cents : Integer ) : Integer;
{
  PRECONDITIONS:
  Cents has been initialized.

  POSTCONDITION:
  Returns the number of ways to pay out the given
  number of cents, using only pennies.
}
BEGIN

   IF Cents < 0 THEN
      P := 0

   ELSE
      P := 1

END; { P }



FUNCTION N( Cents : Integer ) : Integer;
{
  PRECONDITIONS:
  Cents has been initialized.

  POSTCONDITION:
  Returns the number of ways to pay out the given
  number of cents, using only nickels and pennies.
}
BEGIN

   IF Cents < 0 THEN
      N := 0

   ELSE IF Cents = 0 THEN
      N := 1

   ELSE
      N := P( Cents ) + N( Cents - 5 )

END; { N }
```

```
FUNCTION D( Cents : Integer ) : Integer;
{
  PRECONDITIONS:
  Cents has been initialized.

  POSTCONDITION:
  Returns the number of ways to pay out the given
  number of cents, using dimes, nickels, and pennies.
}
BEGIN

   IF Cents < 0 THEN
      D := 0

   ELSE IF Cents = 0 THEN
      D := 1

   ELSE
      D := N( Cents ) + D( Cents - 10 )

END; { D }


FUNCTION Q( Cents : Integer ) : Integer;
{
  PRECONDITIONS:
  Cents has been initialized.

  POSTCONDITION:
  Returns the number of ways to pay out the given
  number of cents, using quarters, dimes, nickels,
  and pennies.
}
BEGIN

   IF Cents < 0 THEN
      Q := 0

   ELSE IF Cents = 0 THEN
      Q := 1

   ELSE
      Q := D( Cents ) + Q( Cents - 25 )

END; { Q }
```

But we immediately notice the great similarities among these functions. In fact, they are all versions of the same general function.

Your job in this lab session is to write a single recursive function that embodies the four particular functions shown above. **Hint:** Add a parameter representing the value in cents of the maximum coin being used to make change. Adapt the CHANGE.PAS driver and use it to test your function. **Hint:** First test the four individual functions as shown above, adding output statements so that you can see the order of recursive calls during test runs. (This is the same method we used in Lab 11.1.) Once you have everything working correctly and you have familiarized yourself with the program's recursive operation, convert the four functions to a single, generalized function and test again.

> Turn in your source-code listing and printouts of testing runs. Show that your program correctly predicts the number of ways to pay out 0 cents, 1 cent, 12 cents, 50 cents, and 99 cents.

References

George Polya. "On Picture-Writing." *American Mathematical Monthly* **63**, 689–697 (1956).

Ronald L. Graham, Donald E. Knuth, and Oren Patashnik. *Concrete Mathematics.* (Addison-Wesley, 1989). Pages 313–316; 330–332.

Harold Abelson and Gerald Jay Sussman, with Julie Sussman. *Structure and Interpretation of Computer Programs* (MIT Press/ McGraw-Hill, 1985). Pages 37–39.

Lab 12.1
Experimenting with Subranges and Enumerations

Concepts: Subrange and enumerated types.

Lab techniques: Using the computer to experiment.

Prerequisites: Chapter 12 of *Structures and Abstractions*.

Pascal differs from older languages in providing several ways for programmers to define their own data types. In Chapter 12, we encounter the first of these: subrange and enumerated types. Like the real and ordinal types we studied earlier, subrange and enumerated types are *simple types*, in which only one value can be stored at a time.

A subrange type is defined as a subrange of the values allowed for a previously-defined ordinal type. (See Section 12.1 of the text.) Thus, we can have subranges of integers, of characters, or of booleans, though the latter is virtually useless. One of the most common subranges of integer values is a type for storing nonnegative integers, which we might choose to call NonNegInt:

```
TYPE
    NonNegInt = 0..MaxInt;
```

Then we can define a variable of the new type:

```
VAR
    NatNum : NonNegInt;
```

This declaration means that NatNum can store only the integer values in the range from 0 through MaxInt, inclusive.

Enumerated types are defined by listing all the values that can be stored, in order from the one with lowest ordinal value to the one with the highest ordinal value. (The lowest ordinal value is always 0.) For example, we can declare a new type for storing the colors of traffic lights:

```
TYPE
    TrafficLightColors = ( Red, Yellow, Green );
```

A variable of this type can then be declared:

```
VAR
    Color : TrafficLightColors;
```

With this definition, Color can be assigned only the values Red,

Yellow, or Blue. Note that Red, Yellow, and Blue are identifiers and not strings: they are names corresponding to the ordinal values 0, 1, and 2, respectively. This is analogous to the way that Pascal's boolean values are named False and True, corresponding to the ordinal values 0 and 1. In fact, the Boolean type can be considered to be a two-valued built-in enumerated type. (The built-in Boolean type, of course, has special properties not shared by programmer-defined enumerated types. For example, boolean expressions are used to determine the paths through decision and looping structures.)

Experimenting with a subrange type

The textbook's first application of a subrange type is in a program that reads a one-byte nonnegative number in decimal notation, then displays it in binary. Here is the program as it appears in Section 12.2 of the text. (It is also provided on disk as DECTOBIN2.PAS.)

```
PROGRAM DecToBin ( Input, Output );
{
  Version 2, using subrange variable.
}

TYPE
    OneByteInteger = 0..255;

VAR
    Number : OneByteInteger;


PROCEDURE ShowPurpose;
BEGIN

    WriteLn( 'CONVERTING 1-BYTE DEC INTEGER TO BINARY' );
    WriteLn

END; { ShowPurpose }
```

```
PROCEDURE ShowOneBitAndGetNext(
                            PowerOfTwo : OneByteInteger;
                            VAR Rem    : OneByteInteger );
{
  PRECONDITIONS:
  0 < PowerOfTwo <= 255;

  POSTCONDITIONS:
  Bit corresponding to PowerOfTwo has been displayed.
  Rem is now the remainder of division by PowerOfTwo.
}
BEGIN

   Write( ( Rem DIV PowerOfTwo ):1 );
   Rem := Rem MOD PowerOfTwo

END; { ShowOneBitAndGetNext }


PROCEDURE ShowBinaryOf( Number : OneByteInteger );
{
  PRECONDITIONS:
  Number is in the range [ 0 .. 255 ];

  POSTCONDITIONS:
  The one-byte binary representation of Number
  has been displayed. Number is unchanged.
}
VAR
   Power, Remainder : OneByteInteger;

BEGIN

   WriteLn;
   Write( Number:3, ' is the same as ' );
   Remainder := Number;
   Power := 128;

   WHILE Power > 1 DO
   BEGIN

      ShowOneBitAndGetNext( Power, Remainder );
      Power := Power DIV 2

   END;

   WriteLn( Remainder:1, ' binary.' )

END; { ShowBinaryOf }
```

```
PROCEDURE GetOneByteInteger( VAR Number: OneByteInteger );
{
  POSTCONDITION:
  0 <= Number <= 255.
}
VAR
   Int : Integer;

BEGIN

   REPEAT

      Write( 'Integer between 0 and 255? ' );
      ReadLn( Int )

   UNTIL ( Int >= 0 ) AND ( Int <= 255 );

   {
     Now that the value of the integer is known to be
     in the one-byte subrange, it can be copied
     into the Number variable.
   }
   Number := Int

END; { GetOneByteInteger }


BEGIN { main program }

   ShowPurpose;
   GetOneByteInteger( Number );
   ShowBinaryOf( Number )

END.
```

We concentrate here on the GetOneByteInteger procedure above. The procedure reads an integer from the keyboard, stores it in an *integer* variable, and checks the value to make sure it is in the subrange 0..255. The value is copied into the Number variable, of type OneByteInteger, only if the value is in that subrange.

You should experiment with this program by altering the procedure so that no check is performed before storing the value in the Number variable. Remove the REPEAT..UNTIL loop, the final assignment statement, and the declaration of Number. In other words, change the procedure to look as shown on the next page.

```
PROCEDURE GetOneByteInteger(VAR Number : OneByteInteger);
{
  POSTCONDITION:
  0 <= Number <= 255.
}
BEGIN

    Write('Integer between 0 and 255? ');
    ReadLn(Number)

END; { GetOneByteInteger }
```

Now compile the program *with range checking turned on* and run it several times, trying to enter the following numbers at the prompt:

-1

0

3

255

256

(*Be sure range checking is turned on when you compile the program!*)

Report what happens in the space below:

_____

_____

_____

_____

_____

_____

_____

_____

_____

Next, recompile the program with range checking turned *off* and report what happens in the five cases:

_____

_____

_____

_____

_____

_____

_____

_____

Now, in your own words, explain the value of the subrange variable in ensuring the validity of the procedure's original postcondition. Does a subrange variable have this value when range checking is turned off?

_____

_____

_____

_____

_____

_____

_____

_____

_____

_____

Experimenting with an enumerated type

An enumerated type is allowed to store only the named values that are listed in the type declaration. Consider, for example, a program that processes U.S. income tax forms, on which the taxpayer lists a Filing Status chosen from the following list:

- Single.

- Married, filing joint return.

- Married, filing separate return.

- Head of household (with qualifying person).

- Qualifying widow(er) with dependent child.

(Let's not go into the details of these categories—this is the way they are listed on a U.S. I.R.S. Form 1040.)

The program might, then, have an enumerated type:

```
TYPE
    Status = ( Single, MarriedJoint, MarriedSeparate,
             HeadOfHousehold, Widowed );
```

Just to give the flavor of the code, we consider the part of the program that accepts filing status data from the keyboard, and the part that asks for further data in selected cases. This will be enough to answer several common questions about the use of enumerations, and enough to test on the computer.

```
PROGRAM IRS ( Input, Output );

TYPE
   NonNegInt = 0..MaxInt;
   Status = ( Single, MarriedJoint, MarriedSeparate,
              HeadOfHousehold, Widowed );

VAR
   FilingStatus  : Status;
   NumDependents : NonNegInt;


PROCEDURE GetStatus( VAR FilingStatus : Status );
VAR
   Answer : Char;

BEGIN

   REPEAT

      WriteLn( 'ENTER FILING STATUS:' );
      WriteLn( 'S for Single;' );
      WriteLn( 'J for married, filing Jointly;' );
      WriteLn( 'M for Married, filing separately;' );
      WriteLn( 'H for Head of Household;' );
      WriteLn( 'W for Widow/Widower.' );
      WriteLn;
      Write( 'Your status? ' );
      ReadLn( Answer );
      WriteLn

   UNTIL ( Answer = 'S' ) OR ( Answer = 'J' )
      OR ( Answer = 'M' ) OR ( Answer = 'H' )
      OR ( Answer = 'W' );

   CASE Answer OF

      'S' :  FilingStatus := Single;
      'J' :  FilingStatus := MarriedJoint;
      'M' :  FilingStatus := MarriedSeparate;
      'H' :  FilingStatus := HeadOfHousehold;
      'W' :  FilingStatus := Widowed

   END

END; { GetStatus }
```

```
PROCEDURE GetNumDependents(
                          FStatus           : Status;
                          VAR NumDependents : NonNegInt );
BEGIN

   IF FStatus = HeadOfHousehold THEN
   BEGIN

      Write( 'Number of dependents: ' );
      ReadLn( NumDependents )

   END;

   {--and so on }

END; { GetNumDependents }


BEGIN { main program }

   GetStatus( FilingStatus );
   GetNumDependents( FilingStatus, NumDependents );

   {--and so on }

END.
```

You might wonder why the `GetStatus` procedure reads a letter indicating filing status, then stores an enumeration constant corresponding to the letter. Why not just store a letter in a character variable and avoid the enumeration code altogether? The reason is that *we want the program to read as clearly as possible*. Do we want procedures like `GetNumDependents` to contain code like the following?

```
IF FStatus = 'H' THEN
```

Or would it be clearer to have code like this?

```
IF FStatus = HeadOfHoushold THEN
```

Surely, the latter is clearer, and therefore, better.

Questions

To answer the following questions, it may help to make the corresponding changes in the program, then compile and run it.

What is the ordinal value of `HeadOfHousehold`?

_____

Give two reasons why the following statement would be illegal in the program:

    HeadOfHousehold := True;

Reason #1: _____

Reason #2: _____

Explain briefly why `GetStatus` did not read a value for `FilingStatus` directly from the keyboard:

_____

_____

What would happen if `FilingStatus` were assigned the string of characters `'MarriedJoint'`?

_____

_____

When range checking is turned *off*, what is the value of

    Pred(Single)?   _____

    Succ(Widowed)?   _____

When range checking is turned *on*, what happens when you try to evaluate

    Pred(Single)?   _____

    Succ(Widowed)?   _____

Completing the program

Your assignment for the remainder of this lab is to complete the IRS program so that it accomplishes the following tasks in addition to those already shown:

- If the taxpayer files for Single status, the number of dependents should be set to zero. (Single taxpayers with dependents should file as heads of households.)

- If the taxpayer files as Married, whether filing jointly with or separately from his/her spouse, or if the taxpayer is filing as Widowed, the program should prompt for the number of dependents.

- A CASE structure should be used to make all these decisions, in place of the IF..THEN structure shown previously.

- The main program should afterwards call a procedure that displays the taxpayer's filing status and number of dependents.

- The GetStatus procedure should accept lowercase letters as well as the corresponding uppercase letters: that is, 'h' should be interpreted the same as 'H', and so on.

> Complete the program as described, then turn in the source-code listing together with printouts of runs showing correct operation with all five possible values of FilingStatus. Also turn in the pages from this lab on which you have written answers to questions.

Lab 13.1
Experimenting with Arrays

Concepts: Array, array element, range error, subrange type.

Lab techniques: Direct experimentation.

Prerequisites: Chapter 13 of *Structures and Abstractions*.

An array is a list of homogeneous storage cells, called the *elements* of the array. The elements all share the name of the array, but are distinguished from one another by subscripts. For example, suppose we declare

```
CONST
    Low  = 1;
    High = 3;

TYPE
    IndexRange = Low..High;
    RealArray  = ARRAY [ IndexRange ] OF Real;

VAR
    A : RealArray;
```

Here we have declared an array named A, which is of type RealArray. The array is a composite of the elements A[1], A[2], and A[3], each of which is of type Real. A itself is called an array variable, but it is different from the variables we used in earlier chapters because it is actually a list of simpler variables. The array is our first example of a composite type—a type of storage composed of simpler types of storage. In this lab, we investigate by experiment some of the subtleties of using arrays.

Arrays and array elements as parameters

An array is often used when we have a list of data of the same type and we want to perform some operation on all the elements of the list. Suppose, for example, we want to find the largest real number in a list. If our only concern is to deal with three elements as declared above, we could use code like that written by Jackson P. Slipshod, in the program ARRAY0.PAS:

```
PROGRAM Array0 ( Output );
{ Another awful program by Jackson P. Slipshod. }

CONST
    Low  = 1;
    High = 3;

TYPE
    IndexRange = Low..High;
    RealArray  = ARRAY [ IndexRange ] OF Real;

VAR
    A : RealArray;


FUNCTION MaxOfThree( X, Y, Z : Real ) : Real;
BEGIN

    IF X > Y THEN
    { Max is either X or Z }
        IF X > Z THEN
            MaxOfThree := X
        ELSE
            MaxOfThree := Z

    ELSE IF Y > X THEN
    { Max is either Y or Z }
        IF Y > Z THEN
            MaxOfThree := Y
        ELSE
            MaxOfThree := Z

    ELSE
    { X = Y }
        IF Z > X THEN
            MaxOfThree := Z
        ELSE
            MaxOfThree := X

END; { MaxOfThree }


BEGIN { main program }

    A[ 1 ] := 1.1;
    A[ 2 ] := 2.2;
    A[ 3 ] := 1.5;
```

```
        WriteLn( 'Largest value is ',
                 MaxOfThree( A[ 1 ], A[ 2 ], A[ 3 ] ) )

END.
```

This program was written by Jackson P. Slipshod, so you shouldn't surprised that it isn't well designed. The input of the array element values is hardwired into assignment statements and the `MaxOfThree` function will only work if we send it three real numbers. If we change value of `Low` or `High`, or if we change the type of data stored in the elements, we will have to rewrite the whole program. We can write a program much more versatile than this, but before we do, run Jackson's program and note how the main program's function call correlates with the `MaxOfThree` function header. The element `A[ 1 ]` is associated with the formal parameter `X`, `A[ 2 ]` is associated with `Y`, and `A[ 3 ]` is associated with `Z`. Note that the array elements (the actual parameters) and the formal parameters all have type `Real`:

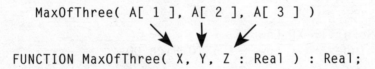

```
        MaxOfThree( A[ 1 ], A[ 2 ], A[ 3 ] )


    FUNCTION MaxOfThree( X, Y, Z : Real ) : Real;
```

To better use the power of the array, we can rewrite Jackson's program so that it sends the entire array to `MaxOfThree` in one swoop and then processes all the elements of the array in a loop that sweeps through the subscripts:

```
PROGRAM Array1 ( Output );
{ An improved version of Jackson's Array0 program. }

CONST
    Low  = 1;
    High = 3;

TYPE
    IndexRange = Low..High;
    RealArray  = ARRAY [ IndexRange ] OF Real;

VAR
    A : RealArray;
```

```
PROCEDURE FillArray( VAR A : RealArray );
VAR
    Index : IndexRange;

BEGIN

    WriteLn( 'Enter the array element values:' );
    FOR Index := Low TO High DO
    BEGIN
        Write( 'Element ', Index:2, ' = ' );
        ReadLn( A[ Index ] )
    END

END; { FillArray }


FUNCTION Maximum( X : RealArray ) : Real;
VAR
    MaxSoFar : Real;
    Index    : IndexRange;

BEGIN

    MaxSoFar := X[ Low ];
    FOR Index := ( Low + 1 ) TO High DO

        IF X[ Index ] > MaxSoFar THEN
            MaxSoFar := A[ Index ];

    Maximum := MaxSoFar

END; { Maximum }


BEGIN { main program }

    FillArray( A );

    WriteLn( 'Largest value is ', Maximum( A ) )

END.
```

Note the correspondence between the actual and formal parameters in the procedure and function calls. In each case, both the actual and formal parameters are of type RealArray:

```
           Maximum( A )
              ↑       ↓
FUNCTION Maximum( X : RealArray ) : Real;
```

A question

What are the two reasons for making FillArray a procedure instead of a function?

1. _____

2. _____

An experiment

In the ARRAY1.PAS program, change the Maximum function's header to read

```
FUNCTION Maximum( X : ARRAY[ IndexRange ] OF Real )
        : Real;
```

What happens when you try to compile the altered program?

_____

Why does this happen?

_____

_____

Common errors

The most common errors with arrays are (1) failing to initialize all needed elements of the array and (2) allowing a subscript to go outside the range declared for the array. The latter is an example of a range error.

Experiencing a range error

Jackson P. Slipshod and his One True Love, Cora Meltdown, are having problems with the following program. Let's take a look at it:

```
PROGRAM Slipshod ( Output );

CONST
    Low  = 1;
    High = 3;

TYPE
    IndexRange = Low..High;
    IntArray   = ARRAY [ IndexRange ] OF Integer;

VAR
    Score : IntArray;


PROCEDURE FillItUp( VAR Score : IntArray );
VAR
    Index : IndexRange;

BEGIN

    WriteLn( 'INITIALIZING SCORE ARRAY' );
    WriteLn( '------------------------' );
    WriteLn;

    FOR Index := Low TO High DO
    BEGIN

        Write( 'Score #', Index:1, ': ' );
        ReadLn( Score[ Index ] )

    END

END; { FillItUp }
```

```
PROCEDURE ShowScores( Sc : IntArray );
VAR
    Index : IndexRange;

BEGIN

    WriteLn;
    WriteLn;
    WriteLn( 'SCORES' );
    WriteLn( '------' );
    WriteLn;

    Index := Low - 1;
    WHILE Index <= High DO
    BEGIN
        Index := Index + 1;
        WriteLn( 'Score #', Index:1, ' = ', Sc[ Index ]:3 )
    END

END; { ShowScores }


BEGIN { main program }

    FillItUp( Score );
    ShowScores( Score )

END.
```

When Jackson and Cora run the program, they get an error message. They have asked you to help them find and fix the error.

Make sure range checking is turned on. What error message appears when you run the program?

_____

Where does the error occur?

_____

What is the error? (Hint: Compare the value being assigned to the range declared for the variable.)

_____

Now replace the loop structure with the following code:

```
Index := Low;
WHILE Index <= High DO
BEGIN
    WriteLn( 'Score #', Index:1, ' = ', Sc[ Index ]:3 );
    Index := Index + 1
END
```

Run the program again with range checking turned on. Now what error message appears?

_____

_____

Where is the error?

_____

_____

Insert a breakpoint at the beginning of the structure in which the error message appears. Then single-step forward until the error occurs, while watching the values of Index and Score[Index] in the Watch/Observe window. What is the nature of the error?

_____

_____

_____

Next, replace the loop with the corresponding FOR structure and test again. Do you still see the error?

_____

_____

Explain this observation.

_____

_____

_____

_____

Turn in a source code listing of the repaired program together with a printout of a successful run.

A two-dimensional array

Jackson and Cora's program has a severe limitation, even when you've got it working correctly. Its array uses only a single subscript, so it stores the scores for only one student. The program would be a lot more useful if it could handle scores for an entire class of students.

To give the program this additional capability, you need to give the Score array a second subscript that represents a student number. For example, if the program is to handle up to five students, each of whom has up to three scores, you might change the declarations to this:

```
CONST
   Low          = 1;
   HighSc       = 3;
   HighStudent = 5;

TYPE
   ScRange = Low..HighSc;
   StRange = Low..HighStudent;
   Array2D = ARRAY [ StRange, ScRange ] OF Integer;

VAR
   Score : Array2D;
```

The array now has two subscripts, and is therefore said to be *two-dimensional*. It is imagined as a table of integers, with the first subscript labelling rows and the second subscript labelling columns. In particular, the element Score[R, C] contains score C for student R.

> Improve Jackson and Cora's program by making its array two-dimensional as described above. Modify the code to make use of this change. (Section 13.5 of the text may be helpful.) Turn in a source code listing of the improved program together with a printout of a successful run.

Lab 13.2
A One-Dimensional Cellular Automaton

Concepts: One-dimensional array, state, state transition, transition rules, cellular automaton.

Lab techniques: Top-down design, choosing a data structure to match a problem.

Prerequisites: Sections 13.1–13.3 of *Structures and Abstractions*.

A system that carries out a task without human intervention, under control of a set of laws or rules, whether natural laws or man-made rules, is called an *automaton*. This is a Greek word that goes back at least to the time of Homer (about 750 B.C.). In the *Iliad*, the sky itself is an automaton:

> Hera lashed her horses; and *moving of themselves* the gates of heaven thundered open, guarded by the Hours in charge of the great sky, and Olympos, empowered to open up the darkness or again to close it.
> (Book V, lines 748–751; italics are mine.)

The *Iliad* even provides a preview of man-made machines. Hephaistos, the blacksmith to the gods, built a squad of robot tea-carts to carry food automatically into the gods' dining hall on Olympos (the Greek spelling):

> [Thetis] found him, sweating, . . . working on twenty tripods, to stand along the walls of his mansion. He had bolted golden wheels to the legs of these so that *of their own motion*, they could roll into the hall of the gods, and return home again: a wonder to behold.
>
> (Book XVIII, lines 373–377; italics are mine.)

Today, we have generalized the meanings of the words "machine" and "automaton." These words now can refer to abstract as well as mechanical machines. For example, an automaton can be a computer program, working under the automatic control of its own instructions.

For our purposes, it will be sufficient to define an automaton as an entity that acts under control of a set of laws or rules and which, once started, can continue to act on its own, without intervention from outside.

Exercise

Indicate whether the following systems are automata according to our definition:

The solar system _____

A society _____

A robot _____

A system for playing blackjack _____

A computer system _____

A computer program _____

A buggy computer program _____

Cellular automata

In this lab session, we encounter *cellular automata.*, which were invented by John von Neumann in 1950, while studying the possibility of self-reproducing machines(!) A cellular automaton is an array of cells, each of which is an automaton in its own right. A single cell can exist in a finite number of *states*, moving between states according to predefined *transition rules*. (Recall that program states and state transitions were introduced in Section 5.5 of the textbook and used again in Section 12.4.)

In this lab session, we deal with cells that exist in either of two states: a cell is either living or dead. If a cell is living, we show it on the screen as an asterisk (*); if it is dead, we display a blank space. Our automaton is one-dimensional, a single row of cells. If we have 40 cells and all of them are alive, our automaton looks like this:

```
****************************************
```

If only every other cell is alive, the same automaton looks like this:

```
* * * * * * * * * * * * * * * * * * * *
```

The state-transition rules

We can make cellular automata simulate the reproductive behaviors of living organisms by designing reasonable state-transi-

I

FIGURE 1. *The neighborhood of cell I includes two cells on either side.*

tion rules for the cells. To begin with, however, we will use a rather arbitrary set of rules that will generate interesting patterns of cell life that are easily checked for correctness. Later, we can invent more realistic rules. Here are our simplistic rules for now:

1. We define the *neighborhood* of a given cell to be the given cell and the two cells on either side of it, five cells in all. (Figure 1.) If the given cell is at the end of the automaton, the neighborhood wraps around to the other end. Thus, the neighborhood of the first cell includes not only the next two cells, but the two cells at the end of the array also. This is shown in Figure 2.

2. If the neighborhood of cell *I* contains either one or three living cells, cell *I* will be alive in the next generation, whether or not it is alive in the current generation. Otherwise, cell *I* is dead in the next generation.

3. Rules 1 and 2 are applied to all cells at the same time, so that the birth or death of one cell does not affect the birth or death of any other cell in the same generation.

FIGURE 2. *If the cells are numbered from 0 to N–1, the neighborhood of cell 0 includes cells N–2 and N–1. If the cells are numbered from 1 to N, the neighborhood of cell 1 includes cells N–1 and N.*

An example of cell generation

Suppose we have a 40-cell automaton obeying these rules. If we start with a single living cell in the middle of the automaton, like this,

*

the second generation will have living cells everywhere within two cells of the original living cell:

*****

But then, the third generation will thin out and spread out:

* *   * *

The fourth generation will spread out even more:

**   * *   **

And little by little, a pattern will appear. (But we won't spoil the fun by revealing it now!)

Question

How will the fifth generation of the example automaton look? Show it below:

Designing the automaton's data structure

In order to build the automaton, we need to structure the data in a way that is appropriate to the problem. The automaton is a row of cells, so it seems natural to represent it by a one-dimensional array. Each cell in the array can have two states, alive and dead, so it is appropriate to represent each cell by a boolean variable. We thus arrive at the idea of using a one-dimensional array of booleans.

Questions

We could also represent a cell by an integer variable, storing 1 for a live cell and 0 for a dead cell. Would this be better or worse than using booleans? Why?

We could represent a cell by a character variable, storing `'*'` for a live cell and `' '` for a dead cell. Would this have any obvious disadvantages over using booleans? What if we packed the array? Would booleans then gain any advantage over characters on your computer system?

Choosing a subscript range

Suppose that there are `NumCells` cells in the array, where `NumCells` is a global constant. Then we could number the cells from `1..NumCells` or from `0..( NumCells - 1 )`, or many other ways. Does any particular choice make more sense than the others?

The key to choosing a subscript range lies in the definition of the neighborhood of a cell. Remember that we said that neighborhoods wrap around at the ends of the array, so that the five-cell neighborhood of the first cell includes the two cells at the end of the array. This means we are going to use `MOD` to compute neighboring cell subscripts. In particular, if the cells are numbered from 0 to `NumCells - 1`, the neighborhood of the cell with subscript I will include the five cells with subscripts

`( I - 2 ) MOD NumCells, ( I - 1 ) MOD NumCells,`

`I, ( I + 1 ) MOD NumCells, and ( I + 2 ) MOD NumCells`

Personally, I prefer this way of computing the neighborhood's subscripts, so I prefer to number the subscripts from 0 to `NumCells - 1`. However, it is possible to number the cells from 1 to `NumCells` if we change the way we compute the subscripts of neighboring cells.

Question

What expressions would we use to calculate the subscripts in a neighborhood if the cells were numbered from 1 to NumCells?

_____

_____

_____

_____

_____

Implementing the third rule

The third reproduction rule says that "the birth or death of one cell does not affect the birth or death of any other cell in the same generation." This means that if we move from left to right across the row of cells, applying the rules, the state of a given cell in the next generation is not affected by the newly-living cells that might have popped to the left of it as part of the that generation. The easiest way to implement this rule is keep two one-dimensional arrays, one representing the older generation and the other representing the next generation. Then we carry out a single generation of reproduction in easy stages:

REPEAT

Apply the reproduction rules to a cell of the older-generation array;

Set the corresponding cell of the next-generation array to "alive" or "dead," according to the result of step 1;

Move on to the next cell

UNTIL all cells have been considered;

Now that the next-generation array contains the next generation of cells, it becomes the current generation, so copy it into the older-generation array.

Building a program

The ideas described on the previous pages are incorporated into the skeleton of a cellular automaton program in the file CELLULAR.PAS. Here it is:

```pascal
PROGRAM CellularAutomaton ( Input, Output );
{ One-dimensional cellular automaton. }

CONST
    HighCell      = 79;
    NumGenerations = 80;

TYPE
    CellRange = 0..HighCell;
    CellArray = ARRAY[ CellRange ] OF Boolean;

VAR
    Cells : CellArray;
    Time  : Integer;


PROCEDURE Initialize( VAR Cells : CellArray );
VAR
    Index : CellRange;

BEGIN

    FOR Index := 0 TO HighCell DO
        Cells[Index] := False;

    Cells[ HighCell DIV 2 ] := True

END; { Initialize }
```

13.2–8   A One-Dimensional Cellular Automaton

```
PROCEDURE ShowCells( VAR Cells : CellArray );
VAR
    Index : CellRange;

BEGIN

    FOR Index := 0 TO HighCell DO
       IF Cells[ Index ] THEN
          Write( '*' )
       ELSE
          Write( ' ' );

    WriteLn

END; { ShowCells }


PROCEDURE Propagate( VAR Cells : CellArray );
VAR
    Index    : CellRange;
    NewCells : CellArray;

BEGIN

    FOR Index := 0 TO HighCell DO
    BEGIN

       {--Compute NewCells[ Index ] from information }
       {   in the Cells array }

    END;

    {--Next generation replaces the older generation }
    FOR Index := 0 TO HighCell DO
       Cells[ Index ] := NewCells[ Index ]

END; { Propagate }
```

```
BEGIN { main program }

    Initialize( Cells );

    WriteLn;
    WriteLn;
    ShowCells( Cells );

    FOR Time := 1 TO NumGenerations DO
    BEGIN
        Propagate( Cells );
        ShowCells( Cells )
    END

END.
```

Now you complete it . . .

Your job is to complete this program by filling in the code to apply the reproduction rules at the indicated location in the first loop of the Propagate procedure. If your Pascal system does not provide a true MOD function, you will need to supply one of your own. (A sample is provided on the accompanying floppy disk.) When completed, your program should produce the pattern shown on the next page.

> Turn in a source-code listing and a printout of a run, showing that your program works correctly.

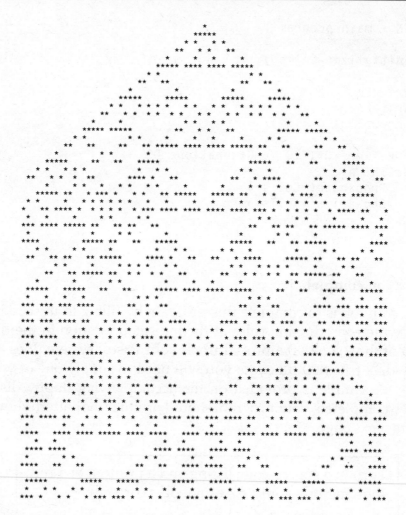

FIGURE 3. Output from the completed program, using the reproduction rules stated in the lab.

Question

With the reproduction rules as stated, do the living cells ever die out, or do they keep on reproducing forever? (Run your program and see.)

Reference: A related automaton is used in the Game of Life, invented by John H. Conway. (See Project 12, Ch. 13 of the text.)

Lab Project 14.1
Drawing High-Resolution Sierpinski Curves

Concepts: Abstract data type, compilation unit.

Lab techniques: Top-down design; using previously-compiled code.

Prerequisites: Chapter 14 of *Structures and Abstractions*. An MS-DOS machine equipped with VGA graphics or an Apple Macintosh, and the compiled high-resolution Turtle ADT file provided on the accompanying MS-DOS or Mac disk.

In mathematics, a *fractal* is a figure whose detailed structure looks the same at any level of magnification. The detail that you can see at one magnification contains still smaller detail of exactly the same structure; and that detail contains still smaller detail of exactly the same structure; and so on, forever. Fractals are useful in modeling certain shapes of nature, like shorelines on maps, pictures of rock formations, leaves, and so on.

In this lab, we will draw a fractal called a *Sierpinski curve*. (But we won't be able to achieve infinitely small detail because of limitations in the computer and in its display.) To understand a Sierpinski curve, it is probably best to look at its detail level-by-level. Consider the square shown in Figure 1. It can be considered the "zeroth" level of a certain Sierpinski curve. At this level, the

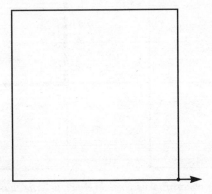

FIGURE 1. *The zeroth level of our Sierpinski curve. At this level, there is none of the recursive detail we will see at higher levels. To draw the zeroth level as shown, the turtle started at the position and heading indicated by the arrow.*

curve has no detail of the type we will introduce, and that's why we refer to it as a zeroth-level curve. Notice that the curve could be drawn as a pair of L-shaped pieces, using the following Turtle Graphics code:

```
PROCEDURE L( Length : NonNegInt );
BEGIN

   Left( 90 );
   MoveForward( Length );
   Left( 90 );
   MoveForward( Length )

END; { L }

PROCEDURE DrawSierpinski( Length : NonNegInt );
BEGIN

   L( Length );
   L( Length )

END; { DrawSierpinski }
```

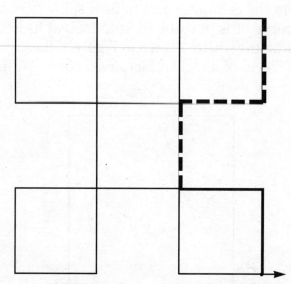

FIGURE 2. Level 1 of our Sierpinski curve. At this level, the characteristic filigree starts to appear. The turtle starts at the position and heading indicated by the arrow and first draws an L with sides half the length used at Level 0, as shown by the heavy solid lines. After the first L, however, the turtle draws a Z-shape as indicated by the heavy dashed line. The whole curve is drawn as four L, Z-combinations.

Level 1

Now let us embellish the curve by adding some filigree, as shown in Figure 2. At this level, the curve looks like a shrunken level-0 curve with a half-sized square added to each corner. The resulting figure is called Level 1. In fact, it is drawn as a half-sized L-shape, followed by a corresponding Z-shape, followed by an L, and so on, as shown in Figure 2. Altogether, there are four L, Z-pairs in the drawing. The code to draw this figure would be

```
PROCEDURE L0( Length : NonNegInt );
BEGIN

   Left( 90 );
   MoveForward( Length );
   Left( 90 );
   MoveForward( Length )

END; { L0 }

PROCEDURE Z0( Length : NonNegInt );
BEGIN

   Right( 90 );
   MoveForward( Length );
   Right( 90 );
   MoveForward( Length );
   Left( 90 );
   MoveForward( Length )

END; { Z0 }

PROCEDURE L1( Length : NonNegInt );
BEGIN

   L0( Length DIV 2 );
   Z0( Length DIV 2 );
   L0( Length DIV 2 );
   Z0( Length DIV 2 );

END; { L1 }
```

```
PROCEDURE DrawSierpinski( Length : NonNegInt );
BEGIN

    L1( Length );
    L1( Length )

END; { DrawSierpinski }
```

Trace through this code to become familiar with it. In the space provided below, describe the sequence of procedure calls and how the figure is drawn:

_____

_____

_____

_____

_____

_____

_____

_____

_____

_____

On to level 2

Level 2 provides even more detail in the drawing, as shown in Figure 3. You will notice that Level 2 is a one-fourth-sized square with a Level-1 drawing at each corner. (Hmmm... There's a pattern here.)

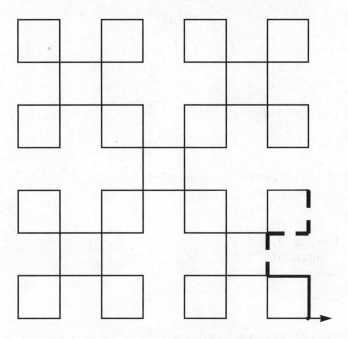

FIGURE 3. *Level 2 of our Sierpinski curve. The turtle starts at the position and heading indicated by the arrow and first draws an L with sides half the length used at Level 1, as shown by the heavy solid lines. After the first L, the turtle draws a Z-shape as indicated by the heavy dashed line. The whole curve is drawn as 16 L, Z-combinations.*

```
PROCEDURE L0( Length : NonNegInt );
BEGIN

   Left( 90 );
   MoveForward( Length );
   Left( 90 );
   MoveForward( Length )

END; { L0 }

PROCEDURE Z0( Length : NonNegInt );
BEGIN

   Right( 90 );
   MoveForward( Length );
   Right( 90 );
   MoveForward( Length );
   Left( 90 );
   MoveForward( Length )

END; { Z0 }
```

```
PROCEDURE L1( Length : NonNegInt );
BEGIN

   L0( Length DIV 2 );
   Z0( Length DIV 2 );
   L0( Length DIV 2 );
   Z0( Length DIV 2 );

END; { L1 }

PROCEDURE Z1( Length : NonNegInt );
BEGIN

   Z0( Length DIV 2 );
   Z0( Length DIV 2 );
   L0( Length DIV 2 );
   Z0( Length DIV 2 );

END; { Z1 }

PROCEDURE L2( Length : NonNegInt );
BEGIN

   L1( Length DIV 2 );
   Z1( Length DIV 2 );
   L1( Length DIV 2 );
   Z1( Length DIV 2 );

END; { L2 }

PROCEDURE DrawSierpinski( Length : NonNegInt );
BEGIN

   L2( Length );
   L2( Length )

END; { DrawSierpinski }
```

By now, you can see the pattern emerging in the code, too. Again, trace through the code to become comfortable with it. In the space provided on the next page, show the sequence of procedure calls and describe how the figure is drawn.

_____

_____

_____

_____

_____

_____

_____

_____

_____

_____

_____

_____

_____

_____

For the general case, we want recursion

What we really want is a pattern of computation that will handle the general case, drawing the Level-n Sierpinski curve. It rapidly becomes obvious that the pattern is that L_x and Z_x call L_{x-1} and Z_{x-1} unless $x = 0$, in which case they carry out the Turtle Graphics instructions shown in L0 and Z0. We thus end up with the recursive program shown below and provided on the disk as SIERPINS.PAS:

```
PROGRAM Sierpinski ( Input, Output );

USES
   TurtleADT;   { Use the high-resolution version   }
                { for your computer. Versions are    }
                { provided for PCs and Macintoshes. }
CONST
   MaxSteps = 128;

VAR
   TopLevel : NonNegInt;
```

```
PROCEDURE GetLevel( VAR TopLevel : NonNegInt );
BEGIN

   WriteLn( 'DRAWING SIERPINSKI CURVES' );
   WriteLn;

   REPEAT
      Write( 'Maximum level? (0-6) ' );
      ReadLn( TopLevel )
   UNTIL ( TopLevel >= 0 ) AND ( TopLevel <= 6 )

END; { GetLevel }


PROCEDURE SetStartingPoint;
{
  Initializes Turtle ADT globals.
  Use values appropriate for your system.
}
BEGIN

   Heading := 0;
   X := +150.0;
   Y := -100.0

END; { SetStartingPoint }


PROCEDURE L( Level, Length : NonNegInt );
FORWARD;


PROCEDURE Z( Level, Length : NonNegInt );
BEGIN

   IF Level > 0 THEN
   BEGIN
      Z( Level - 1, Length DIV 2 );
      Z( Level - 1, Length DIV 2 );
      L( Level - 1, Length DIV 2 );
      Z( Level - 1, Length DIV 2 )
   END
```

```
    ELSE
    BEGIN
       Right( 90 );
       MoveForward( Length );
       Right( 90 );
       MoveForward( Length );
       Left( 90 );
       MoveForward( Length )
    END

END; { Z }


PROCEDURE L; { See previous forward declaration }
BEGIN

    IF Level > 0 THEN
    BEGIN
       L( Level - 1, Length DIV 2 );
       Z( Level - 1, Length DIV 2 );
       L( Level - 1, Length DIV 2 );
       Z( Level - 1, Length DIV 2 )
    END

    ELSE
    BEGIN
       Left( 90 );
       MoveForward( Length );
       Left( 90 );
       MoveForward( Length )
    END

END; { L }


PROCEDURE DrawSierpinski( Level, Length : NonNegInt );
BEGIN

    L( Level, Length );
    L( Level, Length )

END; { DrawSierpinski }
```

```
BEGIN { main program }
    GetLevel( TopLevel );

    Initialize;
    SetStartingPoint;

    DrawSierpinski( TopLevel, MaxSteps );
END.
```

Something new—a forward reference

Pascal requires that a procedure be declared in a program before the place where it is called. In this program, L calls both itself and Z, so in theory, both L and Z should be declared before L. Similarly, Z calls both itself and L, so in theory, both Z and L should be declared before Z. Whoops! There's no way that both L and Z can be declared first. To handle such a case, Pascal allows us to state in a "forward reference" that one of these procedures will be declared later than normal. This is the reason for the code

```
PROCEDURE L( Level, Length : NonNegInt );
FORWARD;
```

just before the declaration of Z. This is called a *forward declaration*. In the completed declaration that appears later, the procedure's parameters are not shown because they were already declared in the FORWARD declaration.

Running the program under Turbo Pascal

To run this program under Turbo Pascal, the linker must be able to find a .TPU file containing the object code for the Turtle ADT. A high-resolution version of the Turtle ADT was written for use with VGA graphics, and saved in a file called VGATURTL.PAS. When compiled to disk, this yielded an object code file called VGATURTL.TPU., which is provided. (The source code is not provided, but an interface file is, so that you can see what identifiers are declared in the ADT.) Make sure this VGATURTL.TPU file is located in the subdirectory containing your Turbo system, or at least along a path that will be searched by the linker. Then, when you compile the provided version of SIERPINS.PAS, which contains the line

```
USES
    VGATurtleADT;
```

the Turbo linker will automatically search for a .TPU file whose

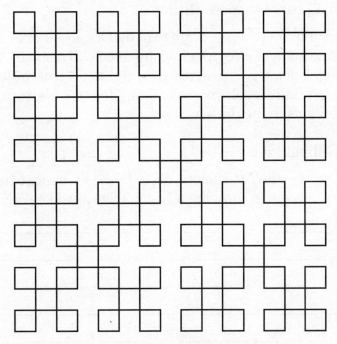

FIGURE 4. The level-3 Sierpinski curve generated by our program.

name consists of the first eight letters of VGATurtleADT and hope-fully, find it. Other than this, you compile the SIERPINS.PAS program normally.

Running the program under THINK Pascal

To use this program on a Macintosh under THINK Pascal, you must include both the MacTurtleADT.intf interface file and the precompiled MacTurtleADT.lib file in your project, followed by the Sierpinski.pas file. The following errors are common when using a precompiled ADT:

- If the client program—here Sierpinski.pas—is not listed *last* in the project, you will get the Wrong build order error message.

- The declarations of labels, constants, types, and variables in the ADT's interface file must be marked off with {$J+}, {$J-} directives to indicate that such identifiers are already declared in the ADT's precompiled .lib file, or you will get an error message reading Link failed: multiply-defined symbols.

A Sierpinski curve is space-filling

When you run your program to higher levels—Level 6 is about as much detail as a VGA or Macintosh screen will resolve—you will notice that the detail gets progressively tighter. If you could run the program at infinite level, you would find that the Sierpinski curve covers *all* points in the drawing area.

What you should do

In the space provided below, describe the sequence of recursive procedure calls when drawing a Level-3 Sierpinski curve:

_____

_____

_____

_____

_____

_____

_____

_____

_____

_____

_____

_____

_____

> Compile and link the Sierpinski program, saving the resulting executable code on a floppy disk. Run the program for all levels up to Level 6 and confirm that the program runs correctly. Turn in a floppy containing your executable code. If possible, also turn in output from your runs.

Lab 15.1
Records

Concepts: Records, fields, WITH statement.

Lab techniques: Direct experimentation.

Prerequisites: Chapter 15 of *Structures and Abstractions*.

The record is our second composite type. It differs from the array in that the components of a record, which are called fields, can be of different types. (The elements of an array must all be of the same type.) For this reason, a record is said to be heterogeneous, while an array is said to be homogeneous.

Trying a record

The following code is found in the file REC1.PAS, and uses an EmployeeRec record type similar to the one in Section 15.1 of the text. Compile, link, and run the program as described below, then answer the following questions.

```
PROGRAM Record1 ( Output );

CONST
    LowNum = 1;
    HiNum  = 2; { It's a very small business! }

TYPE
    {
      Either import String40 from String40 ADT
      or declare
      String40 = PACKED ARRAY [1..40] OF Char.
    }
    EmployeeRec    = RECORD
                         Name   : String40;
                         ID     : String40;
                         Salary : Real
                     END;
    EmployeeRange = LowNum..HiNum;
    EmployeeArray = ARRAY [ EmployeeRange ] OF EmployeeRec;

VAR
    Employees : EmployeeArray;
```

```
{
   Either import String40 and a ReadLnString procedure
   from an ADT as described in Chapter 14 and Appendix H,
   or insert a ReadLnString procedure here.
}

PROCEDURE GetRecords( VAR Employees : EmployeeArray );
{
   POSTCONDITIONS:
   The Employees array has been filled.

   PROCEDURE REQUIRED:
   ReadLnString, from String40 ADT.
}
VAR
   EmplNum : EmployeeRange;

BEGIN

   WriteLn;
   FOR EmplNum := LowNum TO HiNum DO
   BEGIN

      Write( 'Name for #', EmplNum:2, '?        ' );
      ReadLnString( Employees[ EmplNum ].Name );

      Write( 'I.D. code for #', EmplNum:2, '? ' );
      ReadLnString( Employees[ EmplNum ].ID );

      Write( 'Salary for #', EmplNum:2, '?    $' );
      ReadLn( Employees[ EmplNum ].Salary );

      WriteLn

   END;

END; { GetRecords }


BEGIN { main program }

   GetRecords( Employees )

END.
```

Make a run like this:

```
Name of # 1?        Bugs Bunny
I.D. code for # 1? B001497X
Salary for # 1?     $441.95

Name of # 2?        Daffy Duck
I.D. code for # 2? D001223X
Salary for # 2?     $411.00
```

Now answer the following questions:

What is the name of the *field* in which Daffy Duck is stored?

_____

What is the name of the *field* in which B001497X is stored?

_____

What is the type of the *field* in which B001497X is stored?

_____

What is the name of the *array* in which Bugs Bunny is stored?

_____

What is the name of the *record* in which Daffy Duck is stored?

_____

What is the name of the *type* of the array in which Daffy Duck is stored?

_____

Adding to the program

Now modify the GetRecords procedure by adding a WITH structure such that the I/O statements can be simplified to the following form:

```
Write( 'Name for #', EmplNum:2, '?        ' );
ReadLnString( Name );

Write( 'I.D. code for #', EmplNum:2, '? ' );
ReadLnString( ID );

Write( 'Salary for #', EmplNum:2, '?     $' );
ReadLn( Salary );
```

Again, test the program. When you are satisfied that it works the same as before, print out a source code listing to be turned in with your other lab work.

> Turn in a source code listing of the resulting program, along with printout of a test run.

Now add a procedure that prints a list of all the employees' salaries and the total of all the salaries, and call it from the main program.

> Turn in a source code listing of the resulting program, along with printout of a test run.

Helping Ms. Meltdown

Cora Meltdown has gotten herself in trouble again, while trying to write her own version of the journal-article program of Section 15.1 of the text. Her program is in the disk file called JOURNAL.PAS. Here's what Cora has written so far; when she compiles it, she gets error messages at the locations indicated by the arrows:

```
PROGRAM Journal ( Input, Output );
{ From Lab 15.1 }

{ DANGER: This code was written by Cora Meltdown! }

TYPE
    JournalArticle =
        RECORD
            Auth  : String40;     { <=== UNKNOWN IDENTIFIER }
            Title : String40;
            Journ : String40;
            Vol   : Integer;
            Pg    : Integer;
            Yr    : Integer;

VAR                               { <=== IDENTIFIER EXPECTED }
    Art : JournalArticle;


PROCEDURE RdJournArt( VAR Art : JournalArticle );
BEGIN

    WITH JournalArticle DO     { <=== "(" EXPECTED }
    BEGIN

        WriteLn( 'Author(s): ' );
        ReadLnString( Auth );

        WriteLn( 'Title: ' );
        ReadLnString( Title );

        WriteLn( 'Name of journal: ' );
        ReadLnString( Journ );

        WriteLn( 'Volume number: ' );
        ReadLn( Vol );

        WriteLn( 'Page number: ' );
        ReadLn( Pg );

        WriteLn( 'Year: ' );
        ReadLn( Yr );

        WriteLn

    END

END; { RdJournArt }
```

```
PROCEDURE WrJournArt( Art : JournalArticle );
BEGIN

   Write( 'Author(s):  ' );
   WriteLn( Author );          { <=== UNKNOWN IDENTIFIER }
   WriteLn;

   Write( 'Title    : ' );
   WriteLn( Title );
   WriteLn;

   Write( 'Journal  : ' );
   WriteLn( Journ );
   WriteLn;

   Write( 'Volume   : ' );
   WriteLn( Vol:4 );

   Write( 'Page     : ' );
   WriteLn( Pg:4 );

   Write( 'Year     : ' );
   WriteLn( Yr:4 );

   WriteLn

END; { WrJournArt }


BEGIN { main program }

   RdJournArt( Art );
   WrJournArt( Art )

END.
```

In an effort to help Cora, load this program into your Pascal system and try to compile it. Your compiler might give messages somewhat different from what Cora's compiler says, but errors should be marked in about the same places. Now let's debug the program a step at a time.

The first error message appears at the beginning of the record type declaration, and says that an identifier is "unknown." What should be done to correct this error? (Hint: You will either have to get the program to make use of previously-written code, or you will have to add some code to Cora's program.)

_____

_____

Correct the first error in the program and then recompile the code. Now you see an error marked at the global VAR declaration. The message may be confusing because the compiler gets really confused at this point. What is the error? (Hint: Carefully compare Cora's RECORD declaration with the syntax shown in the textbook.)

_____

_____

Correct Cora's mistake in the RECORD declaration and recompile the program. Now you see a message at the beginning of the WITH structure in the RdJournArt procedure. What's wrong with the statement WITH JournalArticle DO?

_____

_____

Fix the error in the WITH statement and recompile yet again. (Whew!) Now you see an error message at the first WriteLn in the WrJournArt procedure—something to the effect that Auth is an unknown identifier. What's the error here?

_____

_____

After fixing these four errors, your program should be working. You may, however, want to improve on Cora's programing style.

> When you have finished repairing and improving this program, turn in a source code listing and output from a test run.

Lab 16.1
Files

Concepts: Text file, nontext file.

Lab techniques: Direct experimentation.

Prerequisites: Chapter 16 of *Structures and Abstractions*.

A file is a composite data structure, like an array or record. Unlike a record, however, a file's components are all of the same type. Unlike both arrays and records, a file's length is not predetermined, but can change while the program is running. And unlike the arrays and records we've studied so far, a file is normally stored in a mass storage medium rather than main memory.

Standard Pascal allows for two kinds of files: text files and nontext files. A text file's components are characters, organized in lines of text, like text on a screen or on paper. A nontext file is allowed to have components of any type whatever, as long as it does not contain a file. Text files are discussed in the textbook in Sections 4.3, 4.4, 10.6, 10.7, and 16.1-16.3; nontext files are discussed in Sections 16.4-16.5. (And in the Turbo edition, 16.6.)

Standard Pascal's files have two limitations. First of all, they are always *sequential*: that is, the data are always written or read in the forward direction, from the beginning of the file, moving toward the end. In other words, there can be no hopping around or going backwards when accessing a Standard Pascal file. Furthermore, a Standard Pascal file can be opened for reading or opened for writing, but not for both at the same time. Both of these limitations are relaxed in many commercial Pascal systems, particularly in those intended for development of commercial software, but such nonstandard provisions vary with the system and are not pursued here.

Writing a text file

It takes only five steps to write a text file:

1. Declare a Text variable.

2. Associate an external file name with the Text file variable.

3. Open the file for writing and place the file pointer at the beginning of the file.

4. Write the lines of characters to the file.

5. Close the file.

Step 1 is easy; it just declares a file variable. As you recall from Section 10.X, the file variable is actually used by Pascal to store the memory address of the file buffer. Suppose we want the file variable to be called OutFile:

```
VAR
    OutFile : Text;
```

Step 2 has no provision in Standard Pascal, which assumes that external file names are the business of the operating system. As a result, step 2 is performed differently in different Pascal systems. For example, if we want to associate the filename LOTSA.DAT with the OutFile file variable in Turbo Pascal, we write

```
BEGIN
    Assign( OutFile, 'LOTSA.DAT' );
```

Turbo Pascal is almost unique in having a special Assign statement just for implementing step 2. Step 3 is then performed by means of a Rewrite statement:

```
    Rewrite( OutFile );
```

In most Pascal systems, including THINK Pascal, steps 2 and 3 are combined in a single Rewrite statement. In one statement, the file variable is associated with an external filename, the file is opened for writing only, and the file pointer is placed at the beginning of the file. For example, if a Macintosh file is called Lotsa Data, the Rewrite statement would be

```
BEGIN
    Rewrite( OutFile, 'Lotsa Data' );
```

How are steps 2 and 3 accomplished in your Pascal system? In the space below, write code for opening a text file associated with the external filename REALGOOD.TXT. Name the file variable OutFile.

_____

_____

_____

Step 4 is performed in the same way as writing to the screen, except that the `Write` and `WriteLn` statements specify the file variable as their first parameter. For example, to write a character variable `Ch` to the file associated with the `OutFile` variable, we would use

```
Write( OutFile, Ch )
```

or

```
WriteLn( OutFile, Ch )
```

In writing the file, remember that a text file must consist of lines of text. Therefore, the file must contain an `<EOLn>` just before the `<EOF>`, in addition to any other desired `<EOLn>`s.

In the space provided below, write Pascal code that will write to an already-opened `OutFile` all the lowercase letters of the alphabet, first in forward order, then in reverse order. (Hint: Use a loop or loops to sweep through the appropriate ASCII codes.) There should be an `<EOLn>` between the two alphabets, and one just before `<EOF>`.

_____

_____

_____

_____

_____

_____

_____

_____

_____

_____

Step 5 is performed automatically in Standard Pascal, when the program terminates. Because there is no provision in Standard Pascal for closing the file during the running of the program, a program cannot write a file, close it, then reopen it for reading during a single run. To get around this, most Pascal systems provide a nonstandard `Close` statement like this one:

```
Close( OutFile )
```

Check whether your Pascal system provides such a statement, and whether the syntax is as shown. Report your findings below:

_____

_____

Building a program to write a text file

Now put together all the pieces of code you wrote in the previous answers. Use them in a `WriteTextFile` procedure, and build a driver program to test the procedure. Run your program and use it to write the forward-and-backward-alphabets file.

> Turn in a source code listing together with a copy of the data file that was written.

Reading a text file

Reading a text file is, of course, analogous to writing one. Again, there are five steps:

1. Declare a `Text` variable.

2. Associate an external file name with the `Text` file variable.

3. Open the file for reading and place the file pointer at the beginning of the file.

4. Read the characters that are in the file.

5. Close the file.

Step 1 is done just as it was when writing the file. There is no need to use the same file variable, so we change the name to reflect the fact that we are now getting input from the file:

```
VAR
    InFile : Text;
```

In Turbo Pascal, step 2 is the same as when writing the file:

```
BEGIN
    Assign( InFile, 'LOTSA.DAT' );
```

In Turbo Pascal, step 3 is performed separately from step 2. To open the file for reading instead of writing, we use

```
    Reset( InFile );
```

In most Pascal systems, including THINK Pascal, steps 2 and 3 are combined in a single `Reset` statement, which associates the file variable with an external filename, opens the file for reading only, and places the file pointer at the beginning of the file. For example, if a Macintosh file is called `Lotsa Data`, the `Reset` statement would be

```
BEGIN
    Reset( InFile, 'Lotsa Data' );
```

In the space below, write code for opening a text file associated with the external file name `REALGOOD.TXT` in your Pascal system. The file variable should be named `InFile`.

_____

_____

_____

Step 4 is like reading from the keyboard, except that the `Read` and `ReadLn` statements specify the file variable as their first parameter. To copy a character from the file associated with the `InFile` variable, into the `Ch` variable, we would use

```
    Read( InFile, Ch )
```

or

```
    ReadLn( InFile, Ch )
```

Remember that the text file consists of lines of text, just like text from the keyboard. You have to organize the control structures that do the reading so that you don't read the `<EOLn>`s into character variables unless you really want to.

In the space provided below and on the next page, write Pascal code that will read from an already-opened `InFile` the two alphabets previously written to that file, echoing the characters to the screen with the same line structure:

_____

_____

_____

_____

An input file is closed automatically by Standard Pascal when the program terminates, but many real-world Pascal systems allow you to close a file manually by means of a statement like

```
Close( InFile )
```

Building a program to read your text file

Now put together all the pieces of code you wrote in the previous answers. Use them in a ReadTextFile procedure, and test it with a driver program. To test the program, read the forward-and-backward alphabets file that you wrote earlier, echoing the characters to the screen with the same line structure they had in the file.

> Turn in a source code listing together with a printout of a sample run.

A nontext file

A nontext file is a file of components of any type that does not contain a file. For example, we could have a file of records:

```
TYPE
   String40    = PACKED ARRAY [ 1..40 ] OF Char;

   EmployeeRec = RECORD
                    Name   : String40;
                    ID     : String40;
                    Salary : Real
                 END;

   EmployeeFile = FILE OF EmployeeRec;
```

Writing a nontext file

You have just seen an example of the declaration of a nontext file variable. Such a file is opened in the same way as a text file.

A nontext file has a big advantage over text files: the components of a nontext file can be written or read directly to or from the file, even if they are of a composite type. Suppose we have the declarations

```
VAR
   Employee : EmployeeRec;
   EmplFile : EmployeeFile;
```

Then we can write an entire record to `EmplFile` by means of `Write( EmplFile, Employee)` and later, after reopening the file for reading, read an entire record from the file by means of `Read( EmplFile, Employee )`. Note that `WriteLn` and `ReadLn` cannot be used with nontext files because such files are not organized into lines of data.

Why can we read and write composite values when using nontext files, but not when using text files? Because a nontext file stores the composite values as the same bit patterns used in main memory, so there is no need to translate to or from a character representation.

A sample program

Here is a program—`NonText.pas` on the disk—that writes such an employee file. Although it calls the nonstandard `Close` procedure, most Pascal systems support this.

```
PROGRAM NonText ( Output );

USES String40ADT;
{
   Imports String40, ReadLnString,
   and WriteString from String40ADT.
}

TYPE
   EmployeeRec  = RECORD
                     Name   : String40;
                     ID     : String40;
                     Salary : Real
                  END;
```

```
           EmployeeFile = FILE OF EmployeeRec;


PROCEDURE GetRecord( VAR Employee : EmployeeRec );
BEGIN

    WriteLn;

    Write( 'Name?        ' );
    ReadLnString( Employee.Name );

    Write( 'I.D. code? ' );
    ReadLnString( Employee.ID );

    Write( 'Salary?     $' );
    ReadLn( Employee.Salary );

END; { GetRecord }


PROCEDURE WriteRecFile;
VAR
   EFile         : EmployeeFile;
   Employee      : EmployeeRec;
   NoMoreRecords : Boolean;
   Ch            : Char;

   PROCEDURE OpenRecFile( VAR EFileVar : EmployeeFile );
   BEGIN

      {
         Insert here whatever code is needed by your
         Pascal system to associate an external file
         named 'EMPL.DAT'with EFileVar, opening the file
         for output.
      }

   END; { OpenRecFile }

BEGIN

   OpenRecFile( EFile );

   NoMoreRecords := False;
   REPEAT

      GetRecord( Employee );
      Write( EFile, Employee );
```

```
        WriteLn;
        Write( 'More? ' );
        ReadLn( Ch );
        IF (Ch <> 'Y') AND (Ch <> 'y') THEN
           NoMoreRecords := True;
        WriteLn

   UNTIL NoMoreRecords;

   Close( EFile )

END; { WriteRecFile }


BEGIN { main program }

   WriteRecFile

END.
```

Which statements in this program would not work with a text file?

_____

_____

_____

Your assignment

Add a ReadRecFile procedure to the program, so that the program will read back the contents of the file written by WriteRecFile. Your program should echo the file's data to the screen, formatted for easy understanding.

> Turn in a source code listing for your completed program, together with a printed copy of the I/O during a sample run.

Lab Project 16.2
Turing Machines

Concepts: Finite-state automata; Turing machines; random-access files.

Lab techniques: Use of a precompiled ADT unit; implementation of an ADT.

Prerequisites: Chapter 16 of *Structures and Abstractions*.

For a change of pace, let's play a game. It's a board game like Monopoly, but with a certain spartan quality. It turns out to be surprisingly important.

For this game, we have a board consisting of a single row of squares, extending indefinitely into the distance in both directions. Each square is either empty or occupied by a single hotel. Let's suppose, the first time we play this game, that all squares are empty except for three contiguous squares in the middle. We start play at the rightmost of these three.

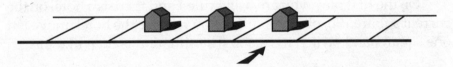

You play this game by yourself, according to a predefined set of rules. On each play or move, there are three kinds of actions you can make, governed by the rules:

- You can remove the hotel if there is one, place a hotel if the square is empty, or leave the square as it is.

- You can then move left or right one square, or stay on the current square;

- You can then adopt a different rule for play, continue to use the old one, or halt.

When the rules say to halt, the game is over.

To see how this game works, let's play from the board position shown above, using two predefined rules:

Rule 1:
If there's a hotel on the current square, then
        remove it, move left one square, and adopt rule 2;
but if there's no hotel, then
        leave the current square empty and halt.

Rule 2:
If there's a hotel on the current square, then
        remove it, move left one square, and adopt rule 1;
but if there's no hotel, then
        place a hotel on the current square and halt.

You start out using rule 1. The initial position is

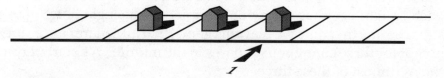

On the first play, you are using rule 1 and there is a hotel on the current square. So, obeying rule 1, you remove the hotel, move left one square, and switch to rule 2. The situation is then like this:

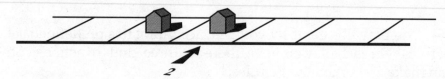

Now you're using rule 2 and again, there's a hotel on the current square. So you remove the hotel, move left one square, and switch back to rule 1. The situation is

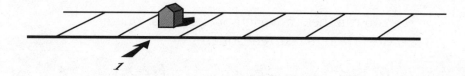

Now you're using rule 1 and there's a hotel on the current square, so you remove the hotel, move left one square, and switch to rule 2. The situation is

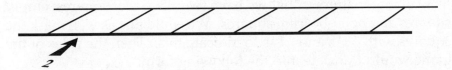

Now you're using rule 2 but there's no hotel on the current square, so you place a hotel on the empty square and halt. The game is over.

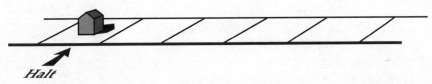

That completes the example. You started with three hotels and removed all of them, but ended up placing a single hotel in the square just to the right of where the original three were.

Now you try it . . .

Now here's something to investigate on your own: what happens if you start with only two hotels? Don't guess; play the game and find out! Then play the game with one hotel, and with four. What happens? (Hint: Make a list showing the results in the four cases, and look for a pattern.) Can you give a general description of what this game accomplishes if you start with *n* hotels, where *n* is any whole number? Write your answer below:

_____

_____

_____

_____

_____

_____

_____

_____

Symbolizing the Game

As you've noticed by now, we never made any use of the fact that the objects occupying some of the squares were "hotels." In fact, all that matters is that we have two flavors of squares: empty squares and hotel-bearing squares. We could just as well mark the squares with '0's and '1's to indicate this. Then the rules of the game would translate into the following form:

Rule 1:
If you read a '1' in the current square, then
       write a '0' there to replace the '1',
       move left one square, and switch to rule 2;
but if you read a '0' there, then
       leave the '0' there and halt.

Rule 2:
If you read a '1' in the current square, then
       write a '0' there to replace the '1',
       move left one square, and switch to rule 1;
but if you read a '0' there, then
       leave the '1' there and halt.

In this language, we have a game equivalent to the one we played before, but now we think of reading and writing the characters '0' and '1' instead of removing and placing hotel icons on a Monopoly board. The game is the same; it's just symbolized differently.

Turing machines

As you probably discovered in the last section, our game actually computes useful information about a numeric property of the initial board state. Not only that; the "game" is actually a rigid set of rules that can be carried out by a machine capable of following the rules. In other words, the game can be played by an automaton. (We defined "automaton" in Lab Project 13.2.)

Such automata were first described in 1936 by Alan Turing, in a famous paper that investigated what is computable. Machines of this kind are now called *Turing machines*, and they can perform text processing, arithmetic, and draw graphics. In fact, *everything that can be done by a von Neumann computer can be done by a Turing machine!*

A Turing machine is usually visualized as a movable read/write head that travels forward and backward along a tape bearing some kind of symbols. It is programmable machine, because we control it by specifying the rules that it uses.

The rules correspond to machine states

Notice that each numbered rule corresponds to a *state* of the Turing machine. In our first example, the machine used rule 1 when it had encountered an even number of hotels so far and used rule 2 when it had encountered an odd number of hotels so far. Therefore, the use of rule 1 corresponds to machine state 1, which is the state of having encountered an even number of hotels, and the use of rule 2 corresponds to state 2, the state of having encountered an odd number of hotels. The "rules" specify the actions in each state, including state transitions.

A shorthand for the state rules

In order to make it easier to work out examples, let's adopt a shorthand for the rules. We'll use a state table containing five columns: for the state number, for the character read from the current square, for the character to write on the square, for the "move," and for the state transition. The two rules in the previous example would look like this:

State	If reading	Then write,	move,	adopt state
1	1	0	L	2
1	0	0	—	Halt
2	1	0	L	1
2	0	0	—	Halt

This notation makes it easier to specify the required actions.

Another Turing machine

To emphasize the generality of Turing machines, let's examine a second machine. This one uses '0's and '1's too, but it manipulates '0's and '1's as part of a binary number. Suppose that the tape is filled with spaces except for a single string of '1's and '0's.

Again, the read/write head starts at the right end of the string, in state 1:

```
01101010
       ^
       1
```

This Turing machine is more complicated than our first example. For one thing, the tape contains three different symbols: '0's, '1's, and blanks (spaces). Also, let's suppose there are three states in addition to the Halt state and that the rules are these:

State	If reading	Then write,	move,	adopt state
1	0	1	L	2
1	1	0	L	3
1	space	—	—	Halt
2	0	—	L	2
2	1	—	L	2
2	space	—	—	Halt
3	0	1	L	2
3	1	0	L	3
3	space	1	L	Halt

We start in state 1, reading a '0':

```
01101010
       ^
       1
```

The rule for state 1 says that we should write a '1', move left, and change to state 2:

```
01101011
      ^
      2
```

Now we are in state 2 and reading a '1', so we do nothing but move left:

```
01101011
      ^
      2
```

This continues until the read/write head reaches the first space to the left of the binary string:

```
01101011
^
2
```

Now we are in state 2 and reading a space, so we halt:

```
01101011
^
Halt
```

The net effect has been to change `'01101010'` into `'01101011'`.

But consider what happens if the initial string is `'01111111'`. We start in state 1 at the right end of the string:

```
01111111
       ^
       1
```

We are in state 1 and read a `'1'`, so we write a `'0'`, move left, and switch to state 3:

```
01111110
      ^
      3
```

In state 3, we read a `'1'`, so we write a `'0'`, move left, and stay in state 3:

```
01111100
     ^
     3
```

This continues until we get to the leading `'0'`:

```
00000000
^
3
```

Now we are in state 3 and reading a `'0'`, so we write a `'1'`, move left, and switch to state 2:

```
10000000
^
2
```

Now we are in state 2 and reading a space, so we halt:

```
10000000
^
Halt
```

The net result has been to change `'01111111'` to `'10000000'`.

Explain in your own words why this Turing machine is useful:

_____

_____

_____

_____

The Turing machine as an abstract data type

Now it's time to build a Turing machine abstract data type. We need a moving read/write head, a tape containing symbols, and a state processor that enacts the rules. In carrying out the rules, the machine is capable of five actions:

1. Write a symbol to the current position on the tape.

2. Read a symbol from the current position on the tape.

3. Move one square to the right.

4. Move one square to the left.

5. Execute a state transition (which may be null).

All of this, except the state transitions, can be expressed as the following ADT interface:

```
INTERFACE

TYPE
   MachineState = ( One, Two, Three, Four, Five, Halt );
   SymbolType   = ( Hotel, Empty );

VAR
   State : MachineState;


PROCEDURE WriteTape( S : SymbolType );
{
  POSTCONDITION:
  The symbol S has been written to the tape at the
  current position of the read/write head.
}
```

```
PROCEDURE ReadTape( VAR S : SymbolType );
{
  PRECONDITION:
  The tape has been initialized with symbols.

  POSTCONDITION:
  S contains a copy of the symbol on the tape at
  the current position of the read/write head.
}

PROCEDURE MoveRight;
{
  POSTCONDITION:
  The head has moved one square to the right.
}

PROCEDURE MoveLeft;
{
  POSTCONDITION:
  The head has moved one square to the left.
}

PROCEDURE InitializeMachine;
{
  POSTCONDITION:
  The tape has been initialized with symbols and the
  read/write head has been given an initial position.
}

PROCEDURE ShowTape;
{
  PRECONDITION:
  The tape has been initialized with symbols.

  POSTCONDITION:
  The symbols on the tape have been displayed in
  sequence, from left to right.
}
```

You will find this interface file on the floppy disks accompanying this book. The MS-DOS disk contains the interface portion of a unit suitable for Turbo Pascal, called TURING.INT, while the Macintosh disk contains an interface file called TuringADT.Intf, for inclusion in a THINK Pascal project. These disks also contain precompiled units for use with the little program we are about to write, so that you can take a Turing machine for a test drive without having to write the implementation yourself.

On the MS-DOS disk, the precompiled unit is called TURINGAD.TPU; make sure this file is in the same directory as your client program or at least in the search paths that will be used by the Turbo software. On the Mac disk, the precompiled ADT is called TuringADT.lib; you add it to your client project, along with the interface file.

Writing a client program to use the Turing ADT

Never mind for now how we can implement the ADT operations shown in the interface. First, let's concentrate on how the operations can be controlled and used. If we have the interface shown above implemented as a Pascal unit and precompiled, we can bring the "hotels" Turing machine to life with the following program, which uses the unit:

```
PROGRAM TuringMachine ( Output );

USES TuringADT;
{
  The following identifiers are imported from TuringADT:
  State, Position, WriteTpe, ReadTape, MoveRight,
  MoveLeft, InitializeMachine, ShowTape.
}

VAR
   Symbol : SymbolType;


PROCEDURE Process( S : SymbolType );
{
  This procedure contains the rules controlling the
  actions of the Turing machine. Normally, this procedure
  would be part of the Turing ADT. It is provided here so
  that you can program the Turing machine without knowing
  how the machine is represented in computer storage.
}
BEGIN

  CASE State OF
  {
    Up to five states, plus Halt, are allowed by the
    Turing ADT, but we are not obligated to use all of
    them in Turbo Pascal or THINK Pascal.
  }
```

```
One : IF S = Hotel THEN
         BEGIN
            WriteTape( Empty );
            MoveLeft;
            State := Two
         END

      ELSE IF S = Empty THEN
            State := Halt

      ELSE
      BEGIN
         WriteLn( '+++ Erroneous symbol on tape +++' );
         State := Halt
      END;

Two : IF S = Hotel THEN
         BEGIN
            WriteTape( Empty );
            MoveLeft;
            State := One
         END

      ELSE IF S = Empty THEN
      BEGIN
         WriteTape( Hotel );
         State := Halt
      END

      ELSE
      BEGIN
         WriteLn( '+++ ERRONEOUS SYMBOL ON TAPE +++' );
         State := Halt
      END;

   {
      The following ELSE is used in Turbo Pascal;
      for THINK Pascal, change ELSE to OTHERWISE.
   }
   ELSE
   BEGIN
      WriteLn( '+++ ERRONEOUS STATE +++' );
      State := Halt
   END

   END { CASE }


END; { Process }
```

```
BEGIN { Main program }

    InitializeMachine;
    ShowTape;

    WHILE NOT ( State = Halt ) DO
    BEGIN

        ReadTape( Symbol );
        Process( Symbol );
        ShowTape

    END

END.
```

If you are using Turbo or THINK Pascal . . .

. . . you should get the `TuringMachine` program running with the precompiled ADT unit and test the program with one, two, three, and four hotels. Confirm that the program's behavior agrees with the results you got by hand earlier in the lab.

> Turn in a disk containing the executable code for your completed program, together with printouts of the four runs.

If you are using another Pascal system . . .

. . . you will not be able to use the precompiled units provided on the disks. In this event, you will have to move on to the final stage of the lab and implement the ADT before you can run the `TuringMachine` program.

Implementing the Turing ADT

In implementing the ADT, you first need to decide on an appropriate representation for the data type itself. The machine consists of two parts. The first part is the read/write head, which has two characteristics: a `State` and a `Position` on the tape. The second part is the tape, which in theory is endless. Of course, you cannot represent an infinitely long tape in a computer's memory, so you will have to compromise this property of the tape.

In terms of size, the obvious choice would be to represent the tape by a Pascal file. But Standard Pascal provides only sequential files in which we can move forward but not backward. Our Turing machine's read/write head must move in both directions. Turbo Pascal and THINK Pascal both provide nonstandard random-access files, in which we can easily move both forward and backward. But a random-access file has a first component, before which there is nothing. This is unlike a Turing machine tape.

You could use an array, but an array is even worse because it is limited in both directions. As long as relatively small data patterns will be processed, and as long as you are careful not to run the read/write head off the end of the array, you can use an array for the purpose of this lab.

The best choice takes us ahead of our story: we could represent the tape as a doubly-linked list, using techniques to be described in Chapter 19. But that's something for the future.

Discuss all these possibilities with your instructor and decide which representation you will use for this lab. Then write an implementation to accompany the interface shown earlier. Get the entire TuringMachine program running and test it with one, two, three, and four hotels.

Turn in a disk containing the executable code for your completed program, together with printouts of the four runs.

Lab 16.3
Eliza

Concepts: Parallel arrays, strings, ADTs, text files.

Lab techniques: Top-down design; use of an ADT.

Prerequisites: Chapters 13, 14 and 16 of *Structures and Abstractions*.

About 1950, the mathematician and computing pioneer Alan Turing proposed a test for machine intelligence. He asserted that if an interactive machine could fool humans into believing they were communicating with another human, the machine should be considered to possess "intelligence," in some sense of the word and within the context of the interaction. He also predicted that, by the year 2000, we would have machines that passed this test, which is now known as the Turing Test. (Turing did not discuss an important related question: Whether there exist humans who, within the context of particular discussions, appear to *fail* the test.)

By the late 1960s, computer scientists working in the area known as artificial intelligence were beginning to produce programs that could, in a limited context, pass the Turing Test. One of the most famous (or infamous) was a program called Eliza, designed by Joseph Weizenbaum at the Massachusetts Institute of Technology.

Weizenbaum noticed that, when people make small talk, they speak in semiautomatic patterns that are almost predetermined, requiring little thought. He thought that such forms of conversation could be easily mimicked by a computer. So Weizenbaum designed a program that would interact with a human according to a set of conversational rules called a *script*. By providing more comprehensive scripts for polite conversation, the program could be made to seem increasingly believable as a conversationalist. Because the program could be taught to speak believably in polite conversations, Weizenbaum named it after the Eliza Doolittle character in George Bernard Shaw's *Pygmalion* and the subsequent Lerner and Loewe musical, *My Fair Lady*.

By limiting the context of a conversation, Weizenbaum was able to make Eliza seem to respond intelligently to a wide range of user inputs. The most famous (and controversial) script for Eliza was called `Doctor`. It mimicked the conversational responses of a nondirective psychotherapist during the initial interview of a patient.

In fact, `Eliza` was a rather primitive natural-language processor. It responded to keywords in the user's inputs, analyzed a few parts of speech, and assembled its responses from pieces of the user's sentences. Weizenbaum vehemently denied that `Eliza` was intelligent. He described "her" as an actress who could repeat lines, but who had no idea what she was saying. Despite this, many users found themselves pouring out their hearts to the `Eliza` script, and some even claimed that it helped them with their personal problems! With people calling him on the phone begging to be helped by `Eliza` and psychiatrists asking to use it as a diagnostic tool, Weizenbaum repudiated the whole project and became an opponent of the claim that computers can be intelligent. To this day, people still debate whether `Eliza` was intelligent in any sense.

In this lab, we take a brief look at the kind of simple language processing that can give a superficial appearance of intelligence. When we finish, you may want to discuss the concept of "intelligence" with your classmates and instructor. Language processing in particular and artificial intelligence in general are important research areas in computer science.

A session with the Eliza

Here is a sample of the kind of dialogue that can occur when a human "talks" to `Eliza`. In the following example, the computer's output is in uppercase, while the "patient's" inputs are in lowercase:

```
HELLO. WHAT SEEMS TO BE THE PROBLEM?
I can't sleep at night, and I have weird dreams.

WHAT DO YOU DREAM ABOUT?
I usually dream about sex and alarm clocks.

DOES SEX REMIND YOU OF DEATH?
Not particularly.

ARE YOU SURE?
Yes.

YOU SEEM QUITE CERTAIN.
I am.
```

TELL ME MORE ABOUT YOUR DREAMS.
Once I dreamed that my father ate my goldfish.

WAS YOUR FAMILY A HAPPY ONE?
Well, my mother often wore a propeller beanie.

DID YOUR MOM AND DAD GET ALONG TOGETHER?
Yes.

ARE YOU SURE?
Very sure.

TELL ME ABOUT YOUR JOB.
I hate my boss.

SOMETIMES OUR HATES CONCEAL OUR ATTRACTIONS.
You're being silly.

WE WERE TALKING ABOUT YOU, NOT ME. TELL ME MORE.
My dog and cat told me to move out of their apartment.

DOES THE WORD "BOSS" REMIND YOU OF THE WORD "DOG"?
You are supposed to be helping me.

I AM SUPPOSED TO BE HELPING YOU?
Yes. Goodbye.

GOODBYE. PLEASE PAY THE RECEPTIONIST ON YOUR WAY OUT.

Most people are intrigued by a program that responds like this—at least, for a few minutes. However, the program is responding according to only a few simple rules, arranged in a hierarchy of levels:

1. The program first checks the user's input string for top-priority keywords like "hate," "love," "sex," or "death." If it finds such a word, it responds with a predetermined reply suited to that keyword. For the sake of variety, the program can have a set of fixed responses for each keyword and choose one of them at random. In the dialogue shown above, an example of level-1 response occurred in the exchange

    I usually dream about sex and alarm clocks.

    DOES SEX REMIND YOU OF DEATH?

Similarly, when the user mentioned "father," Eliza responded with an answer involving "family"; when the user mentioned "mother," Eliza responded in terms of "Mom and Dad."

2. If there is no top-priority keyword in the user's input string, the program looks for second-priority keywords. If it finds any, it stashes them away for later use. When the stash accumulates at least three keywords, the program can choose to use one or more of these in a "surprise" response. For example, if the stash contains the words "dog" and "boss," but the user's input contains no words that would trigger an immediate top-priority response, the program can, apparently out of the blue, ask something like

    ```
    HOW DO YOU FEEL ABOUT YOUR BOSS?
    ```

    or, as in the example above, it can paste together a sentence from two keywords the user supplied earlier:

    ```
    DOES THE WORD "BOSS" REMIND YOU OF THE WORD "DOG"?
    ```

3. If levels 1 and 2 have not provided Eliza with a response, she can simply reverse all the pronouns in the user's input, turning it into a question. In the example dialogue, the user wrote

    ```
    You are supposed to be helping me.
    ```

    Eliza responded

    ```
    I AM SUPPOSED TO BE HELPING YOU?
    ```

    This particular response not only reversed the pronouns, but also recognized that the original sentence was in second person, and changed "are" to "am" in the response.

    If this kind of response appears too frequently, the user will sense the pattern and Eliza's tricks will be exposed. So the program decides randomly whether to use this strategy when the opportunity arises. Sometimes it does, sometimes it doesn't.

4. If levels 1–3 fail to produce a suitable response, `Eliza` can look for third-priority keywords that might reasonably lead to a fixed response. For example, in the sample dialogue, the user writes

    ```
    You're being silly
    ```

   and `Eliza` replies

    ```
    WE WERE TALKING ABOUT YOU, NOT ME. TELL ME MORE.
    ```

   The purpose here is to get the user to supply more information, which should supply more keywords for level-1 and level-2 responses. Again, this strategy shouldn't be overused, so `Eliza` decides randomly whether to use it in a given case.

5. If steps 1–4 all fail to generate a suitable response, `Eliza` will have to fall back on responses that are suitable for any occasion, and which can be used to elicit more data for later responses. In the sample dialogue,

    ```
    TELL ME ABOUT YOUR JOB.
    ```

   was such a response. Here are some other general-purpose responses:

    ```
    TELL ME MORE ABOUT YOUR FAMILY.
    PLEASE GO ON.
    MANY PEOPLE FEEL THAT WAY. PLEASE GO ON.
    ```

   The program chooses at random from a number of such responses provided for it in the script.

Even with a good script and good programming, the patterns eventually become apparent in the program's responses and the user either gets angry or loses interest in the conversation. The fun for the programmer lies in providing `Eliza` with enough variety and randomness to make her unpredictable for a while. (Also, if the user gets angry, the program can be scripted to reply in funny ways to profanity!)

Choosing data structures

Before programming Eliza, we have to decide how the program's data should be organized and stored. Eliza reads input strings from the "patient," then replies with a string of her own. Although we don't know the lengths of these strings ahead of time, it should be sufficient to allow up to one line (80 characters) in a string. We will need to use a number of string operations as we pull apart strings and reassemble Eliza's replies, so we will use the String80 ADT that was built in Chapter 14.

Several of the response strategies involve recognizing a substring in the patient's input, then replying with a corresponding preset response string. This means that the program will have to look up keywords in a table, then use a corresponding string in the output. One way to handle this would be to use parallel arrays, as in Section 13.4. Another would be to have a keyword stored together with its preset response as fields in a record. However, for the sake of readers who haven't yet covered Chapter 15, we will use parallel arrays here. Furthermore, for our first attempt at programming Eliza, we will skip level 3, with its pronoun reversals. Here's a list of the arrays we will need for the various response strategies:

Level 1: A Keywords1 array for first-priority keywords, and a Responses1 array for the corresponding responses. The current number of stored keyword/response pairs is stored in NumKywds1.

Level 2: A Keywords2 array for second-priority keywords, which are copied to a Stash array when found in the patient's inputs. The number of keywords stored in Keywords2 is stored in NumKywds2; the number of keywords stashed from the patient's inputs is stored in NumStashed.

Level 3: (Skipped in our first Eliza program.)

Level 4: A Keywords3 array for third-priority keywords, and a Responses3 array for the corresponding responses. The current number of stored keyword/response pairs is stored in NumKywds3.

Level 5: A `Universals` array for general-purpose responses, the number of which is stored in `NumUniversals`.

Here are the declarations:

```
CONST
   Size = 15;  { Max. number of strings in an array }

TYPE
   NonNegInt = 0..MaxInt;
   StrList   = ARRAY [1..Size] OF String80;

VAR
   Keywords1, Keywords2, Keywords3,
   Universals, Stash, Responses1,
   Responses3                     : StrList;
   NumKywds1, NumKywds2, NumKywds3,
   NumUniversals, NumStashed      : NonNegInt;
```

The data are stored in a text file

Once we have declared the arrays, we have to decide how the program will load data into the arrays. It is best to have the program read the preset keywords and responses from a text file, because we can re-edit a text file without re-editing or recompiling the program. This way, we can improve the behavior of `Eliza` without doing any programming.

We might as well put the data into the file in the same order as the strategies have been described in the preceeding discussion. For level 1, we can start with six keyword/response pairs, stored one after another; first comes the number of data pairs (here `NumKywds1`), followed by the data:

```
6
DEATH
DOES DEATH REMIND YOU OF SEX?
SEX
DOES SEX SOMETIMES SEEM UNREAL TO YOU?
DREAM
DO YOUR DREAMS SOMETIMES SEEM MORE REAL THAN BEING AWAKE?
HATE
SOMETIMES OUR HATES CONCEAL OUR ATTRACTIONS.
LOVE
WHAT IS THE STRONGEST LOVE OF YOUR LIFE?
```

```
JOB
HOW DO YOU FEEL ABOUT YOUR BOSS?
```

The data for other stratgies are stored similarly. See the `DOCTORO.DAT`
file on the accompanying disk.

A skeleton for the program

As usual, we start by writing a skeleton for the program, using
our hierarchical outline as a guide:

```
PROGRAM Eliza ( Input, Output );

{
  REQUIRES THE DATA FILE, DOCTORO.DAT,
  THE STRING80 ADT, AND A PSEUDORANDOM NUMBER GENERATOR.

  This version does not use pronoun reversal.
}

USES String80ADT;
{
  The following identifiers are imported from String80ADT:
  String80, ReadLnString, WriteString, LengthOfString,
  ToUpperCase, StripString, Position, MakeEmptyString,
  AppendChar.
}

CONST
   Size = 15;  { Max. number of strings in an array }

TYPE
   NonNegInt = 0..MaxInt;
   StrList   = ARRAY [1..Size] OF String80;

VAR
   Keywords1, Keywords2, Keywords3,
   Universals, Stash, Responses1,
   Responses3                          : StrList;
   NumKywds1, NumKywds2, NumKywds3,
   NumUniversals, NumStashed           : NonNegInt;
```

```
PROCEDURE InitializeLists;
VAR
   ListsFile : Text;
   Count     : NonNegInt;

BEGIN

   {
     Adjust the following instruction to suit your
     compiler, so that it will open the DOCTOR0.DAT file.
   }
   Reset( ListsFile );

   ReadLn( ListsFile, NumKywds1 );
   FOR Count := 1 TO NumKywds1 DO
   BEGIN
      ReadLnString( ListsFile, Keywords1[ Count ] );
      ReadLnString( ListsFile, Responses1[ Count ] )
   END;

   ReadLn( ListsFile, NumKywds2 );
   FOR Count := 1 TO NumKywds2 DO
      ReadLnString( ListsFile, Keywords2[ Count ] );

   ReadLn( ListsFile, NumUniversals );
   FOR Count := 1 TO NumUniversals DO
      ReadLnString( ListsFile, Universals[ Count ] );

   ReadLn( ListsFile, NumKywds3 );
   FOR Count := 1 TO NumKywds3 DO
   BEGIN
      ReadLnString( ListsFile, Keywords3[ Count ] );
      ReadLnString( ListsFile, Responses3[ Count ] )
   END;

   NumStashed := 0

END; { InitializeLists }


PROCEDURE ListenToPatient( VAR PatientSays : String80 );
BEGIN

   { This is only a stub. }

END; { ListenToPatient }
```

```
PROCEDURE ReplyAtLevel1( PatientSays : String80;
                        VAR NoReply : Boolean );
BEGIN

   { This is only a stub. }
   NoReply := True

END; { ReplyAtLevel1 }


PROCEDURE ReplyAtLevel2( PatientSays : String80;
                        VAR NoReply : Boolean );
BEGIN

   { This is only a stub. }
   NoReply := True

END; { ReplyAtLevel2 }


PROCEDURE ReplyAtLevel4( PatientSays : String80;
                        VAR NoReply : Boolean );
BEGIN

   { This is only a stub. }
   NoReply := True

END; { ReplyAtLevel4 }


PROCEDURE ReplyWithUniversal;
BEGIN

   { This is only a stub. }

END; { ReplyWithUniversal }
```

```
PROCEDURE MakeReply( PatientSays    : String80;
                     VAR DoctorSays : String80 );
VAR
   NoReply : Boolean;

BEGIN

   WriteLn;

   ReplyAtLevel1( PatientSays, NoReply );

   IF NoReply THEN
      ReplyAtLevel2( PatientSays, NoReply );

   { Level 3 is not used in this program. }

   IF NoReply THEN
      ReplyAtLevel4( PatientSays, NoReply );

   IF NoReply THEN
      ReplyWithUniversal

END; { MakeReply }


PROCEDURE SayHello;
BEGIN

   WriteLn;
   WriteLn( 'HELLO. WHAT SEEMS TO BE THE PROBLEM?' )

END; { SayHello }


FUNCTION TimeToSayGoodbye( S : String80 ) : Boolean;
BEGIN

   { This is only a stub. }
   TimeToSayGoodbye := True

END; { TimeToSayGoodbye }
```

```
PROCEDURE SayGoodbye;
BEGIN

    WriteLn;
    WriteLn( 'GOODBYE.' );
    WriteLn( 'PLEASE PAY THE RECEPTIONIST AS YOU LEAVE.' )

END; { SayGoodbye }


PROCEDURE Consult;
VAR
    PatientSays, DoctorSays : String80;

BEGIN

    SayHello;
    REPEAT
        ListenToPatient( PatientSays );
        MakeReply( PatientSays, DoctorSays )
    UNTIL TimeToSayGoodbye( PatientSays );

    SayGoodbye;

END; { Consult }


BEGIN { main program }

    InitializeLists;
    Consult

END.
```

As usual, you should test the skeleton before adding code to implement the procedures.

Handling the patient's inputs

The program must be able to recognize particular words in the patient's inputs, and these words must be recognized no matter what case they are in. In other words, 'Death', 'death', and 'DEATH' should be treated the same by the program. For this reason, it is convenient to have the program translate the patient's input to upper case and strip punctuation from it as soon as it comes in. Furthermore, the program should prompt the patient if the patient tries to enter an empty string:

```
PROCEDURE ListenToPatient( VAR PatientSays : String80 );
VAR
    LenStr : Integer;

BEGIN

    REPEAT

        ReadLnString( Input, PatientSays );

        LenStr := LengthOfString( PatientSays );
        IF LenStr = 0 THEN
        BEGIN
            WriteLn;
            WriteLn(
                'I CAN''T HELP IF YOU DON''T SAY ANYTHING.' )
        END

    UNTIL LenStr > 0;

    ToUpperCase( PatientSays );
    StripString( PatientSays );

END; { ListenToPatient }
```

Note that all of the string operations needed here are imported from String80ADT, a special version of which is supplied on the disk accompanying this manual.

Implementing the TimeToSayGoodbye function

First consider how the program should terminate. One simple choice is to have TimeToSayGoodbye return True whenever it detects the substring BYE in the patient's input. (I know, I know—this isn't an infallible way of determining when the patient wants to quit. But we have to start with something simple!) If we have previously stored the string 'BYE' in a global variable called Bye, we can implement TimeToSayGoodbye with a single two-way decision structure:

```
IF Position( Bye, S, 1 ) > 0 THEN
    TimeToSayGoodbye := True
ELSE
    TimeToSayGoodbye := False
```

The only remaining problem is how to initialize a `String80` variable named `Bye`. We insert in the `InitializeLists` procedure the following code:

```
MakeEmptyString( Bye );
AppendChar( 'B', Bye );
AppendChar( 'Y', Bye );
AppendChar( 'E', Bye );
```

Processing level-1 replies

The first step in formulating a response to the patient's input is to check for first-priority keywords in the input. The program does this by looking for each of the `Keywords1` elements in the `PatientSays` string. If such a word is found, the program displays the corresponding response. If the procedure can make such a response, it sets `NoReply` to `False`; otherwise, `NoReply` is `True`:

```
PROCEDURE ReplyAtLevel1( PatientSays : String80;
                         VAR NoReply : Boolean );
VAR
   Num : NonNegInt;

BEGIN

   NoReply := True;
   Num := 1;
   WHILE ( Num <= NumKywds1 ) AND NoReply DO
   BEGIN

      IF Position( Keywords1[ Num ], PatientSays, 1 )
         > 0 THEN
      BEGIN
         WriteString( Output, Responses1[ Num ] );
         WriteLn;
         NoReply := False
      END

      ELSE
         Num := Num + 1

   END

END; { ReplyAtLevel1 }
```

Processing level-2 responses

At level 2 of the processing of inputs, the program checks for second-priority keywords, and if they are found, adds them to a stash of such words, from which they can be pasted into later responses.

A level-2 response can be made if there are more than two words stashed away. In making such a response, the program chooses two stashed words at random, using the RandomInt function shown below. But for the sake of variety in Eliza's behavior, she doesn't always make such a response when she is able to. Here is where a new note appears in the program: Eliza "flips a coin" to decide whether to make a level-2 response. More specifically, Eliza calls a Random procedure, which returns a pseudorandom real number R, such that $0 \leq R < 1.0$. If this number is greater than some preset threshold, Eliza goes ahead and makes a level-2 response; otherwise, she skips it. This randomness is an important factor in making the program seem human, and adjusting the randomness threshold is touchy business. The following code assumes that we have a Random function, either built into the Pascal system or written into the program. (See Appendix I.)

```
FUNCTION RandomInt( N : NonNegInt ) : NonNegInt;
{
  PRECONDITION:
  0 <= N < MaxInt.

  POSTCONDITION:
  0 <= RandomInt <= N.

  Function required: Random.
}
BEGIN

  RandomInt := Round( N * Random )

END; { RandomInt }
```

```
PROCEDURE ReplyAtLevel2( PatientSays : String80;
                            VAR NoReply : Boolean );
{ Function required: RandomInt. }
CONST
    Threshold = 0.6;

VAR
    Num, RandInt1, RandInt2 : NonNegInt;

BEGIN

    NoReply := True;
    FOR Num := 1 TO NumKywds2 DO
    BEGIN

        IF Position( Keywords2[ Num ], PatientSays, 1 )
            > 0 THEN
        BEGIN

            IF NumStashed < Size THEN
            BEGIN
                NumStashed := NumStashed + 1;
                Stash[ NumStashed ] := Keywords2[ Num ]
            END

        END

    END;

    IF ( Random > Threshold ) AND ( NumStashed > 2) THEN
    BEGIN

        REPEAT
            RandInt1 := RandomInt( NumStashed );
            RandInt2 := RandomInt( NumStashed )
        UNTIL RandInt1 <> RandInt2;

        Write( 'WHEN I SAY ''' );
        WriteString( Output, Stash[ RandInt1 ] );
        Write( ''', DOES IT REMIND YOU OF ''' );
        WriteString( Output, Stash[ RandInt2 ] );
        WriteLn( '''?' );

        NoReply := False

    END

END; { ReplyAtLevel2 }
```

Before using the random-number generator, we must seed it by calling the `Randomize` in the `InitializeLists` procedure. If your Pascal system doesn't supply `Random` and `Randomize`, you can use the ones shown in Appendix I.

What's left?

Your assignment now is to complete the `DOCTOR0.PAS` program by inserting the implementations shown above, then completing the `ReplyAtLevel4` and `MakeUniversalReply` procedures. Adjust the program and the `DOCTOR0.DAT` file until you have gotten them working as well as you can.

> Turn in your source code, data file, and printouts of sample runs.

An advanced assignment

If you're feeling ambitious, you should try to implement level 3, in which pronouns are reversed and Eliza turns the patient's reply into a question. In doing this, you may find it helpful to use the `FirstWord` and `WordsAfterFirst` procedures in the special `String80ADT` provided on the accompanying disk. Furthermore, you will finmd on the disk a `Doctor` program and `Doctor.DAT` file which, together, show how a more elaborate `Eliza` behaves.

References

Joseph Weizenbaum: *Computer Power and Human Reason* (W.H. Freeman, 1976)

Pamela McCorduck: *Machines Who Think* (W.H. Freeman, 1979)

Lab 18.1
Animating Sorting

Concepts: Sorting.

Lab techniques: Using the computer to animate the actions of sorting procedures, as an aid to visualization.

Prerequisites: Chapter 18 of *Structures and Abstractions*.

Chapter 18 describes two very different sorting procedures in great detail, and mentions several others in passing. In order to fully appreciate the differences among the various useful sorting algorithms, it helps to be able to visualize them at work. In this project, we work out a rudimentary animation program to go with our sorting procedures. The program can be embellished as an out-of-class project.

The idea

Most sorting algorithms, including selection sort and quicksort, operate by swapping pairs of keys. We start with the keys in some initial order, perhaps random, and by swapping a pair of keys, then another, and then another, the list of data becomes progressively ordered. To picture the operation of the algorithm, then, we must be able to picture the way in which order grows in the list of keys.

Suppose, for the sake of this lab, we start with the keys in random order in an array Key[1], Key[2], ..., Key[N]. And suppose that the keys are integer numbers. Then we can picture the list of keys as a sequence of bar graphs. Such a picture will be called a *snapshot* of the array. An example of random-valued keys is shown in Figure 1.

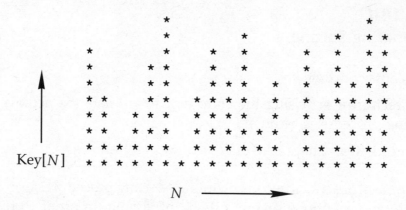

FIGURE 1. *A snapshot of 20 keys with values in random order. Each vertical bar graph represents a single key.*

Suppose that the goal is to put the keys in nondecreasing order, so that the final snapshot should look like Figure 2.

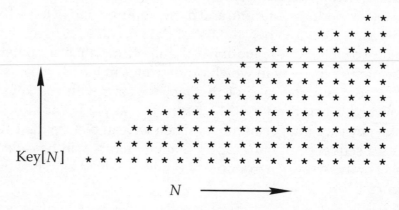

FIGURE 2. *A snapshot of the same 20 keys after being sorted into nondecreasing order.*

In order to graphically display the process of sorting, we want a program that carries out the following steps:

1. Initialize an array of 20 keys. (More than 20 would be hard to display clearly on the screen.)

2. Show a snapshot of the initial sequence of keys.

3. Carry out the sorting process by repeating three steps until the array is sorted:

   a. Choose two keys to be swapped. (How this is done depends on the sorting algorithm.)

   b. Swap the chosen two keys.

   c. Display a snapshot of the new sequence of keys.

The skeleton of the program then follows directly. Never mind right now how we will implement some of the procedures. To start with, just get the skeleton running.

```
PROGRAM ShowSort ( Output );

CONST
   Size  = 20;

TYPE
   IndexRange = 1..Size;
   IntArray   = ARRAY [ IndexRange ] OF Integer;

VAR
   Key : IntArray;  { The array of keys to be sorted }


PROCEDURE Initialize( VAR Key : IntArray );
BEGIN

   { Stub only; we'll fill it in later. }

END; { Initialize }
```

```
PROCEDURE ShowArray( VAR Key : IntArray );
BEGIN

    { Stub only; we'll fill it in later. }

END; { ShowArray }


PROCEDURE Swap( VAR Key : IntArray;
                    I, J    : IndexRange );
VAR
    Temp : Integer;

BEGIN

    Temp      := Key[ I ];
    Key[ I ]   := Key[ J ];
    Key[ J ] := Temp

END; { Swap }


PROCEDURE Sort( VAR Key : IntArray );
{
  Selection sort from Section 18.4 of the text.

  PRECONDITION:
  Key array has been initialized.

  POSTCONDITION:
  Key[1] <= Key[2] <= ... <= Key[Size]
}
VAR
    I, J, Position : IndexRange;
    Minimum : Integer;

BEGIN

    ShowArray( Key );
    FOR I := 1 TO ( Size - 1 ) DO
    BEGIN

        Minimum  := Key[ I ];
        Position := I;
```

```
        FOR J := ( I + 1 ) TO Size DO
           IF Key[ J ] < Minimum THEN
           BEGIN
               Minimum := Key[ J ];
               Position := J
           END;

        Swap( Key, I, Position );
        ShowArray( Key )

    END

END; { Sort }


BEGIN

    Initialize( Key );
    Sort( Key )

END.
```

Initializing the array

First there is the question of how we will fill the array initially. One choice that makes the program more fun to watch is to fill the array with random integers. Because we intend to use bar graphs to represent the keys visually, let's have all the keys be nonnegative. Also, since we don't want the bar graphs to be taller than the screen, let's make the largest key equal to the size of the array, which is 20. Thus we need 20 keys, each of which is in the range from 0 through 20. We can generate such numbers by means of a pseudorandom number generator like the ones built into Turbo and THINK Pascal, or the one described in Appendix I of the textbook. Such generators are initialized by calling a Randomize procedure, then they produce a sequence of pseudorandom real numbers, r, such that $0 \le r < 1.0$. In order to get our desired integers from 0 through 20, all we have to do is to multiply by 20, then round to the nearest integer. Here, then, is the procedure completed:

```
PROCEDURE Initialize( VAR Key : IntArray );
{
  POSTCONDITIONS:
  For all all I from 1 through Size,
     0 <= Key[ I ] <= 20.
  The values in this array are in pseudorandom order.
}
VAR
    Index : IndexRange;

BEGIN

  { Seed the random-number generator. }
  Randomize;

  {
    Generate and store a sequence of Size
    pseudorandom numbers in the desired range.
  }
  FOR Index := 1 TO Size DO
  BEGIN

    Key[ Index ] := Round( Random * Size );

    {
      The following is for testing purposes only,
      and can be removed when the program is running
      correctly.
    }
    WriteLn( Key[ Index ] )

  END

END; { Initialize }
```

Displaying the array of keys

It would be really nice if there were a way to do high-resolution graphics in Standard Pascal. If there were, we could draw our sequence of bars graphs, wait a moment, erase the screen, swap a pair of keys, draw the new sequence of bar graphs, and so on. Visually, each "snapshot" of the array would appear to be replaced by the next one.

But the best we can do in Standard Pascal is to draw crude pictures by writing rows of characters on the screen, so that a snapshot will scroll onto the screen line by line. In particular, if the keys have values between 0 and 20, we will draw bars up to 20 rows high. We might as well display the bars as columns of asterisks (stars) and separate the bars by columns of spaces. (See the sample snapshots shown earlier.)

The sequence of actions in the ShowArray procedure will then go something like this:

For Rows 20, 19, 18, ..., 0 of the snapshot, do this:
  Sweep across the current row by sweeping through the twenty keys of the array. For each key, do this:
    If Row ≤ Key[Column], then
      draw part of a bar by writing '* ' (star, space) to the screen;
    otherwise, the bar doesn't reach this row,
      so write '   '. (Two spaces)

Here, then, is the completed ShowArray procedure:

```
PROCEDURE ShowArray( VAR Key : IntArray );
VAR
   Row   : Integer;
   Index : IndexRange;

BEGIN

   WriteLn;
   FOR Row := Size DOWNTO 0 DO
   BEGIN
      FOR Index := 1 TO Size DO
         IF Row <= Key[ Index ] THEN
            Write( '* ' )
         ELSE
            Write( '  ' );
      WriteLn
   END;
   WriteLn

END; { ShowArray }
```

Whoops!

Insert the completed procedures in the program skeleton and run the program a number of times. You can see, I hope, how the array becomes progressively ordered, starting at the left (the low-numbered indices). Unfortunately, each snapshot scrolls off the screen so fast, it's hard to see what's happening. We need a way to hold a snapshot on the screen briefly before it's replaced by the next.

One solution would be to make the user press return when ready to see the next snapshot. This could be accomplished by inserting a ReadLn at the end of the ShowArray procedure.

But it isn't fun to press return many times during a run. Wouldn't it be better to have the program use an automatic time delay between snapshots? To do this, we insert a do-nothing procedure that runs a time-consuming loop. Just have ShowArray call, as its last action, the following TimeDelay procedure:

```
PROCEDURE TimeDelay;
{ This procedure does nothing but chew up time. }

CONST
   Delay = 500;

VAR
   Time : Integer;
   X    : Real;

BEGIN

   FOR Time := 1 TO Delay DO
      X := Ln( Exp( X ) )

END; { TimeDelay }
```

Note that the Delay constant may need to be adjusted to suit your computer system.

Clearing the screen

Now you should have no trouble watching the array as it is sorted. However, you'll probably become dissatisfied with the program after running it a few times. For one thing, it is annoying that the snapshots scroll onto and off of the screen. The results would look better if we could clear the screen rapidly after each time delay. There is no way to do this nicely in Standard Pascal, but your Pascal system may provide a way to do it. Check with your instructor or your system's reference manual. If your system provides a way to clear the screen without scrolling, use it in your program.

Showing the swaps

Another nice touch would be to have the snapshots display the keys involved in each swap. For example, if the second and seventh keys are to be swapped next, we can show this with an arrow:

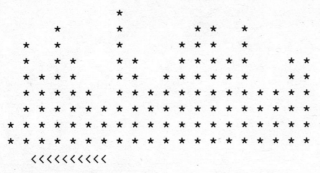

Insert code for such an embellishment into the program.

> Turn in a source-code listing of the completed program.

Compare selection sort with quicksort

Once your program is running and you have gotten a feel for how selection sort builds order in the array, make a second version of the program in which the Sort procedure implements the quicksort algorithm described in Section 18.5 of the text. After running quicksort a number of times, describe in your own words how the order in the array grows differently under quicksort than it does under selection sort:

_____

_____

_____

_____

> If possible, turn in both source code and executable files for this program, so that your instructor can run your program and check your code.

Lab 19.1
Pointers and Linked Lists

Concepts: Pointers, dynamic storage, linked lists.

Lab techniques: Using an interactive debugger to check pointer values; animation.

Prerequisites: Sections 19.1–19.3 of *Structures and Abstractions*.

A pointer variable is used to store the memory address of a storage cell. A pointer is never a generic pointer; it is always a pointer to some particular type. For example, we can declare

```
TYPE
   IntPointer  = ^Integer;
   CharPointer = ^Char;

VAR
   IPtr : IntPointer;
   CPtr : CharPointer;
```

With these declarations, IPtr is a variable that can contain only the address of an integer storage cell, while CPtr can contain only the address of a character storage cell.

The importance of pointers lies in their use when creating *dynamic storage cells*. Dynamic storage is storage that is allocated, and possibly deallocated, while a program is running. Such storage can therefore be set aside as needed during a run, as the program learns how much storage is required by the data being manipulated. Contrast this to the *static allocation* used in previous chapters, in which we had to preallocate the maximum storage that would ever be required by a program, with much of it unused during typical runs.

Initializing a pointer to NIL

Initially, a pointer variable like IPtr or CPtr contains garbage, so we have to initialize it. There are two ways to do this in Pascal. First of all, when we want to indicate that the pointer points to nothing—that is, when it contains no meaningful address—we assign it the Pascal standard constant value called NIL:

```
   IPtr := NIL;
   CPtr := NIL;
```

The NIL constant is a generic pointer constant predefined in Pascal to mean "pointer to nothing meaningful." Its actual value depends on the Pascal system being used: it is not, for example, necessarily a zero address value. As you can see from the examples, the NIL value can be assigned to any kind of pointer variable: pointer to integer, pointer to character, or pointer to anything.

A first experiment with initialization

You should try out pointer declaration and initialization to see their effects with your own eyes. Load into your Pascal system the following program, which is provided on the accompanying floppy disk as TESTPTRO.PAS:

```
PROGRAM TestPointers;
TYPE
   DataType = Integer;
   List = ^Node;
   Node = RECORD
               Value : DataType;
               Link  : List
           END;

VAR
   L : List;

BEGIN

{  L := NIL  }

END.
```

As you can see, this program declares L to be a pointer to a Node, where a Node is defined to be record containing an integer and another pointer to a Node. This is similar to the kind of nodes used in Section 19.3 of the text.

Open the **Watch** or **Observe** window in your debugger and observe the value of L as you single-step through the program. (We use the Watch/Observe window to check the value of L because most Pascal systems will not allow us to write the value to the screen by normal means.)

What value does L have during the first run? Does L have the same value during successive runs? Why does it have this value or these values?

_____

_____

_____

_____

Now remove the curly braces from around the line that assigns a value to L. Again, single-step through the program. What value does the Watch/Observe window show in L this time? Is the value the same during successive runs?

_____

_____

_____

_____

Initializing a pointer by dynamic allocation

The other way that a pointer variable can receive a value is during dynamic allocation, when the program calls on the Pascal's New procedure to create dynamically a new storage cell of the kind that the pointer can point to. The syntax for calling New is

```
New( PointerIdentifier )
```

The New procedure is discussed in Section 19.1 of the text.

Experimenting with New

To better understand what New does, it helps to watch it work with your own eyes. Load into your Pascal system the file called TESTPTR1.PAS, which contains the code shown on the next page.

```
PROGRAM TestPointers ( Input, Output );
TYPE
    DataType = Integer;
    List = ^Node;
    Node = RECORD
               Value : DataType;
               Link  : List
           END;

VAR
    L : List;


PROCEDURE GetNode( VAR L : List );
{
  PRECONDITION:
  L has a value.

  POSTCONDITION:
  L points to a new node, in which the data value
  has been initialized from the keyboard,
  and the link points to the old L.
}
VAR
    OldL : List;

BEGIN

    OldL := L;
    New( L );

    Write( 'Integer value? ' );
    ReadLn( L^.Value );

    L^.Link := OldL

END; { GetNode }


BEGIN

    L := NIL;
    GetNode( L )

END.
```

Single-step through this program, using the **Step Into** or **Trace Into** command, so that you can single-step through the GetNode procedure as well. As you do so, watch the values of L, OldL, L^.Value, and L^.Link. Then answer the following questions:

As execution enters the GetNode procedure, what are the values of L, OldL, L^.Value, and L^.Link? Why do they have these values?

_____

_____

_____

_____

_____

_____

Right after New(L) has been executed, what are the values of L, OldL, L^.Value, and L^.Link? Why do they have these values?

_____

_____

_____

_____

_____

_____

Are ther values of L the same in successive runs?

_____

Draw a diagram of the dynamically-allocated storage as execution reaches the end of the GetNode procedure.

Building a linked list

Finally, we try out an embellishment of the previous program that allows us to build a linked list of as many nodes as we want. The code below is from disk file LINKLIST.PAS:

```pascal
PROGRAM LinkedList ( Input, Output );
TYPE
   DataType = Integer;
   List = ^Node;
   Node = RECORD
              Value : DataType;
              Link  : List
          END;

VAR
   Head : List;



PROCEDURE ShowList( L : List );
BEGIN

   { This is only a stub. }

END; { ShowList }


PROCEDURE GetNode( VAR Head : List );
{
  PRECONDITION:
  Head has a value.

  POSTCONDITION:
  Head points to a new node, in which the data value
  has been initialized from the keyboard,
  and the link points to the old value of Head.
}
VAR
   OldHead : List;

BEGIN

   OldHead := Head;
   New( Head );

   Write( 'Integer value? ' );
   ReadLn( Head^.Value );
```

```
        Head^.Link := OldHead

END; { GetNode }


PROCEDURE GetList( VAR Head : List );
VAR
    Answer  : Char;

BEGIN

    REPEAT

        GetNode( Head );
        ShowList( Head );
        WriteLn;

        Write( 'Another? <Y/N> ' );
        ReadLn( Answer );
        WriteLn

    UNTIL ( Answer <> 'y' ) AND ( Answer <> 'Y' )

END; { GetList }


BEGIN

    Head := NIL;

    GetList( Head )

END.
```

Single-step through this program while observing the values of Head, OldHead, Head^.Value, and Head^.Link in the Watch/ Observe window of your debugger. Enter data as shown in the exchange below:

```
Integer? 11
Another? <Y/N> Y
Integer? 22
Another? <Y/N> Y
Integer? 33
Another? <Y/N> N
```

Answer the following questions about this run:

Show the values of the variables just before GetNode terminates *for the last time*:

      Head contains   _____

      OldHead contains   _____

      Head^.Value contains   _____

      Head^.Link contains   _____

Draw a diagram of the dynamically-allocated storage in use just before the program terminates:

A final assignment

Now implement the ShowList procedure recursively so that it displays a linked list. If Head points to a list containing the integers 101, 102, and 103, in that order as we traverse the list from head to tail, your ShowList procedure should display

```
101 ---> 102 ---> 103 ---> NIL
```

> Turn in your source code and printouts of sample runs.

Credit: Jack Mostow, of Rutgers, The State University of New Jersey, made suggestions that improved this lab.

Appendix A:
Operator Precedence

Operators	Category	Precedence level
( )	parentheses	Highest: 1
NOT	negation	2
*, /, DIV, MOD, AND	multiplicative	3
+, -, OR	additive	4
=, <>, <, <=, >, >=, IN	relational	Lowest: 5

Appendix B:
ASCII Character Codes

Standard Pascal uses the International Standards Organization (ISO) character code, of which the American variant is the American Standard Code for Information Interchange (ANSI X3.41977), called ASCII (ass'-key) for short. ASCII is a 7-bit code, yielding 128 possible values from 0 through 127 decimal. The eighth bit (the most significant one) is either set to zero, used as a parity (error-checking) bit, or used for some system-specific purpose.

MS-DOS personal computers use the eighth bit in ASCII, and character codes from 128 to 255 correspond to special characters and graphics symbols. This extended ASCII is not shown here; see the Turbo Pascal edition of *Structures and Abstractions* for further details.

The following page lists ASCII character code numbers in decimal (base 10), octal (base 8), and hexadecimal (base 16) notation, along with the corresponding characters. As an example of the use of these tables, Chr(65) is the letter 'A', so that Ord('A') is 65.

ASCII:
AMERICAN STANDARD CODE FOR INFORMATION INTERCHANGE

Dec	Oct	Hex	Char	Dec	Oct	Hex	Char
0	000	00	Null	67	103	43	C
1	001	01	^A = SOH	68	104	44	D
2	002	02	^B = STX	69	105	45	E
3	003	03	^C = ETX	70	106	46	F
4	004	04	^D = EOT	71	107	47	G
5	005	05	^E = ENQ	72	110	48	H
6	006	06	^F = ACK	73	111	49	I
7	007	07	^G = BEL	74	112	4A	J
8	010	08	^H = Backspace	75	113	4B	K
9	011	09	^I = Horiz Tab	76	114	4C	L
10	012	0A	^J = Line Feed	77	115	4D	M
11	013	0B	^K = Vert Tab	78	116	4E	N
12	014	0C	^L = Form Feed	79	117	4F	O
13	015	0D	^M = Car Return	80	120	50	P
14	016	0E	^N = Shift Out	81	121	51	Q
15	017	0F	^O = Shift In	82	122	52	R
16	020	10	^P = DL Esc	83	123	53	S
17	021	11	^Q = Dev Ctl 1	84	124	54	T
18	022	12	^R = Dev Ctl 2	85	125	55	U
19	023	13	^S = Dev Ctl 3	86	126	56	V
20	024	14	^T = Dev Ctl 4	87	127	57	W
21	025	15	^U = Neg Ack	88	130	58	X
22	026	16	^V = Synch Idle	89	131	59	Y
23	027	17	^W = ETB	90	132	5A	Z
24	030	18	^X = Cancel	91	133	5B	[
25	031	19	^Y = EM	92	134	5C	\
26	032	1A	^Z = Substitute	93	135	5D	]
27	033	1B	Escape	94	136	5E	^
28	034	1C	File Sep	95	137	5F	_
29	035	1D	Group Sep	96	140	60	`
30	036	1E	Record Sep	97	141	61	a
31	037	1F	Unit Sep	98	142	62	b
32	040	20	Space	99	143	63	c
33	041	21	!	100	144	64	d
34	042	22	"	101	145	65	e
35	043	23	#	102	146	66	f
36	044	24	$	103	147	67	g
37	045	25	%	104	150	68	h
38	046	26	&	105	151	69	i
39	047	27	'	106	152	6A	j
40	050	28	(	107	153	6B	k
41	051	29	)	108	154	6C	l
42	052	2A	*	109	155	6D	m
43	053	2B	+	110	156	6E	n
44	054	2C	,	111	157	6F	o
45	055	2D	-	112	160	70	p
46	056	2E	.	113	161	71	q
47	057	2F	/	114	162	72	r
48	060	30	0	115	163	73	s
49	061	31	1	116	164	74	t
50	062	32	2	117	165	75	u
51	063	33	3	118	166	76	v
52	064	34	4	119	167	77	w
53	065	35	5	120	170	78	x
54	066	36	6	121	171	79	y
55	067	37	7	122	172	7A	z
56	070	38	8	123	173	7B	{
57	071	39	9	124	174	7C	|
58	072	3A	:	125	175	7D	}
59	073	3B	;	126	176	7E	~
60	074	3C	<	127	177	7F	Delete
61	075	3D	=				
62	076	3E	>				
63	077	3F	?				
64	100	40	@				
65	101	41	A				
66	102	42	B				

Frequently Used Hot Keys in Turbo Pascal (MS-DOS)

Key Strokes	Command	Description
Alt-*Letter*	Pull Down Menu	Pulls down the menu whose name begins with the given letter.
F3	Open file	Opens existing source-code file in new window.
Alt-F3	Close file	Closes the active source-code window.
F2	Save	Saves the contents of the active source-code window.
F1	Help	Asks for on-line help.
Alt-X	Exit	Exit from Turbo Pascal.

Editing:

Shift-*ArrowKeys*	Select	Selects text for cutting or copying.
Shift-Del	Cut	Removes selected text, placing it in the Clipboard.
Ctrl-Insert	Copy	Copies the selected text to the Clipboard.
Shift-Insert	Paste	Copies the contents of the Clipboard into the active text window, at the location of the insertion point.

Searching:

Alt-S,F	Find	Finds a specified string.
Alt-S,R	Replace	Replaces first occurrence of specified string with another string.
Ctrl-L	Search Again	Repeats previous Find or Replace.

Running:

Ctrl-F9	Run	Compiles, links, and runs.
Alt-F9	Compile	Compiles program.
F7	Trace Into	Single-steps through execution, including subprograms.
F8	Step Over	Single-steps through execution, but runs subprograms in one step.
Ctrl-F8	Toggle breakpoint	Sets or clears a breakpoint on the line containing the cursor.

Frequently Used Hot Keys in THINK Pascal (Macintosh)

Key Strokes	Command	Description
Cmd-N	New File	Opens a new source-code window.
Cmd-O	Open File	Opens existing source-code file in new window.
Cmd-P	Open Project	Opens an existing project file.
Cmd-W	Close Window	Closes the active source-code window.
Cmd-S	Save	Saves the contents of the active source-code window.
Cmd-Q	Quit	Exit from THINK Pascal.

Editing:

Key Strokes	Command	Description
Cmd-Z	Undo	Reverses the previous edit command.
Cmd-X	Cut	Removes selected text, placing it in the Clipboard.
Cmd-C	Copy	Copies the selected text to the Clipboard.
Cmd-V	Paste	Copies the contents of the Clipboard into the active text window, at the location of the insertion point.

Searching:

Key Strokes	Command	Description
Cmd-F	Find	Finds a specified string.
Cmd-A	Find Again	Finds next occurrence of string.
Cmd-R	Replace	Replaces first occurrence of specified string with another string.
Cmd-D	Replace and Find Again	Replaces first occurrence of target string with another string, then searches for next occurrence of target string.

Running:

Key Strokes	Command	Description
Cmd-G	Go	Compile, link, and run.
Cmd-I	Step Into	Single-steps through execution, including subprograms.
Cmd-J	Step Over	Single-steps through execution, but runs subprograms in one step.